## A Gudiña to Ourense: variant via Verín

| Stage number | Title | Distance | Total ascent | Total descent | Duration | Difficulty | Page |
|---|---|---|---|---|---|---|---|
| 35A | A Gudiña to Verín | 40.3km | 775m | 1380m | 10½hr | Very hard | 251 |
| 36A | Verín to Xinzo de Limia | 37.2km | 820m | 585m | 9¾hr | Very hard | 256 |
| 37A | Xinzo de Limia to Allariz | 22.3km | 270m | 425m | 5½hr | Easy | 261 |
| 38A | Allariz to Ourense | 23.4km | 370m | 755m | 6hr | Easy | 266 |
| **Total** | | **123.2km** | **2235m** | **3145m** | **31¾hr** | | |

## Extension to Astorga

| Stage number | Title | Distance | Total ascent | Total descent | Duration | Difficulty | Page |
|---|---|---|---|---|---|---|---|
| Extension | Granja de Moreruela to Astorga | 94.6km | 705m | 545m | 22¼hr | Easy | 179 |

T0340997

*A modern mile marker leads pilgrims along the long dirt tracks (Stage 26)*

# ROUTE SUMMARY TABLES

| Stage number | Title | Distance | Total ascent | Total descent | Duration | Difficulty | Page |
|---|---|---|---|---|---|---|---|
| 1 | Sevilla to Guillena | 21.8km | 105m | 110m | 5½hr | Easy | 47 |
| 2 | Guillena to Castilblanco de los Arroyos | 18.2km | 445m | 120m | 4¾hr | Easy | 53 |
| 3 | Castilblanco de los Arroyos to Almadén de la Plata | 29.5km | 605m | 480m | 7½hr | Very hard | 57 |
| 4 | Almadén de la Plata to El Real de la Jara | 13.9km | 315m | 300m | 3½hr | Easy | 62 |
| 5 | El Real de la Jara to Monesterio | 21.2km | 470m | 195m | 5½hr | Easy | 65 |
| 6 | Monesterio to Calzadilla de los Barros | 27.3km | 280m | 465m | 6¾hr | Moderate | 69 |
| 7 | Calzadilla de los Barros to Zafra | 18.3km | 155m | 215m | 4¼hr | Easy | 74 |
| 8 | Zafra to Villafranca de los Barros | 20.8km | 240m | 340m | 5hr | Easy | 78 |
| 9 | Villafranca de los Barros to Torremejía | 27.3km | 105m | 220m | 6¼hr | Moderate | 82 |
| 10 | Torremejía to Mérida | 16.4km | 85m | 180m | 3¾hr | Easy | 86 |
| 11 | Mérida to Aljucén | 16.3km | 240m | 185m | 4hr | Easy | 95 |
| 12 | Aljucén to Alcuéscar | 19.3km | 285m | 110m | 4¾hr | Easy | 99 |
| 13 | Alcuéscar to Valdesalor | 26.5km | 150m | 210m | 6¼hr | Moderate | 103 |
| 14 | Valdesalor to Casar de Cáceres | 23.3km | 245m | 260m | 5½hr | Easy | 107 |
| 15 | Casar de Cáceres to Cañaveral | 33.2km | 425m | 440m | 8¼hr | Very hard | 113 |
| 16 | Cañaveral to Galisteo | 28.7km | 440m | 510m | 7hr | Hard | 117 |
| 17 | Galisteo to Carcaboso | 10.8km | 105m | 125m | 2½hr | Easy | 123 |
| 18 | Carcaboso to Hotels Asturias and Jarilla | 28.4km | 330m | 200m | 7hr | Hard | 127 |
| 19 | Hotels Asturias and Jarilla to Puerto de Béjar | 24.2km | 570m | 105m | 6¼hr | Moderate | 131 |
| 20 | Puerto de Béjar to Fuenterroble de Salvatierra | 29.8km | 460m | 400m | 7½hr | Hard | 136 |
| 21 | Fuenterroble de Salvatierra to San Pedro de Rozados | 27.8km | 420m | 400m | 6¾hr | Hard | 142 |
| 22 | San Pedro de Rozados to Salamanca | 25.3km | 260m | 430m | 6hr | Easy | 147 |

| Stage number | Title | Distance | Total ascent | Total descent | Duration | Difficulty | Page |
|---|---|---|---|---|---|---|---|
| 23 | Salamanca to Calzada de Valdunciel | 16.7km | 160m | 165m | 4hr | Easy | 153 |
| 24 | Calzada de Valdunciel to El Cubo de Tierra del Vino | 20.7km | 190m | 150m | 5hr | Easy | 157 |
| 25 | El Cubo de Tierra del Vino to Zamora | 31.9km | 170m | 370m | 7¼hr | Very hard | 162 |
| 26 | Zamora to Montamarta | 19.6km | 170m | 120m | 4½hr | Easy | 168 |
| 27 | Montamarta to Granja de Moreruela (Astorga extension begins here) | 22.3km | 225m | 210m | 5¼hr | Easy | 172 |
| 28 | Granja de Moreruela to Tábara | 26.2km | 450m | 305m | 6½hr | Hard | 201 |
| 29 | Tábara to Santa Marta de Tera | 23.0km | 230m | 260m | 5½hr | Easy | 205 |
| 30 | Santa Marta de Tera to Rionegro del Puente | 28.6km | 250m | 200m | 6¾hr | Hard | 210 |
| 31 | Rionegro del Puente to Asturianos | 26.3km | 385m | 210m | 6½hr | Moderate | 215 |
| 32 | Asturianos to Requejo | 27.8km | 375m | 365m | 6¾hr | Moderate | 219 |
| 33 | Requejo to Lubián | 16.2km | 505m | 495m | 4½hr | Moderate | 224 |
| 34 | Lubián to A Gudiña | 24.5km | 635m | 670m | 6¾hr | Hard | 228 |
| 35 | A Gudiña to Laza (variant via Verín starts here) | 34.9km | 770m | 1270m | 8½hr | Very hard | 233 |
| 36 | Laza to Alberguería | 11.8km | 495m | 75m | 3½hr | Easy | 238 |
| 37 | Alberguería to Xunqueira de Ambía | 21.9km | 275m | 635m | 5¼hr | Easy | 240 |
| 38 | Xunqueira de Ambía to Ourense | 22.2km | 220m | 605m | 5¼hr | Easy | 244 |
| 39 | Ourense to Oseira | 31.9km | 940m | 435m | 8hr | Very hard | 273 |
| 40 | Oseira to Botos | 23.4km | 585m | 760m | 6¼hr | Moderate | 279 |
| 41 | Botos to Dornelas | 27.6km | 550m | 730m | 7hr | Moderate | 283 |
| 42 | Dornelas to Deseiro | 18.8km | 500m | 575m | 5hr | Easy | 288 |
| 43 | Deseiro to Santiago de Compostela | 10.7km | 295m | 240m | 2¾hr | Easy | 293 |
| **Total** | | **995.3km** | **15,110m** | **14,845m** | **245¼hr** | | |

# WALKING LA VÍA DE LA PLATA AND CAMINO SANABRÉS

## THE CAMINO DE SANTIAGO FROM SEVILLE TO SANTIAGO DE COMPOSTELA AND ASTORGA

by Nicole Bukaty

JUNIPER HOUSE, MURLEY MOSS,
OXENHOLME ROAD, KENDAL, CUMBRIA LA9 7RL
www.cicerone.co.uk

© Nicole Bukaty 2023
First Edition 2023
ISBN: 978 1 78631 080 4
Replaces Via de la Plata by Alison Raju
ISBN: 978 1 85284 444 8

Printed in Singapore by KHL Printing on responsibly sourced paper
A catalogue record for this book is available from the British Library.

Route mapping by Lovell Johns www.lovelljohns.com
All photographs are by the author unless otherwise stated.
Contains OpenStreetMap.org data © OpenStreetMap
contributors, CC-BY-SA. NASA relief data courtesy of ESRI

*For my father who walks with me each and every day, I love you*

### Updates to this guide

While every effort is made by our authors to ensure the accuracy of guidebooks as they go to print, changes can occur during the lifetime of an edition. Any updates that we know of for this guide will be on the Cicerone website (www. cicerone.co.uk/1080/updates), so please check before planning your trip. We also advise that you check information about such things as transport, accommodation and shops locally. Even rights of way can be altered over time. We are always grateful for information about any discrepancies between a guidebook and the facts on the ground, sent by email to updates@cicerone.co.uk or by post to Cicerone, Juniper House, Murley Moss, Oxenholme Road, Kendal, LA9 7RL.

**Register your book:** To sign up to receive free updates, special offers and GPX files where available, create a Cicerone account and register your purchase via the 'My Account' tab at www.cicerone.co.uk.

*Front cover: Pilgrims stroll along the tracks on the way to Faramontaos de Tábara on Stage 28 (photo: Carla Gotardello and Mattia Locrati)*

# Symbols used on maps

- **(S)** start point
- **(F)** finish point
- **(SF)** start/finish point
- **(S)** alternative start point
- **(F)** alternative finish point
- **11.1** distance marker
- ～ main route
- ～ alternative route
- ～ main route (alternative stage)
- ～ alternative route (alternative stage)
- ～ international/regional boundary
- ▬ station/railway
- woodland
- urban areas
- ▲ ⏑ summit/pass
- ⏑ bridge

- ■ building
- **P** parking
- 🏰 ⊞ castle/cemetery
- ⛪ ✝ church/cathedral
- ⛪ † monastery/cross
- ⊥ wind turbines
- ✳ viewpoint
- ☆ • point of interest/other feature

Relief
in metres

| 2400–2600 |
| 2200–2400 |
| 2000–2200 |
| 1800–2000 |
| 1600–1800 |
| 1400–1600 |
| 1200–1400 |
| 1000–1200 |
| 800–1000 |
| 600–800 |
| 400–600 |
| 200–400 |
| 0–200 |

## FACILITIES
- ⊕ groceries
- ⊞ ATM
- ☻ rest/picnic area
- ⊙ vending machine
- ⬤ drinking water
- ⊕ pharmacy
- Ⓗ hospital
- ⊕ medical clinic
- ⓘ tourist/pilgrim information
- ■ ⬤ bus stop/bus station
- ■ ⬤ railway station
- ■ tram stop
- ⬛ accommodation
- 🏠 albergue
- 🏠 hotel
- 🏠 casa rural
- ▲ camping
- 🍴 café/bar/restaurant
- 🍞 bakery

### MAP SCALES
Route maps at 1:100,000
Town maps at 1:25,000 unless otherwise stated (see scale bar)

SCALE: 1:100,000

0 kilometres 1   2
0 miles 1

**GPX files** for all routes can be downloaded free at www.cicerone.co.uk/1080/GPX.

## Acknowledgements

Thank you to the brilliant team at Cicerone for the opportunity to make a dream come true: Joe and Jonathan Williams for their confidence in me and for lunches in the Lakes; my editor, Nicole Spray, for her enthusiasm and constant assistance; Natalie Simpson and Maddy Williams for their expertise; Clare Crooke for the fabulous design; and Sandy Brown, my wonderful mentor, guidebook writing inspiration and true pilgrim. I will forever be grateful to my copyeditor, Pat Dunn, for her patience, exceptional suggestions and kindness. Locally, the librarians at Crieff Library always save me a computer and have become colleagues: thank you to Rowena, Janice, Dorothy and Wilma. Loving thank yous to my family: my fiancé, Nicholas; my beautiful, brave mother, Lidia, for being there always and for trusting me to guide her on long-distance walks; my uncle, Darek, who always looks out for us; and Patty, my sister and best friend, who walked with me in ridiculous conditions and has consistently come up with better wording. The gratitude I have for the affection and compassion received on Caminos is what inspired me to write this book. *Gracias, merci, grazie* to my pilgrim friends: Xavi (Camino del Norte); Federica, Edward, Dave and all the volunteers in Viana, Vilamayor de Monjardín and Luquín (Camino Francés); Filip, Fabien, Romain and Henri (Chemin du Puy); and Marisol, Juan Pablo, Alberto, Paco, Miguelito, and Eduardo from Tábara (Vía de la Plata). Endless thanks to the pilgrims who captured those fabulous good-weather shots that I didn't manage to get on the Vía and Sanabrés: Carla, Mattia, Juan Carlos, and Marta.

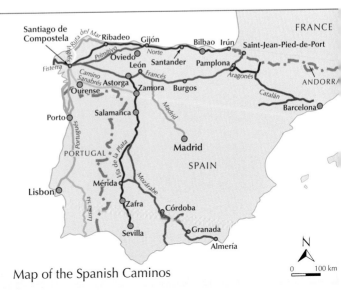

Map of the Spanish Caminos

# CONTENTS

Route summary tables . . . . . . . . . . . . . . . . . . . . . . . . . . . . . . . . . . . . . . . . . . . 1
Map key . . . . . . . . . . . . . . . . . . . . . . . . . . . . . . . . . . . . . . . . . . . . . . . . . . . . . . . 7
Map of the Spanish Caminos . . . . . . . . . . . . . . . . . . . . . . . . . . . . . . . . . . . . . . 8
Overview profile . . . . . . . . . . . . . . . . . . . . . . . . . . . . . . . . . . . . . . . . . . . 10–11
Foreword . . . . . . . . . . . . . . . . . . . . . . . . . . . . . . . . . . . . . . . . . . . . . . . . . . . . 13

**General introduction** . . . . . . . . . . . . . . . . . . . . . . . . . . . . . . . . . . . . . . . . . . 15
A brief history of the Camino de Santiago. . . . . . . . . . . . . . . . . . . . . . . . . . . . 16
The Vía de la Plata and the Camino Sanabrés . . . . . . . . . . . . . . . . . . . . . . . . . 17
Landscape, economy, cultures and languages . . . . . . . . . . . . . . . . . . . . . . . . . 21

**Planning your Camino: before and during** . . . . . . . . . . . . . . . . . . . . . . . . . . . 24
The pilgrim experience. . . . . . . . . . . . . . . . . . . . . . . . . . . . . . . . . . . . . . . . . . 24
Route and schedule options . . . . . . . . . . . . . . . . . . . . . . . . . . . . . . . . . . . . . . 25
Getting there and back . . . . . . . . . . . . . . . . . . . . . . . . . . . . . . . . . . . . . . . . . . 26
When to go . . . . . . . . . . . . . . . . . . . . . . . . . . . . . . . . . . . . . . . . . . . . . . . . . . 27
Planning your day to day on the Camino . . . . . . . . . . . . . . . . . . . . . . . . . . . . 30
Accommodation. . . . . . . . . . . . . . . . . . . . . . . . . . . . . . . . . . . . . . . . . . . . . . . 31
Food. . . . . . . . . . . . . . . . . . . . . . . . . . . . . . . . . . . . . . . . . . . . . . . . . . . . . . . . 32
Budget planning . . . . . . . . . . . . . . . . . . . . . . . . . . . . . . . . . . . . . . . . . . . . . . 34
Preparation and training . . . . . . . . . . . . . . . . . . . . . . . . . . . . . . . . . . . . . . . . 34
What to pack . . . . . . . . . . . . . . . . . . . . . . . . . . . . . . . . . . . . . . . . . . . . . . . . . 35
Baggage and storage services . . . . . . . . . . . . . . . . . . . . . . . . . . . . . . . . . . . . . 36
Local facilities and practical information . . . . . . . . . . . . . . . . . . . . . . . . . . . . . 37
Waymarking, shells and symbols . . . . . . . . . . . . . . . . . . . . . . . . . . . . . . . . . . 39
Safety and health . . . . . . . . . . . . . . . . . . . . . . . . . . . . . . . . . . . . . . . . . . . . . . 41

**How to use this guide** . . . . . . . . . . . . . . . . . . . . . . . . . . . . . . . . . . . . . . . . . . 42
GPX download. . . . . . . . . . . . . . . . . . . . . . . . . . . . . . . . . . . . . . . . . . . . . . . . 44

**SECTION 1: SEVILLA TO MÉRIDA** . . . . . . . . . . . . . . . . . . . . . . . . . . . . . . . . . 45
Stage 1      Sevilla to Guillena . . . . . . . . . . . . . . . . . . . . . . . . . . . . . . . . . . . . 47
Stage 2      Guillena to Castilblanco de los Arroyos . . . . . . . . . . . . . . . . . . . . . . 53
Stage 3      Castilblanco de los Arroyos to Almadén de la Plata . . . . . . . . . . . . . 57
Stage 4      Almadén de la Plata to El Real de la Jara . . . . . . . . . . . . . . . . . . . . . 62
Stage 5      El Real de la Jara to Monesterio . . . . . . . . . . . . . . . . . . . . . . . . . . . 65
Stage 6      Monesterio to Calzadilla de los Barros . . . . . . . . . . . . . . . . . . . . . . 69
Stage 7      Calzadilla de los Barros to Zafra. . . . . . . . . . . . . . . . . . . . . . . . . . . 74
Stage 8      Zafra to Villafranca de los Barros . . . . . . . . . . . . . . . . . . . . . . . . . . 78

Stage 9       Villafranca de los Barros to Torremejía ........................ 82
Stage 10      Torremejía to Mérida ....................................... 86

**SECTION 2: MÉRIDA TO GRANJA DE MORERUELA** ................ 93
Stage 11      Mérida to Aljucén ......................................... 95
Stage 12      Aljucén to Alcuéscar ....................................... 99
Stage 13      Alcuéscar to Valdesalor .................................... 103
Stage 14      Valdesalor to Casar de Cáceres .............................. 107
Stage 15      Casar de Cáceres to Cañaveral ............................... 113
Stage 16      Cañaveral to Galisteo ...................................... 117
Stage 17      Galisteo to Carcaboso ...................................... 123
Stage 18      Carcaboso to Hotels Asturias and Jarilla ...................... 127
Stage 19      Hotels Asturias and Jarilla to Puerto de Béjar (Colonia la Estación) . . . 131
Stage 20      Puerto de Béjar (Colonia la Estación) to Fuenterroble de Salvatierra . . 136
Stage 21      Fuenterroble de Salvatierra to San Pedro de Rozados ............. 142
Stage 22      San Pedro de Rozados to Salamanca .......................... 147
Stage 23      Salamanca to Calzada de Valdunciel ........................... 153
Stage 24      Calzada de Valdunciel to El Cubo de Tierra del Vino ............. 157
Stage 25      El Cubo de Tierra del Vino to Zamora ......................... 162
Stage 26      Zamora to Montamarta ..................................... 168
Stage 27      Montamarta to Granja de Moreruela .......................... 172

**SECTION 3: EXTENSION TO ASTORGA** ........................... 177
Extension     Granja de Moreruela to Astorga and the Camino Francés ......... 179

**SECTION 4: CAMINO SANABRÉS TO OURENSE** .................... 199
Stage 28      Granja de Moreruela to Tábara ............................... 201
Stage 29      Tábara to Santa Marta de Tera ............................... 205
Stage 30      Santa Marta de Tera to Rionegro del Puente ................... 210

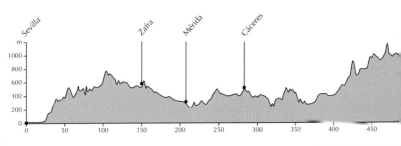

Stage 31    Rionegro del Puente to Asturianos . . . . . . . . . . . . . . . . . . . . . . . . . 215
Stage 32    Asturianos to Requejo . . . . . . . . . . . . . . . . . . . . . . . . . . . . . . . . . . 219
Stage 33    Requejo to Lubián . . . . . . . . . . . . . . . . . . . . . . . . . . . . . . . . . . . . . 224
Stage 34    Lubián to A Gudiña . . . . . . . . . . . . . . . . . . . . . . . . . . . . . . . . . . . . 228

**A Gudiña to Ourense via Laza** . . . . . . . . . . . . . . . . . . . . . . . . . . . . . . . . . . . 233
Stage 35    A Gudiña to Laza . . . . . . . . . . . . . . . . . . . . . . . . . . . . . . . . . . . . . . . 233
Stage 36    Laza to Alberguería . . . . . . . . . . . . . . . . . . . . . . . . . . . . . . . . . . . . 238
Stage 37    Alberguería to Xunqueira de Ambía . . . . . . . . . . . . . . . . . . . . . . . . 240
Stage 38    Xunqueira de Ambía to Ourense . . . . . . . . . . . . . . . . . . . . . . . . . . . 244

**A Gudiña to Ourense: variant via Verín** . . . . . . . . . . . . . . . . . . . . . . . . . . . 249
Stage 35A   A Gudiña to Verín . . . . . . . . . . . . . . . . . . . . . . . . . . . . . . . . . . . . . 251
Stage 36A   Verín to Xinzo de Limia . . . . . . . . . . . . . . . . . . . . . . . . . . . . . . . . . 256
Stage 37A   Xinzo de Limia to Allariz . . . . . . . . . . . . . . . . . . . . . . . . . . . . . . . . 261
Stage 38A   Allariz to Pereiras (connection with Stage 38 to Ourense) . . . . . . . . 266

**SECTION 5: OURENSE TO SANTIAGO DE COMPOSTELA** . . . . . . . . . . . . . . . 271
Stage 39    Ourense to Oseira . . . . . . . . . . . . . . . . . . . . . . . . . . . . . . . . . . . . . 273
Stage 40    Oseira to Botos (Estación de Lalín) . . . . . . . . . . . . . . . . . . . . . . . . . 279
Stage 41    Botos (Estación de Lalín) to Dornelas . . . . . . . . . . . . . . . . . . . . . . . 283
Stage 42    Dornelas to Deseiro (Sergude) . . . . . . . . . . . . . . . . . . . . . . . . . . . . 288
Stage 43    Deseiro (Sergude) to Santiago de Compostela . . . . . . . . . . . . . . . . 293

**Appendix A**    Stage planning tables . . . . . . . . . . . . . . . . . . . . . . . . . . . . . . . 300
**Appendix B**    Spanish–English glossary of key terms . . . . . . . . . . . . . . . . . . . 309
**Appendix C**    Useful contacts and links . . . . . . . . . . . . . . . . . . . . . . . . . . . . 314
**Appendix D**    Bibliography . . . . . . . . . . . . . . . . . . . . . . . . . . . . . . . . . . . . . . 317

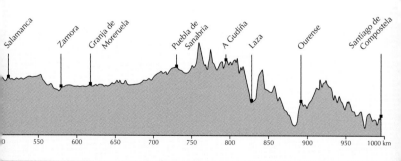

Pilgrims can attend Mass at the magnificent Catedral de Santiago de Compostela (Stage 43)

# FOREWORD

When Theresa and I met Nicole Bukaty on a cloudy, July day in Santiago de Compostela, we both felt that immediate bond that unites experienced pilgrims. Although we'd never walked together, we sensed a camaraderie forged by countless footsteps on paths under the Iberian sun and recollections of laughter-filled conversations over glasses of wine and a *menú del peregrino*. At the time, Nicole was in the early stages of her explorations for this book, and over lunch in the shadow of the Cathedral we talked and laughed about some of the joys and hardships of researching and writing a Camino guide. I was taken by Nicole's love of pilgrim walking, and by the excitement she felt to lead others onto a new route she was already beginning to love.

With this book Nicole now unfolds the Vía de la Plata and Camino Sanabrés for an expectant pilgrim community, a community ready to take a fresh look at a seemingly intimidating itinerary. Nicole made an important and wise choice: since the Roman Via de la Plata aimed at Asturias rather than Santiago, a strict adherence to that itinerary would put Santiago-bound pilgrims onto the more crowded Camino Francés at the intersection of the two paths in Astorga. While offering the Astorga route to her readers, Nicole aptly focuses on the left fork route through the Sanabrés region that affords a unique and uncrowded entry to Santiago through Ourense.

Nicole's descriptions linger on the astounding and ancient monuments that mark the way, the weathered Roman aqueducts and amphitheaters and temples that make the route special. She also describes the blessed emptiness in between; the vast, sparse stretches that give space for the soul to breathe. Smartly guiding the way is Nicole's youthful, genial, and joyful voice.

To pilgrims who follow this way: you have a path of wonders ahead. You've chosen wisely and well to follow Nicole as your guide. *Buen camino*.

*Sandy Brown*

*Guidebook author*

*In summer, many pilgrims start at dawn, even in Galicia, where temperatures can rise to over 45°C (Stage 37)*

# GENERAL INTRODUCTION

Although stages can be long, pilgrims find an immediate welcome and help if needed on arrival in a town (Stage 22)

Stepping onto the extraordinary Vía de la Plata is to embark on a journey that first took place two millennia ago, that of the military voyage made by Roman legionaries between the south and north of Roman Hispania. Centuries later, pilgrims began to follow in their footsteps towards Santiago de Compostela.

Immersion into pilgrim life holds many marvels and delights, with tradition, spirituality, nature and culture combining to make up the beauty of any Camino. The Vía de la Plata bestows even more on the traveller, tracing the historic route of this ancient Roman road and embracing its legacy. Every day, every place, every nook and cranny reveal a wonderful relic of the Vía's epic past. For those who remain mindful that

this path is even older than the original pilgrimage to the tomb of Santiago Apóstol, the trek becomes doubly rewarding: march as the Romans did and contemplate as the pilgrims do.

Crossing four very distinct autonomous regions of Spain, this Camino winds through beautiful solitary landscapes dotted with pretty little towns. Approximately once a week, it lands in a grandiose city with treasures that take you back in time and where all pilgrim comforts are to be found.

Yet take care, as this is not an easy Camino and should not be underestimated. Distances between accommodation options can be extensive, provisions are often scarce, the heat of the sun and downpours of rain can be severe, and there are fewer pilgrims around. It involves walking a minimum of 20km per day self-sufficiently, carrying your own provisions. This is no Camino Francés, del Norte, Inglés or Portugués. Instead, it is a pilgrimage through serene regions where wanderlust pilgrims will find their most happy inner place.

Walking the Vía de la Plata, it is natural to start cherishing every mile marker, whether it be an original Roman one (*miliario*) or a lovely modern replica, and pilgrims often become engrossed in the history of the Romans, looking for signs of their presence. They inevitably fall for the bewitching *dehesas* (oak-planted meadows) of Andalucía and Extremadura, the magnitude of Castilla y León's immense Meseta plateau, and the sumptuous greens of Galicia's hills and forests. At the end of it all, pilgrims will be overwhelmed by enduring memories of the many weeks of walking, the warmth of local people and the modest *albergues* (pilgrim hostels). Even stronger will be the friendships created with other pilgrims and *hospitaleros* (hostel hosts), as together they overcome the Vía's challenges and remedy everything over that delicious, hearty dish of the day. Such bonds will last a lifetime.

## A BRIEF HISTORY OF THE CAMINO DE SANTIAGO

After the death and resurrection of Jesus Christ, his twelve disciples travelled the world to tell of his story and sacrifice. James (Santiago) went to Roman Hispania, now the Iberian peninsula (Spain and Portugal), to spread the Gospel from the Andalucian coast up to Fisterra. He returned to Jerusalem at a time when King Herod started persecuting Christians. Santiago was condemned to death and executed in AD44, becoming the first disciple to be martyred. Because apostles were buried where they had evangelized, James's body was taken to Spain and forgotten about for 750 years.

According to tradition, the first documentation narrating the discovery of the tomb of the apostle is in San Isidoro's 1077 *De ortu et obitu patrum*. In the first half of the 9th century, around 813, a hermit monk called Pelayo saw an abundance of lights dancing above the mountain situated where the Cathedral of Santiago is now. The name Compostela stems from this sighting: Latin *campus stellae* means 'field of stars'. Alerted, Bishop Teodomir investigated and unearthed a tomb containing three bodies, identifying one as that of Santiago.

Soon after, King Alfonso II made his journey from Oviedo in Asturias to the tomb. He built a church and small monastery over it, and pilgrimages towards a setting sun began, bringing expansion and prosperity to the town. The surrounding lands of Galicia, having been left vacant during the ongoing expulsion of Muslims from the north of Spain, were once again filled. For the Catholic monarchs of Spain, the symbol of the apostle was a decisive factor in establishing their politics and fighting the Iberian Muslims, a battle that lasted until the 11th century. In 1078, following the Turkish seizure of the Holy Sepulchre in Jerusalem, pilgrimages to Santiago increased further.

After an apogee lasting until the 13th century, the number of pilgrims

Santiago de Compostela from the rooftops of the cathedral (Stage 43)

started to decline and memories began to fade. It was not until the 20th century that interest in the Camino resurfaced and, in October 1987, the Council of Europe declared the Camino de Santiago as the first European Cultural Route. In 1993 and 2015, the Camino Francés and Camino del Norte respectively gained their UNESCO World Heritage titles.

## THE VÍA DE LA PLATA AND THE CAMINO SANABRÉS

### History

The 2000-year-old history of a path that was used and reused is told at every turn and in the magnificent UNESCO World Heritage cities of Sevilla, Mérida, Cáceres, Salamanca and Santiago de Compostela.

Based on the itineraries created by the Emperor Antoninus, the *Itinerarium Provinciarum Antoni(ni) Augusti*, comprehensive details of names and locations of Roman sites and roads across the Roman Empire have been established. The collection contains 225 lists, or *iters*, each reporting the start, end and total Roman mileage of a route as well as intermediate points along it (called *mansios*) and the distance between those points, similar to a Camino guidebook. The Vía de la Plata, denominated *iter ab emerita asturicam* in Antoninus's publication, verifies the Vía's precise itinerary. The Vía de la Plata is only the stretch between Mérida and Astorga, whereas there were other Roman roads linking Sevilla to Itálica and Itálica to Mérida.

Prior to the Romans' arrival in the Iberian peninsula, the south to north corridor that became the Vía de la Plata was already the general artery taken for journeys and trade during pre-Palaeolithic times, it being the easiest possible passage through the landscape. The Romans, true pioneers of engineering, put in place infrastructure, imprints of which can be seen along the entire Camino. They built the cobblestone roads, some of which are extremely well preserved. They also set up their *mansios* in the form of surveillance camps, pit stops for rest and food, villas and Roman cities fit for emperors: Emerita Augusta (Mérida), capital of the Roman province of Lusitania, and Asturica Augusta (Astorga).

Rome first set eyes on and invaded Iberia in 218BC, seeing victory at Ilipa, near Sevilla, in 206BC and founding Itálica near the battlefield soon after. At the end of the 1st century BC, the Vía de la Plata started to become an addition to the military network of Roman roads, yet it was not until 19BC, during the reign of Emperor Augustus, that the conquest of Iberia and the Vía were completed.

Latin became the official language and Roman Hispania was founded, becoming the birthplace of three Roman emperors, including Hadrian. Hispania flourished and the Roman legacy brought with it Christianity and a Jewish population. Through the process of pacification of the territory and exploitation of coveted mineral resources, especially gold, the Vía de la Plata and her tributaries became commercial and administrative roads.

The entire route was waymarked by cylindrical stone mile markers inscribed with dedications to the emperors and interspaced exactly by a Roman mile, the equivalent of 1.48km. These *miliarios* can regularly be found on the Camino, measuring your progress. The Vía de la Plata preserves the largest number of these itinerary indicators of the ancient Roman world.

The period of stability under the Romans started to crumble in AD409

*The Roman Acueducto de los Milagros in Mérida brought water to the city from the Proserpina reservoir (Stage 11)*

following the invasion of Hispania by Germanic tribes, including the Visigoths. They brought the earliest representations of Christ known to exist in Spain, although their impact generally is less easy to observe.

In the early 8th century, the Vía's importance resurfaced as a key channel for the Muslim invasion of the Iberian peninsula at a time when the Visigoths were weakened by famine and disease. In 711, Tariq ibn Ziyah, the Muslim governor of Tangier, docked with his Berber army in Gibraltar. With the surviving Visigoth nobility fleeing north, it was an easy feat for the African Muslims, the Moors, to conquer the Iberian peninsula within a few years.

They established the Islamic civilization known as Al-Andalus, which would last well into the 11th century. The excellent communication network of the Vía de la Plata and other Roman roads facilitated their advance, and it is precisely from the Arabic word *balata* (meaning 'paved' or 'cobblestone') that the name *la Plata* for the Mérida–Astorga road came into being. Islamic cities, such as Sevilla, thrived, boasting beautiful mosques, palaces, universities, gardens and public baths.

Christians and Jews had the freedom to continue their worship and were known as *Mozárabes*. As Christians had to pay a special tax, many converted to Islam or moved to the north (Asturias), which, due to its hideout behind the Cantabrian mountains, was the sole area that remained Christian. The Camino Sanabrés is often referred to as the Camino Mozárabe, because the latter starts in Almería or Málaga (the strongest region of Al-Andalus) then coincides with the Sanabrés for the final two or so weeks to Santiago de Compostela.

In the late 10th century, Al-Mansour, a general from Córdoba, the capital of Al-Andalus, attacked the Christian north and destroyed the Catedral de Santiago de Compostela in 997. Christian slaves carried the doors and bells to the great mosque in Córdoba, most likely along a similar line to the Camino Sanabrés, Vía de la Plata and Camino Mozárabe.

In the early 11th century, due to ongoing internal struggles between different sects in the north of Africa and within Spain, the emirate started to break up into small kingdoms, with Sevilla being one of the strongest. Despite the Almoravid and Almohad sects joining forces in the early 12th century, the Christian armies of the *Reconquista* (Reconquest) were beginning to see the end of their 400-year quest to drive the Muslims out. Zamora, for example, had been recaptured relatively early on, which explains the abundance of Romanesque churches there. The Almohad's successors, the Nasrids, retreated to Granada, and the Catholic Kingdom of León proceeded southwards to take key towns, again using the old Roman roads to their advantage. It was Castilla's King Fernando III, el Santo, who took Córdoba in 1236 and Sevilla in 1248. Almost 200 years later, the Catholic monarchs (*Reyes Católicos*) Isabela of Castilla and Fernando of Aragón launched the final crusade. They entered the city of Granada in 1492, thus forcing Boabdil, the last emir, to surrender and thereby ending the existence of Al-Andalus.

The ruling of the Catholic monarchs left a considerable mark on

Spain's heritage. On the one hand, it led to the founding of the Spanish Inquisition, which forced Muslims and Jews to convert to Catholicism. Refusal resulted in forced expatriation or being burnt at the stake. On the other hand, it brought an end to the eight centuries of battles, expulsions and devastations that had left many regions of Spain empty of people or preserved buildings, an effect which is felt strongly along the Vía de la Plata.

It was time for something big to happen, and so it was that in 1492, Cristóbal Colón, sponsored by the *Reyes Católicos*, sailed to the Americas. This kicked off a domino-effect for Spain, bringing with it a whole new world of opportunity and transforming the country into one of Europe's wealthiest.

Yet the country was divided. During Spain's finest hour, ruling much of the known world, all the fabulous wealth was squandered on luxurious royal lifestyles, neglecting the needs of ordinary Spaniards. Nonetheless, Spain's Golden Age brought outstanding new buildings in late Gothic style, such as in Salamanca, Renaissance masterpieces as seen in Sevilla, and Baroque wonders, including the reconstructed Catedral de Santiago de Compostela.

With Spain's monarchs creating marital ties with foreign monarchs, the country experienced centuries of constant battles of royal succession and external wars. The weakened old-fashioned monarchs and conservative church allowed the economy to stagnate, creating further inequalities.

*Not a cloud in the sky as the Camino winds towards the Ermita de la Virgen del Castillo (Stage 27)*

| Style | Years | Characteristics |
|-------|-------|-----------------|
| Roman | 210BC–AD409 | Examples include roads, bridges, waterworks, amphitheatres and baths |
| Visigoth | 409–711 | Simple stone churches and horseshoe arches |
| Moorish | 711–1492 | Horseshoe arches, square minarets, intricate tiled geometric patterns, floral motifs and exquisite colours |
| Romanesque | 1100–1300 | Modest angular decorations and proportions, perfect semicircular arches influenced by Byzantine churches |
| Mudéjar | 1100–1700 | Adaptations of Moorish traditions by Islamic craftsmen incorporated into Romanesque, Gothic and Renaissance buildings, especially post-*Reconquista* and using inexpensive materials |

Following the death of France's Louis XVI in the aftermath of the 1789 French Revolution, Spain declared war on France, then made peace with the French Republic two years later. However, in 1807, under the excuse that they were heading to Portugal, French forces poured into Spain and occupied it as part of the Napoleonic Wars. Many ruins in the Zamora province are a result of these battles. King Carlos IV was forced to abdicate, making way for Napoleon's brother, Joseph Bonaparte. The French were finally driven out in 1813 by Spain and her allies: the Duke of Wellington and British forces.

The 20th century did not by any means bring peace to Spain until the very end. Following the February 1936 election of the left-wing Popular Front, Nationalist plots against the government exploded, leading to a brutal and bloody civil war that lasted until 1939. One of the leaders of the plot was Francisco Franco who, after the Nationalist victory, ruled Spain under his dictatorship until 1975.

Appendix D suggests further reading material on the Vía de la Plata.

## Architecture

The Vía de la Plata and Camino Sanabrés display a richness of early and late Gothic, Renaissance and Baroque monuments, as well as an array of specific additional styles mentioned in this book.

## LANDSCAPE, ECONOMY, CULTURES AND LANGUAGES

Spain's landscapes have been shaped by history, economy and culture.

### Landscapes

The Vía and Sanabrés pass through the four autonomous regions of Andalucía, Extremadura, Castilla y León and Galicia, and their nine provinces: Sevilla, Badajoz, Cáceres, Salamanca, Zamora, León, Ourense, Pontevedra and A Coruña.

The diverse sumptuous landscapes encountered are unique to Spain; by serving as windows to the country's soul, they tell stories of the past. The *cañadas* are a recurring feature. Somewhat similar to drover's tracks, they were first established in the 13th century by royal decree for the purpose of transhumance, a biannual process of livestock migration between wheatfields and mountains, in this case mainly involving merino sheep. The Vía de la Plata Roman road made way for these very wide tracks, which were used until the late 20th century. The old royal drover's tracks that the Vía often coincides with are the Cañada Real de la Plata and Cañada Real de la Vizana.

History determined the land designated for agriculture and economic growth. Many efforts were made in the past to fill the big empty parts of Extremadura and Castilla y León, including a now-disused railway that ran between Astorga and Plasencia. Roman and Moorish *acequias* (water irrigation channels) were repurposed during Franco's land reforms in the 1950s

and 1960s, which introduced irrigation schemes for massive agricultural plots. These are still in use today. The middle sections of the Vía take pilgrims up to the Meseta, an enormous flat plateau at an average elevation of 750m. Again, the Meseta is a consequence of history. The Romans were the first to cut down the extensive forests that once grew atop the plateau, for use as timber. Although attempts to populate the land succeeded to an extent, the bigger cities were the most fortunate, leaving the small villages and towns to their own devices.

Each landscape truly presents its own characteristics. In addition to the dense forests of the Sanabria and Ourense regions, the eucalyptus of Galicia, the undulating wheatfields between Salamanca and Astorga, the

*Pilgrims cross the dehesas of Andalucía and Extremadura (Stage 3)*

*The majority of the Vía de la Plata crosses unavoidable long stages with little shade, zero provisions and no shelter*

olive trees and vineyards of Andalucía and Extremadura, the extensive farming along the entire way, there is a specific type of forest which is only found on this Camino, the *dehesa*. Covering three million hectares, these forests of Andalucía and Extremadura are home to evergreen, holm and cork oak trees, distanced approximately 30–40 metres apart to provide the ideal grazing territory for cattle and the famous Iberian pig. Livestock enjoys shade from the sun, feasting on acorns and the lush green grass of the meadows. The oldest trees in this agroecological system are 3000 years old.

Whether it be in the *dehesas* or fields, up the mountain passes of Béjar or on top of the Meseta, through Galicia's forests or along a flowing river, the scale of the emptiness, married with Spain's cloudless skies, grants joyful walking during the day and spectacular stargazing at night.

## Languages

While on the trail, you will find yourself having to use at least basic Spanish to communicate with the locals, apart perhaps from in some of the major cities. In rural locations, life flows calmly, local café/bars are busy in the mornings, and only Spanish is spoken, so be sure to take your time as no one else will be in a rush. In Galicia, locals speak both Spanish and Gallego/Galego (Galician), a Romance language more similar to Portuguese. Note that information will always be in Galician, although often it is given in both Galician and Spanish. A useful Spanish–English glossary is provided in Appendix B.

23

# PLANNING YOUR CAMINO:
# BEFORE AND DURING

*A highlight on the Camino Sanabrés is the overnight in the Monastery of Oseira (Stage 39)*

The Vía is known as the most difficult of Caminos, and the Sanabrés presents its challenges too. All adversities are surmountable with careful planning and preparation. A list of useful contacts and sources of information for pilgrims is provided in Appendix C.

### THE PILGRIM EXPERIENCE

To access the amenities that will support your walk, you will need to carry a *credencial*.

#### The credencial (pilgrim passport)
The *credencial* is a pilgrim's identity card. It is a booklet that must be shown in order to register at each lodging, usually upon arrival, along with your official identity document (passport or national identity card). The host then stamps the *credencial* with a unique design and adds the date. Stamps are also available in café/bars, restaurants and some churches and cathedrals. The *credencial* is a superb reminder of your journey, but it is also an essential document that you can present at the Pilgrim Office in Santiago de Compostela in order to receive your *compostela* certificate. From Ourense on the Camino Sanabrés or Sarria on the Camino Francés, you must ensure that you have two stamps from two different establishments per day.

To purchase your *credencial* (usually €3 in cash) in Sevilla, there are three options:
- Next door to the cathedral by the Giralda tower, on Plaza Virgen de los Reyes, find the Diocesan Book Shop in the Archbishop's Palace (Mon–Fri 09:00–14:00).

- At Cl. Castilla 82 in the Triana neighbourhood (on the Camino), visit the Amigos del Camino de Santiago en Sevilla, but call ahead first to check opening times (tel 954 335 274 or 696 600 602, www.via-plata.org).
- Pop into Albergue Triana (Cl. Rodrigo de Triana 69, tel 954 459 960, www.trianahostel.com).

In other locations, some albergues sell the *credencial*, so check accommodation listings in the stages.

## The compostela (certificate of completion)

Upon completion of the Camino, even if you don't attempt it all in one go and as long as you have walked the last 100km or cycled the last 200km, the Pilgrim Office in Santiago de Compostela provides you with an exquisite scroll called the *compostela*. Written in Latin and incorporating your name, the certificate features beautiful calligraphy and images, resembling the original document handed to pilgrims in days of yore. You may also be tempted to request a distance certificate confirming the number of kilometres you have covered, which in the case of the Vía is an extremely impressive amount.

## ROUTE AND SCHEDULE OPTIONS

Selecting your starting point and the best schedule for you depends entirely on your own circumstances. Often, pilgrims see the 1000km that make up the Vía as definitive; however, sections can be completed individually and pilgrims can start out from various places.

The most popular section is from Ourense northwards (totalling just over 100km and allowing a pilgrim to receive their *compostela*), yet many commence in Zamora, opting to complete the Camino Sanabrés section in 18 days. In brief, Sevilla to Mérida takes 10 days, Mérida to Salamanca 12 days, and Salamanca to Granja de Moreruela (where there's a choice between the Astorga extension and the Camino Sanabrés) 5 days. Granja de Moreruela to Santiago de Compostela along the Camino Sanabrés will take up to 17 days, five of which would be between Ourense and Santiago.

For ease, the best starting points are major transport hubs such as Sevilla, Mérida, Salamanca, Zamora, A Gudiña (the AVE high-speed Galicia–Madrid railway line stops here, 10 days from Santiago through Galicia) and Ourense.

Once you reach Granja de Moreruela, you encounter two tempting options: to continue via Astorga, or to proceed through Ourense.

The first option keeps to the Vía de la Plata via Astorga where, after 4 days, you join the Camino Francés and follow it for the final 11 days to Santiago; this makes a total of 42 stages from Sevilla, depending on your pace. This is the traditional Vía de la Plata route, so the infrastructure for pilgrims between Granja de Moreruela and Astorga is excellent. However, at the time of writing (2023) it is the less common choice for pilgrims, so you may find yourself alone in the albergues on this section. This changes dramatically once you reach Astorga and the bustling Camino Francés. The Astorga extension leads you through fields and *fincas* (farming and

*In Granja de Moreruela, pilgrims choose between the Camino Sanabrés through Ourense or the Camino Francés via Astorga (Stage 27)*

hunting estates), and alongside rivers, with the N-VI national highway nearby, visiting the historic towns of Benavente, La Bañeza and Astorga.

The second option from Granja de Moreruela is along the Camino Sanabrés. This takes around 16 days to complete and totals 43 stages from Sevilla, making it slightly longer than the Astorga option. On the Sanabrés, you walk through fields and *fincas*, accompanied by rivers and reservoirs, before entering more wooded and hilly landscapes from Requejo onwards (Stage 33). You travel through the historic towns of Puebla de Sanabria and Ourense, enjoy excellent bread from Cea (Stage 39), and visit the Monastery of Oseira and its albergue. Upon reaching Galicia, there are two options: to walk through Laza or through Verín. Laza tends to be more popular as it is 32.4km shorter and crosses hills with outstanding views, yet the towns on the Verín option are more historic.

For journeys around Spain, see www.renfe.com for trains and www.alsa.es for coaches. There are only four airports close to the Vía: Sevilla (SVQ), Madrid (MAD), Santiago de Compostela (SCQ) and A Coruña (LCG); you will need to use trains or coaches if starting anywhere other than Sevilla. Journey duration times provided below are the minimum to be expected. Note that trains get booked up quickly during national and school holidays.

### Getting to Sevilla

A bus service runs regularly from the airport to the centre (¾hr). Santa Justa railway station serves the AVE high-speed rail line, with trains from Madrid taking 2½hr. Alsa coaches also connect Sevilla to other major cities.

## Getting to Mérida

It is best to fly into Sevilla and take the train (3¼hr) or coach (2¼hr). Alternatively, fly into Madrid and take a train (3¾hr) or coach (4¾hr).

## Getting to Cáceres

From Sevilla, the train takes 4hr and the coach 3¼hr. The coach from Mérida takes 55min.

## Getting to Salamanca

From Madrid, the train takes 1¾hr and there is no direct coach. There are coach options from Sevilla (7hr), Mérida (4hr) and Zamora (3½hr).

## Getting to Zamora

Direct trains run from Madrid (1¼hr), Santiago de Compostela (2hr) and A Coruña (2½hr).

## Getting to Granja de Moreruela

The only option is to take a coach from Zamora on the Zamora–Astorga line (½hr). Check the Alsa website, as timings vary during the year. In January 2023, there is only one coach a day as follows: Monday–Thursday at 16:25, Friday at 17:25, Saturday at 13:10, and Sunday at 10:55.

## Getting to A Gudiña

Direct trains run from Madrid (2hr), Zamora (50min), Santiago de Compostela (1½hr) and A Coruña (2hr).

## Getting to Ourense

Direct trains run from Madrid (2½hr), Santiago de Compostela (40min) and A Coruña (1hr).

## Leaving Santiago de Compostela

Trains to A Coruña take ½hr, and 3hr to Madrid. City buses leave from Praza Galicia and the train station for SCQ airport every 30 minutes. The journey can take between 35 and 55 minutes and costs around €3 (www.tussa.org).

## WHEN TO GO

This is perhaps the most asked question and most important consideration, since the Vía is infamous for its extreme weather patterns.

Summer along the entire Vía is very hot, prone to wildfires, and potentially dangerous due to lack of regular drinking water and shade. Walking in July and August is only recommended with prior experience of walking in 40°C or more. During heatwaves, such as that of 2022, temperatures can rise to almost 50°C and albergues can be stifling, with night temperatures exceeding 35°C. There is no air conditioning, and rarely has a fan been sighted. Even an early morning start entails 30°C by 09:00.

In winter, Andalucía and the southern parts of Extremadura are often sunny and remain dry. Galicia is cold, rainy and even snowy, and the elevation on the Castilla y León Meseta brings glacial wind and rain as well as very cold nights. From November through to February, river/stream crossings and flooding on certain sections indicated in this book can cause further complications and hindrances. There is rarely any heating in albergues.

The best months for walking are mid to end of September, October, March, April, May and June, as shown in Tables 1 and 2.

Table 1: 2021 indicative average high/low temperatures in °C, rain days (R) and daylight hours (S)

| Elevation | Sevilla 8m | | | Mérida 224m | | | Salamanca 804m | | | Ourense 143m | | | Santiago de Compostela 261m | | |
|---|---|---|---|---|---|---|---|---|---|---|---|---|---|---|---|
| | °C | R | S | °C | R | S | °C | R | S | °C | R | S | °C | R | S |
| Jan | 16/6 | 6 | 10 | 13/1 | 6 | 10 | 9/0 | 5 | 10 | 12/5 | 11 | 10 | 12/5 | 13 | 9 |
| Feb | 18/7 | 5 | 11 | 15/2 | 5 | 11 | 11/0 | 4 | 11 | 13/5 | 9 | 11 | 13/5 | 9 | 11 |
| Mar | 21/9 | 5 | 12 | 18/5 | 5 | 12 | 15/2 | 5 | 12 | 16/7 | 9 | 12 | 15/6 | 10 | 11 |
| Apr | 23/11 | 5 | 13 | 21/7 | 6 | 13 | 16/4 | 6 | 13 | 17/8 | 10 | 13 | 16/7 | 11 | 12 |
| May | 27/14 | 3 | 14 | 26/11 | 5 | 14 | 20/8 | 6 | 15 | 20/11 | 9 | 15 | 18/9 | 9 | 14 |
| Jun | 32/18 | 1 | 15 | 31/15 | 2 | 15 | 26/11 | 4 | 15 | 25/14 | 5 | 15 | 22/12 | 6 | 15 |
| Jul | 35/20 | 0 | 14 | 34/17 | 1 | 15 | 29/13 | 2 | 15 | 28/15 | 3 | 15 | 24/14 | 4 | 15 |
| Aug | 35/20 | 0 | 14 | 34/17 | 1 | 14 | 29/13 | 2 | 14 | 28/16 | 4 | 14 | 24/14 | 4 | 15 |
| Sep | 31/18 | 2 | 12 | 30/14 | 4 | 12 | 25/10 | 4 | 12 | 25/14 | 6 | 12 | 22/13 | 6 | 12 |
| Oct | 26/15 | 6 | 11 | 23/10 | 7 | 11 | 19/7 | 7 | 11 | 20/11 | 11 | 11 | 18/11 | 12 | 11 |
| Nov | 20/10 | 6 | 10 | 18/5 | 6 | 10 | 13/3 | 6 | 10 | 15/8 | 12 | 10 | 14/8 | 13 | 10 |
| Dec | 17/7 | 7 | 10 | 14/2 | 7 | 10 | 9/0 | 6 | 9 | 12/6 | 12 | 9 | 12/6 | 12 | 9 |
| Best | Feb, Mar, Apr, Oct, Nov | | | Mar, Apr, May, Oct, Nov | | | May, Jun, Sep, Oct | | | May, Jun, Sep | | | May, Jun, Jul, Aug, Sep | | |

**Table 2: 2021 indicative maximum high/low temperatures in °C**

| Elevation | Sevilla 18m | | Mérida 224m | | Salamanca 804m | | Ourense 143m | | Santiago de Compostela 261m | |
|---|---|---|---|---|---|---|---|---|---|---|
| | Max °C | Min °C | Max °C | Min °C | Max °C | Min °C | Max °C | Min °C | Max °C | Min °C |
| Jan | 23 | -4 | 14 | -3 | 19 | -12 | 15 | -5 | 23 | -4 |
| Feb | 21 | 0 | 22 | 3 | 19 | -3 | 19 | 0 | 21 | 0 |
| Mar | 25 | 2 | 32 | 3 | 29 | -6 | 26 | 2 | 25 | 2 |
| Apr | 24 | 3 | 33 | 5 | 29 | -2 | 23 | 3 | 24 | 3 |
| May | 30 | 2 | 34 | 5 | 30 | 2 | 27 | 1 | 30 | 2 |
| Jun | 34 | 9 | 36 | 9 | 33 | 7 | 30 | 6 | 34 | 9 |
| Jul | 39 | 13 | 39 | 11 | 35 | 6 | 34 | 10 | 39 | 13 |
| Aug | 43 | 13 | 43 | 14 | 39 | 8 | 31 | 10 | 43 | 13 |
| Sep | 34 | 13 | 38 | 11 | 33 | 4 | 30 | 9 | | 34 |
| Oct | 29 | 6 | 30 | 6 | 27 | -3 | 26 | 4 | 29 | 6 |
| Nov | 21 | -1 | 25 | 0 | 21 | -5 | 17 | 3 | 21 | -1 |
| Dec | 22 | 0 | 20 | 0 | 21 | -4 | 18 | 3 | 22 | 0 |
| Most extreme heat | Jun, Jul, Aug, Sep | | May, Jun, Jul, Aug, Sep | | Jul, Aug | | Jul | | Jun, Jul, Aug, Sep | |
| Most extreme cold | Jan | | Jan | | Jan, Feb, Mar, Oct, Nov, Dec | | Jan | | Jan | |

*Pilgrims take to the road early to complete the longer days (Stage 35)*

Weather is a deciding factor for many pilgrims on the Vía and determines how busy it is at any given time. Overall, the most popular months are March, April and May.

Note that several albergues close over winter and, although there are alternative lodgings, winter walking incurs a bigger budget.

## PLANNING YOUR DAY TO DAY ON THE CAMINO

Unlike on other Caminos, it is essential to look at and plan stages in advance to ensure that you get the most out of your trip and can manage the distance.

### Stage planning

Some stages are unavoidable and very hard, such as Stages 3 (29.5km) and 15 (33.2km). Other long stages, including Stages 18, 20, 21, 39 and 40, are suggested in order to offer walkers an opportunity to stay at recommended albergues. Stages 35A and 36A may appear daunting but both can easily be divided exactly into two. Before every stage, inspect the distances, ascent and descent, and the availability of provisions. If a section is unmanageable, ask your albergue or in a café for local up to date public transport and taxi services.

### Provisions along the stage

There are times when it is vital to prepare and shop for the walk the day before, for example ahead of Stage 3. If a drinking fountain or service is not mentioned in the route description, assume there isn't one. Checking what lies ahead will make all the difference and can be life-saving.

### Provisions at stage end

Stages have been organized with access to provisions in mind. The only location without 100% reliable food options at stage end is Santa Marta de Tera (Stage 29); however, there are eateries in the town before it, 1km away.

## Accommodation closures

Details of accommodation are included in each listing and, where possible, the stages end at albergues that are open year-round. Where an albergue is closed at any time, alternative accommodation options are suggested, the only exceptions being Puerto de Béjar (Stage 19) and Alberguería (Stage 36), where the albergues close over winter. Both stages can easily be rearranged: for example, on Stage 19, you can finish 3km early and stay in the excellent albergue in Baños de Montemayor.

## ACCOMMODATION

There are different types of accommodation along the Vía de la Plata and Camino Sanabrés, but the majority will be albergues since many towns do not see any tourists except for pilgrims. Indeed, the location of albergues will define the choice of stage/distance to be accomplished on any one day.

During winter months, bearing in mind Spain's lovely spontaneous lifestyle, many pilgrims find it reassuring to call in advance to check that a place is open, even if hosts have confirmed precise dates for this guidebook. Booking ahead, where possible, is a personal preference.

## Albergues

Sometimes still known as *refugios* (shelters), albergues are pilgrim hostels. Many are *albergues municipales*, meaning they are run by the local authority, and booking ahead is usually not an option. There are also some privately run albergues that sometimes have private rooms in addition to dormitory accommodation and where reservations are possible.

All albergues offer low-cost accommodation in dorms (usually in bunk beds) and, unlike on the more traversed Caminos, the ones on the Vía are very modest. They tend not to have heating or air conditioning, no bedding or towels are provided, and only some have kitchens. There is always a mattress and pillow.

In Galicia, *albergues municipales* are run by the Xunta de Galicia (the government of Galicia) and cost €8. They hand out paper covers for mattresses and pillows, but no bedding. At best there may be a fridge and/or microwave. Before Galicia, some *albergues donativos* offer a true pilgrim experience, community dinners and breakfasts, and rely solely on donations to run.

Be sure to check for updates at www.cicerone.co.uk/1080/updates, as albergues may close or new ones may open.

## Hotels

On the Vía and Camino Sanabrés, there are three types of hotels: *hoteles*, *hostales* and *pensiones*. They do not differ hugely, although *hoteles* are usually bigger and the other two are smaller family-run businesses. Hotels often offer pilgrim rates. Some *casas rurales* (holiday lets) are included, where relevant, on the stages; although ordinarily these are entire homes/apartments, they also offer individual rooms and discounts to pilgrims with the *credencial*. In all these establishments, private rooms with

either a private or shared bathroom can be reserved in advance.

### Camping

There are few campsites along the Vía de la Plata and wild camping is illegal in these four regions of Spain. In fact, it is particularly difficult on the Vía due to lack of water sources and pitching places. Under no circumstances should fires be lit.

### FOOD

If you have been to Spain, and especially if you have walked a Camino, you already know what to expect when eating out.

Breakfast options tend to be a sweet pastry such as a croissant, toast with butter and jam or, if you have more of a savoury tooth, toasted baguette with olive oil and tomato purée topped with ham and/or cheese. Snacks available throughout the day are *tortilla* slices, olives (usually stuffed with anchovies), or sandwiches filled with options such as cheese, ham, *chorizo* or pork fillet.

Lunchtime and evening *menús del día* (dishes of the day) are an affordable three-course copious event. The Vía and Sanabrés do not yet have a trend for *menús peregrinos* (pilgrim menus) so pilgrims eat like locals and, because many towns are not tourist destinations, prices are low. Starter options tend to be: salads with lettuce, tomatoes, white asparagus, sweetcorn, grated carrots, olives, eggs and tuna, so specify if you want to remove any of those items; pasta with a tomato and meat sauce; or a stew usually made from chickpeas and meat or spinach. Main courses almost always involve fries and a choice between beef, pork or fish. Common desserts are flan, ice cream and canned fruit. Set menus always include bread, a soft or alcoholic beverage, water and coffee. For vegan and vegetarian pilgrims, and generally all those who like to incorporate fruit and vegetables into their daily diet, supermarkets are convenient because *menús del día* have few such items.

There are many à la carte dishes to pick from and it is common in Spain to order a spread and share. These sharing sizes are called *raciones*, whereas *tapas* are in fact mostly individual portions served with a soft or alcoholic drink.

All the above applies to the entire Vía and Sanabrés, but there are also some alluring specialities. Andalucía is known for fish and seafood, usually deep-fried with light batter. *Gazpacho*, a blended soup of tomatoes, peppers, cucumber, garlic, olive oil and bread, is especially refreshing on a hot day, as is its egg-and-ham-topped variation called *salmorejo*. Depending on your preference, you may wish to try the Iberian ham, *jamón de bellota*, either in Andalucía or Extremadura. In Alcuéscar (Stage 12) locals enjoy *ancas de rana*, battered frogs' legs with a vinegar dressing, and further up through Extremadura a spread made of pork, potato and heaps of paprika, called *patatera*, is very popular. *Migas extremeñas* are another Extremaduran speciality: breadcrumbs fried with pork, peppers and garlic.

Cáceres and Salamanca have delicious *tapas* of all sorts, from toast with cuttlefish to black pudding to barbecued Mediterranean vegetables. It is enough

*Traditional Galician food: Padrón green peppers, and octopus covered in paprika and olive oil*

to step up to the counter and witness the sweep of goodies to know that you will be in gastronomical bliss. In Castilla y León, pork products and beef steak are most common, for example pigs' ears in Santa Croya de Tera (Stage 29). Throughout Galicia, eating *pulpo* (octopus) and other sautéed seafood platters is almost unavoidable.

Once in Santiago, treat yourself to the *Tarta de Santiago*: made of ground almonds, almost frangipane-like, this soft buttery cake is decorated with Santiago's cross.

## BUDGET PLANNING

The Vía is one of the less expensive Caminos, which is helpful, considering the number of weeks involved. Accommodation is available at prices ranging from €5 to €12. Eating out is affordable and portions are very generous. The *menú del día* usually costs between €8 and €13, and breakfasts, snacks and drinks can easily cost under €5 per day. With a soft beverage or a glass of wine or beer, there is almost always a snack provided (such as olives, crisps or *tortilla* slice). Several albergues have kitchen facilities, and the reasonable prices in supermarkets benefit budgeting further.

Expect a daily budget of between €15 and €40 per day if you plan on staying in dorms, cooking or eating a *menú del día*, and enjoying pre-dinner drinks (*aperitivos*) and snacks. Private single rooms range from €15 to €70, depending on location, and doubles from €30 to €100.

## PREPARATION AND TRAINING

Although pilgrims embark on many of the popular Caminos with little to no experience of long-distance walking and do not encounter any major difficulties, the Vía de la Plata is a completely different story. Preparation (or lack of it) could end up being a deciding factor in whether you complete the trek or have to abandon it. The main concern is the ability to carry sufficient water and food on long stretches where you may not meet a soul. For some, on a warm 30km+ day, 4 litres of water may not suffice.

Many pilgrims who take on the Vía tend to have already done other Caminos and/or long-distance backpacking routes. Camino novices can undeniably have a brilliant problem-free time, but only with a thorough understanding of what challenges may arise. To help avoid stress and situations that can lead to abandoning the trek, physical injury or worse, this guidebook aims to provide the knowledge of what to expect, as well as recommendations to help you have the loveliest of Caminos. Thanks to the serene landscapes, with no sections requiring any technical skills, there are many opportunities for reflection, which is what helps to make the Vía such a wonderful experience.

Training for the Camino builds muscle strength and is necessary for breaking in the shoes and backpack that you plan to wear. Absolutely essential is blister prevention, so try to purchase your walking shoes, including spares, six months in advance and wear them as often as possible. An ideal programme to start at least three months before departure is:

*A pilgrim crosses over rocks above Río Esla on Stage 28 (photo: Marisol Canovas)*

- Wear your main shoes as often as possible.
- Start walking at least 10–15km two/three times per week.
- Start walking two days in a row and with a packed backpack + 2 litres of water.
- Try to fit in a 25–30km+ walk once a week (ideally with the backpack).
- Walk a route of 35–40km to see how it feels.

Additional strengthening exercises might include: using a cross trainer at the gym (wearing your backpack); Pilates for core work, glutes and quads; sit-ups and crunches; shoulder and back exercises such as push-ups and dead lifts; stretching; and regular ankle and neck rotations.

Two helpful articles are www.cicerone.co.uk/how-to-get-hill-fit-and-train-for-long-distance-walking and www.cicerone.co.uk/how-to-walk-a-camino-without-blistering-pain.

Generally, the aim of the packing game is to ensure that your bag weighs a maximum of 10% of your bodyweight, including provisions. Variations on this depend on the season, region and a pilgrim's size or experience. On the Vía and Camino Sanabrés, always consider that you will need to leave space for water and some food. Essential items are:

- 40-litre capacity backpack
- Year-round: rain cover for your pack, poncho/waterproof jacket
- Waterproof trousers (except June–September)

- Walking shoes (lightweight trail for summer, waterproof trail for winter) and hiking sandals for switching into and for evenings
- Clothes: two quick-dry T-shirts, a long-sleeved layer (light for summer, fleece or thermal for winter), two pairs of shorts, one pair of trousers; gloves and a neck buff are also helpful in the colder months. (Clothes depend on the season: many parts of the Vía are walked at an altitude close to 700–900m above sea level, making mornings and evenings cool, and even freezing, during late autumn, winter and early spring.)
- Bedding: in summer, a light two-season sleeping bag is largely sufficient; in winter, since albergues rarely have heating, a bag that goes down to at least 0°C will help to ensure a good night's sleep; a large pillowcase is also a nice luxury, but a T-shirt suffices for some pilgrims. (Most albergues, apart from a small handful, do not provide blankets.)
- Reusable water bottles, preferably with an insulation system to keep your water cool: two 1.5-litre bottles in summer are advisable, even if not kept filled to the top; they can be used to quench your thirst and to soak your hat or hair
- Protection: summer or winter hat, sunscreen and sunglasses
- Insect repellent
- Basic first-aid kit, including blister plasters
- Quick-dry lightweight towel
- Toiletries, including shampoo that works as body wash and for washing clothes by hand
- Some toilet paper/tissues with a few small plastic bags, for when nature calls en route
- Hiking poles
- Phone (and camera) and chargers with European adaptors
- Debit/Credit cards and cash (most places only accept cash)
- Travel/Identity documents (originals and photocopies) in a plastic wallet/ziplock sandwich bag
- Head torch for reading in bed, getting up in the night and early morning starts
- Earplugs
- *Credencial* (pilgrim passport)
- Some personal favourites for summer are a head net for protection against mosquitoes and other insects, and/or a fan, to not only swipe those pests away but also cool down
- Another preferred item is an umbrella for winter or parasol for summer
- For picnicking pilgrims: a knife, fork and plastic container (which also helps store that delicious cheese) can come in handy

## BAGGAGE AND STORAGE SERVICES

In contrast to the affordable options for luggage transfers on the Camino Francés and Camino del Norte, the Vía does not have a backpack transfer service for individual pilgrims until Ourense (Stage 38) or Astorga (extension route), which emphasizes the importance of packing light. Local taxi services will help, although they charge for the journey as though carrying a passenger, not as a luggage transfer service, so a distance of 10km can cost anywhere between €15 and €20.

From Ourense, the existing (2023) baggage transfer service is called MochilaTrans and is run by José Angel (tel 629 035 774). The service only runs from April until October and costs €5 per stage, payable in cash. It is important to book via message/WhatsApp or phone. You must then fill in your details (name, contact information and destination) and pay using the envelopes available in albergues. Between Zamora and Ourense, MochilaTrans will also do transfers at €5–7 depending on location and distance, but only if they receive a minimum of five requests at any one time. From Easter until 31 October, the Spanish postal service provides bag transfers between Ourense to Santiago at a total cost of €55. You must

reserve this online with all your stages planned and accommodation booked in advance. The webpage is available in English: www.elcaminoconcorreos.com

To send items ahead and store them in Santiago de Compostela, take them to a local post office. (Post office locations can be searched for on the Spanish postal service website: www.correos.es/es/es/herramientas/oficinas-buzones-citypaq/detalle.) Ivar Revke, who hosts the largest English-speaking Camino Forum (www.caminodesantiago.me) and has been helping pilgrims in Santiago since 2004, offers luggage storage in Santiago. Address your parcel to Casa Ivar in Santiago (ivar@casaivar.com, https://casaivar.com), as follows:

Casa IvarATT: [Your name goes here] Travesía da Universidad 115704 Santiago de Compostela España

*A quick detour on the way down to Almadén offers a moment of reflection at the Cruz de la Paz (Stage 3)*

## LOCAL FACILITIES AND PRACTICAL INFORMATION

Getting to know the ins and outs of Spain's services helps you to plan ahead, particularly regarding access to drinking water and food.

**Drinking water** is regularly available in villages, towns and cities. Often there is a sign stating *agua potable* (drinking water) or *agua tratada* (treated water), to confirm that the water is drinkable. Warnings for untreated water are also given: *agua no tratada*. If there is no sign, inspect the tap: if you have to turn it on for the water to flow, it can be considered safe to drink. All of them have been tested by the author but, of course, it is an individual decision. Make sure that the tap is turned off before you leave.

Opening hours for **shops**, **small supermarkets** and **pharmacies** are straightforward. On weekdays, they tend to open between 08:00 and 14:00 and then from 16:00–20:00 (big supermarkets close around 22:00). On Saturdays, they only open in the mornings, and on Sundays and national or local holidays they are closed all day. Usually, there is an emergency 24/7 pharmacy in the vicinity, but it will probably require taking a taxi. They are called *farmacias de guardia* and can be located by province at www.farmaceuticos.com/farmacias-de-guardia. It is best to ask in the albergue or local bar.

**Eating out** is very popular in Spain, and food can be found somewhere in town at most times. Café/bars may open as early as 07:00 but usually not before 08:00. They serve hot and cold drinks and snacks (*tortilla*, sandwiches, crisps, chocolate bars) throughout the day and into the evening. Restaurants with more substantial meals and *menús del día* tend to open between 13:00 and 16:00, and then from 20:00 (or later) until very late. On more remote sections of the route, the cafés and restaurants on the national highways (usually part of a petrol station complex) will be the most reliable source of nourishment. Note that all petrol stations have basic snacks and drinks. A handy trick for those who like their coffee/tea and/or breakfast before setting out is to purchase it the night before as a takeaway, especially if your lodgings have a microwave.

**Public transport** and **taxis** are few and far between on this Camino but, if required, the albergue or local bar will have the most up-to-date details. You will find out from them that bus services do exist even though they may not always be listed online or appear on your phone's map.

**Paying by cash** is still the only method in the majority of albergues and café/bars along the way. **ATMs** for cash withdrawals are indicated by a symbol in municipal information boxes (see 'How to use this guide', Figure 1), so plan accordingly.

In addition to being useful in emergencies, the benefits of carrying a **mobile phone** are twofold. Firstly, they are useful for digital maps and for the GPX files available with this guidebook. Additionally, some albergue hosts leave their phone numbers on the door, so calling them may make all the difference between waiting around in unbearable weather conditions for hours or speedily making yourself at home. Mobile data access and phone reception is available almost constantly on the trail.

Throughout summer, in many of the towns on the Camino local **outdoor swimming pools** are open in the afternoons and evenings. They are called *piscina municipal* and the fee ranges between €1-€5.

## Taking your dog

The Vía is a hostile environment for dogs: the burning heat in the air and off the ground is life-threatening, and drinking fountains are scarce on long days. To add to this, if you have a dog with you, local dogs will become more of a nuisance. Most albergues do not accept dogs under any conditions, and in Spain only dogs weighing under 10kg and inside a pet carrier are permitted in the luggage compartments of coaches and on trains.

## WAYMARKING, SHELLS AND SYMBOLS

The Vía is well signed with various traditional Camino symbols, such as yellow scallop shells and yellow arrows on road ramps, road signs, trees, rocks, gates, walls and lamp posts, and on the ground. Original Roman mile markers (*miliarios*) also provide excellent waymarking tools as well as historical interest, whether standing proudly intact or in pieces, often *in situ*. To compensate for the missing ones, many modern mile markers have been erected, particularly on the way in and out of towns in Castilla y León; they are often inscribed with 'Camino Mozárabe', named after the Camino that unites with the Vía in Mérida. Helpful information boards are positioned along the way throughout.

In addition, some regions have their statement waymarking. For example, the Sierra Norte, just after Sevilla, has its own waymarking bollards. The Extremadura region uses a cube featuring a carving of the Arco de Cáparra, with colour-coded directions: the yellow directs pilgrims on the Camino, whereas the turquoise-green is more specific to the route defined by the old Roman road.

Nearing Salamanca, a yellow triangle on a silver plaque directs the way, while in Castilla y León the villages have unique stone slabs welcoming pilgrims. Galicia is undoubtedly the best-signed region, with its iconic distance-waymarking blocks, so getting lost is almost impossible.

Major highways and local roads also lead the way, and it is extremely useful to get to know how they work. For safety, when the Camino merges with a major road, pilgrims are informed by a sign stating *tramo común con* (shared section with); when the Camino crosses a road, the sign says *intersección con* (junction with).

Walking routes in Spain often lie alongside and even on national highways, equivalent to A roads in the UK. This may seem unpleasant, but on the Vía there is always space on either side for pedestrians and cyclists. Reassuringly, there is next to no traffic at most times, as the parallel toll-free motorways are preferred by locals and tourists alike. On the Vía de la Plata up to Benavente, the Camino consistently follows the quiet N-630 national highway and keeps near the A-66 motorway. From Benavente to Astorga it follows the N-VI and A-6. The Camino Sanabrés traces a line alongside the N-525 as well as motorways A-52 to Ourense and then the AP-53 to Santiago.

Finally, it is important to understand local road codes. The first two letters represent the province, for example OU relates to Ourense. On the Sevilla–Astorga route, roads are coded as follows: SE for Sevilla; EX for Extremadura, throughout the region; BA for Badajoz, from just after El Real de la Jara (Stage 4); CC for Cáceres, just before Alcuéscar (Stage 12); SA for Salamanca, from Puerto de Béjar (Stage 19); ZA for Zamora, from El Cubo de Tierra del Vino (Stage 25); LE for León, from just before Alija del Infantado (extension to Astorga).

On the Camino Sanabrés, the road code is ZA until the route enters Galicia after Lubián (Stage 34). Then the Camino follows OU for Ourense; PO for

*Waymarks include Camino yellow shells and arrows, hiking route signs, local and regional signage, and original or replica mile markers*

Pontevedra, from Castro Dozón (Stage 39 or 40); and AC for A Coruña, from Ponte Ulla (Stage 42) until Santiago de Compostela.

## SAFETY AND HEALTH

For all emergencies in Spain, dial 112.

### Crime

Violence and crime are low in Spain but, in the unlikely event of witnessing or experiencing such behaviour, report it immediately to your host and the police.

### Animals

The creatures you will come across most often will be cattle, pigs and dogs. None present problems, although the dogs do tend to bark, which can feel uncomfortable or just a nuisance. It is best to ignore them and continue on your merry way, as they are simply guarding livestock and sending out a warning. Even though most are friendly or uninterested, it is essential that you report an aggressive dog immediately to the police who quickly react in order to ensure pilgrims are kept safe. If you are concerned, carry a dog deterrent whistle, hold your hiking poles up high and avoid walking alone.

There are wolves and snakes at several points on the Vía. The former are very rarely seen. Regarding snakes, it is important to use a head torch when walking in the dark, particularly in the morning on asphalt, as they enjoy the warmth from the ground; but again, it is unlikely that you will come across a snake.

Bedbugs have not caused any issues on the Vía or Sanabrés, but there have been occasional fleas, which are easy to spot and are dealt with immediately by the hostel hosts. The most problematic beasts you will encounter are mosquitoes and flies.

### Avoiding injuries

The trail has no technical sections requiring scrambling, climbing or specialist equipment. To avoid complications, top tips include:

- Judge the amount of paved walking on a stage and select your shoes accordingly.
- On hot days, drink plenty, but also use fountains to cool down your body, for example dampen your hair and hat.
- If the weather is slowing you down, avoid the temptation to run, as this places unnecessary pressure on your knees and feet.
- Zigzag up and down steep hills.
- Walk facing the oncoming traffic.
- Use grassy or gravel edges alongside asphalted sections, where possible.
- Prevent blisters by applying blister plasters to high-risk areas, rather than allowing the blister to form.

# HOW TO USE THIS GUIDE

*Wide dirt tracks make for comfortable walking along the Vía de la Plata (Stage 1)*

This guidebook aims to provide thorough descriptions, maps, accommodation listings and stage suggestions to enable pilgrims to find exact locations and feel reassured along what is a solitary route. Appendix A supplies helpful **stage planning tables** to help you determine your own stages, although the Vía and Sanabrés do not always allow for much imagination or flexibility.

Each stage begins with a summary of key information:

**Stage starts and finishes** tend to be at albergues, so that pilgrims have an opportunity to refresh before exploring a town.

**Distance** statistics show the precise total distance between accommodation options at the start and finish points of the recommended route.

**Ascent and descent figures** show the total amount of ascent and descent for the stage, and should be examined in conjunction with **elevation profiles**. Data was gathered using Gaia GPS.

The **difficulty** of each stage is rated as easy, moderate, hard or very hard,

taking into account length, duration, steepness, terrain and frequency of services.

The **duration** excludes breaks and is calculated using a formula based on 4.5km per hour. For every 100m of ascent, 10min are added.

Precise **percentages of paved surfaces** are given, since paved and asphalted surfaces can be harder on your feet and may determine your shoe selection.

Distances to **albergues** and other **accommodation** options are rounded to the nearest 0.1km, so there may be slight variations between stage totals and cumulative intermediate distances.

A **stage overview** gives an overall description and tips with regard to provisions and the type of terrain covered.

Within the walking directions, **distances** between specific features aid with navigation, and **bold** is used to highlight **places and landmarks** that are labelled on the corresponding route maps. For ease, the following abbreviations are used:

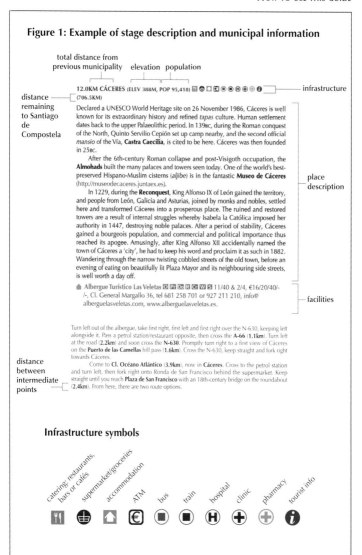

## Figure 1: Example of stage description and municipal information

total distance from
previous municipality   elevation   population

**12.0KM CÁCERES** (ELEV 388M, POP 95,418) 🍴 🛒 🏠 € ▣ ▣ H ✚ ✚ ❶ ☐ ⟵ infrastructure
distance ⟶ (706.5KM)
remaining
to Santiago
de
Compostela

Declared a UNESCO World Heritage site on 26 November 1986, Cáceres is well known for its extraordinary history and refined *tapas* culture. Human settlement dates back to the upper Palaeolithic period. In 139BC, during the Roman conquest of the North, Quinto Servilio Cepión set up camp nearby, and the second official *mansio* of the Vía, **Castra Caecilia**, is cited to be here. Cáceres was then founded in 25BC.

After the 6th-century Roman collapse and post-Visigoth occupation, the **Almohads** built the many palaces and towers seen today. One of the world's best-preserved Hispano-Muslim cisterns (*aljibe*) is in the fantastic **Museo de Cáceres** (http://museodecaceres.juntaex.es).

In 1229, during the **Reconquest**, King Alfonso IX of León gained the territory, and people from León, Galicia and Asturias, joined by monks and nobles, settled here and transformed Cáceres into a prosperous place. The ruined and restored towers are a result of internal struggles whereby Isabela la Católica imposed her authority in 1447, destroying noble palaces. After a period of stability, Cáceres gained a bourgeois population, and commercial and political importance thus reached its apogee. Amusingly, after King Alfonso XII accidentally named the town of Cáceres a 'city', he had to keep his word and proclaim it as such in 1882. Wandering through the narrow twisting cobbled streets of the old town, before an evening of eating on beautifully lit Plaza Mayor and its neighbouring side streets, is well worth a day off.

⟵ place description

🏠 Albergue Turístico Las Veletas ◎ 🄿 🄴 🅁 🄶 🅆 🅂 11/40 & 2/4, €16/20/40/-/-, Cl. General Margallo 36, tel 681 258 701 or 927 211 210, info@alberguelasveletas.com, www.alberguelasveletas.es.

⟵ facilities

Turn left out of the albergue, take first right, first left and first right over the N-630, keeping left alongside it. Pass a petrol station/restaurant opposite, then cross the **A-66** (**1.1km**). Turn left at the road (**2.2km**) and soon cross the **N-630**. Promptly turn right to a first view of Cáceres on the **Puerto de las Camellas** hill pass (**1.6km**). Cross the N-630, keep straight and fork right towards Cáceres.

distance
between
intermediate
points

Come to **Cl. Océano Atlántico** (**3.9km**), now in Cáceres. Cross to the petrol station and turn left, then fork right onto Ronda de San Francisco behind the supermarket. Keep straight until you reach **Plaza de San Francisco** with an 18th-century bridge on the roundabout (**2.4km**). From here, there are two route options.

## Infrastructure symbols

catering; restaurants, bars or cafés   supermarket/groceries   accommodation   ATM   bus   train   hospital   clinic   pharmacy   tourist info

🍴 🛒 🏠 € ▣ ▣ H ✚ ✚ ❶

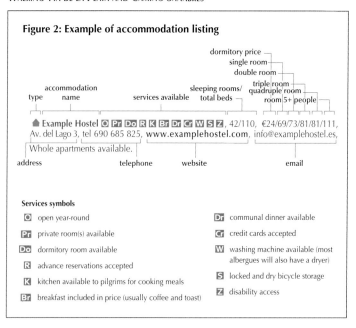

Figure 2: Example of accommodation listing

**Services symbols**

| | | | |
|---|---|---|---|
| **O** | open year-round | **Dr** | communal dinner available |
| **Pr** | private room(s) available | **Cr** | credit cards accepted |
| **Do** | dormitory room available | **W** | washing machine available (most albergues will also have a dryer) |
| **R** | advance reservations accepted | **S** | locked and dry bicycle storage |
| **K** | kitchen available to pilgrims for cooking meals | **Z** | disability access |
| **Br** | breakfast included in price (usually coffee and toast) | | |

| Abbreviation | Spanish | English |
|---|---|---|
| Av. | *avenida* | avenue/boulevard |
| Cl. | *calle* | road |
| Ctra. | *carretera* | road |
| Tr. | *travesía* | alley |

**Accommodation listings** are accurate at the beginning of 2023. Hotel prices may vary from those listed, which are the minimum rates to be expected. Several albergues tend to increase their rates slightly every year.

**Telephone numbers** are provided in their local form. If you are calling from outside Spain, use the international access code for the country you are calling from, followed by the country code for Spain (34) and then the number provided. For example, to call 677 588 499 from the UK, use 00 34 677 588 499.

### GPX DOWNLOAD

Free GPX tracks for the routes in this guidebook are available to download at www.trailblazer.co.uk/1080/GPX.

# SECTION 1:
# SEVILLA TO
# MÉRIDA

*Leaving the Sierra behind, the Camino winds through olive groves on the way to Calzadilla de los Barros (Stage 6)*

*Autumnal walking on red clay tracks on the way to La Almazara (Stage 8)*

The Camino leaves the city of Sevilla through the lively Triana neighbourhood, heading north to Guillena along mostly flat dirt tracks before entering the hillier Sierra Norte de Sevilla. Pilgrims are then immersed in the natural park's oak-planted pastures, the *dehesas*, for three days to Extremadura. Leaving the mountains and Andalucía behind, the route crosses 'los Barros', a land of olive groves, vineyards and red clay tracks.

Although the Vía de la Plata itself begins in Mérida, other Roman roads linked Sevilla with Mérida (Roman Emerita Augusta). Along the way there were intermediate stopping points, called *mansios*, in Santiponce (Itálica), Almadén de la Plata (Monte Mariorum), Monesterio (Curica) and Villafranca de los Barros (Perceiana).

Excitement builds on the approach to Mérida, which pilgrims eventually reach after some straightforward yet monotonous walking near Torremejía.

<hr>

### PLANNING

1   Most pilgrims follow the same first three stages and then start to tackle different distances after Almadén de la Plata.

2   Be sure to stock up on provisions in Castilblanco de los Arroyos, the day before Stage 3.

3   On Stage 8, the albergue in Villafranca de los Barros closes at unpredictable times of the year so a good alternative is to stay in La Almazara.

<hr>

### WHAT NOT TO MISS

On Stage 1, make time to visit Iberia's oldest Roman town, Itálica, in Santiponce, before the last 12.5km to Guillena. Walking through the Finca El Berrocal on Stage 3, look out for deer between oak trees on the slopes. Then, on Stage 5, go to the Museo del Jamón, Spain's best ham museum, in Monesterio. The town of Zafra (Stage 7) is a welcome comfort after the first week on the road, and preserves numerous buildings in Mudéjar style.

To fully enjoy the scale of Mérida's historic monuments, consider taking a day off from walking (Stage 10). Visit the glorious Roman remains, such as the amphitheatre, theatre, Temple of Diana, circus, thermal baths and aqueduct, to suggest but a few.

# STAGE 1
*Sevilla to Guillena*

| | |
|---|---|
| **Start** | Sevilla Cathedral |
| **Finish** | Guillena |
| **Distance** | 21.8km |
| **Total ascent** | 105m |
| **Total descent** | 110m |
| **Difficulty** | Easy |
| **Duration** | 5½hr |
| **Percentage paved** | 37% |
| **Albergues** | Santiponce 9.3km; Guillena 21.8km |

The adventure begins with a perfect introduction to the defining traits of the Vía de la Plata Camino route: the majestic UNESCO World Heritage sites of Sevilla, Roman ruins en route, comfortable dirt tracks, empty countryside, and the companionship of the almost traffic-free N-630 and the A-66 motorway. It is an ideal warm-up for the walking and presents no difficulties, although some parts may be very muddy after rainfall. Visiting the Roman ruins of Itálica and having a snack in Santiponce, midway through the stage, are both highly recommended.

**0KM SEVILLA (ELEV 18M, POP 684,234)** 🏨 ⊕ 🛆 Ⓒ Ⓜ Ⓜ Ⓗ ⊕ ⊕ ❶ **(995.3KM)**

Sevilla, Roman Hispalis, has always been a majestic and exciting city. Its streets lined with orange trees are constantly bathed in sunshine, and innumerable monuments amaze on every corner. A minimum of two days' sightseeing, and eating, are recommended to discover the home of flamenco, *Don Juan*, *Carmen* and *The Barber of Seville*. The magnificent **Catedral de Sevilla** takes centre stage, occupying the place where the great mosque once stood. When Sevilla was captured by the Christian armies, the mosque was used by Christians as a church until 1402, after which it was reconstructed in undeniable Gothic style to become the world's largest cathedral. Within the cathedral rest the remains of Christopher Columbus, and there is a fine art gallery with works by Zurbarán, Murillo and Goya, among others. In the north-eastern corner, climb the **Giralda tower**, a beautiful decorative minaret built at the height of Almohad power. The uppermost parts of the tower were added in the 16th century and at the very top, representing faith,

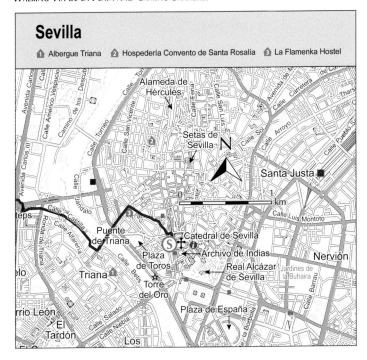

# Sevilla

1 Albergue Triana    2 Hospedería Convento de Santa Rosalía    3 La Flamenka Hostel

stands the symbol of Sevilla: El Giraldillo, a 16th-century bronze weathervane. There is a Pilgrim Mass at 08:30.

The **Alcázar** was built initially as a fort for the Cordoban governors of Sevilla in 913. It saw many expansions and reconstructions, including the 'blessed' palace and another palace that was added by the Almohads in the 12th century. Upon capturing Sevilla, King Fernando III, followed by other Christian monarchs in subsequent years, replaced much of the original with Gothic styles. The sublime Mudéjar palace seen today was the work of King Pedro I between 1364 and 1366.

The **Archivo de Indias** contains 80 million historical documents on Spain's American empire, dating from 1492 to the 19th century. Other irresistible treasures include the **Plaza de España**, the old **Jewish quarter** in the Santa Cruz neighbourhood, the **Torre del Oro**, the Arab baths, the **Andalucian Centre for Contemporary Art**, the huge mushroom structure called **Las Setas**, the **Royal**

**Shipyards**, the **Alameda de Hércules** square and tower, and the many churches and convents, gardens and riverside walks.

🛏 Albergue Triana ⬛⬛⬛⬛⬛⬛⬛ 11/50, €15, Cl. Rodrigo de Triana 69, tel 954 459 960, sevillatriana@gmail.com, **www.trianahostel.com**. Includes breakfast. Reservations recommended. Rents out bikes to pilgrims and sells the *credencial*. Open all year except 8 Jan–7 Feb inclusive.

🛏 Hospedería Convento de Santa Rosalía ⬛⬛⬛⬛ 30/56, €-/25/50, Cl. Cardenal Spínola 8, tel 954 383 209 or 682 313 072, casadeoracion. capuchinas@gmail.com. Essential to book two weeks in advance. Prices vary.

🛏 La Flamenka Hostel ⬛⬛⬛⬛⬛⬛ 7/45 & 10/24, €16/45/55/65, Cl. Reyes Católicos 11, tel 954 104 018, **https://laflamenkahostel.com**. Closed first fortnight in Aug.

The Vía commences at the west face of Sevilla Cathedral at the Puerta de la Asunción. Head north on Av. de la Constitución, left onto Cl. García de Vinuesa, where the first wall waymark appears, and right on Cl. Jimios. Keep straight at the fork, merging with Cl. Zaragoza, and turn left at the end of the road following tourist signs for Puente de Triana. Follow waymarks on the ground to cross the river via the **Puente de Triana** into the Triana neighbourhood (**1.1km**). The Puente de Triana, also called the Puente de Isabel II, spanning Río Guadalquivir, is the oldest bridge in Sevilla, completed in 1852.

Turn right onto Cl. San Jorge, right onto Cl. Calao and bend left, passing apartments. Stay on the tree-lined right-hand side of the road to take the **steps** on the right up to busy roads (**1.3km**). Cross the avenue at the lights ahead, then cross again using those to the left. Turn right behind bushes, and promptly turn left downhill towards a **car park**. Take the bridge over the **river**, along the cycle lane, with Camas ahead (**1.2km**). Adding 400 metres to the stage, an option in bad weather or for refreshments is to reach Santiponce via Camas (🍴⬤⬤⬤⬤).

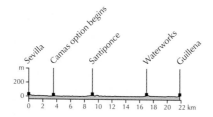

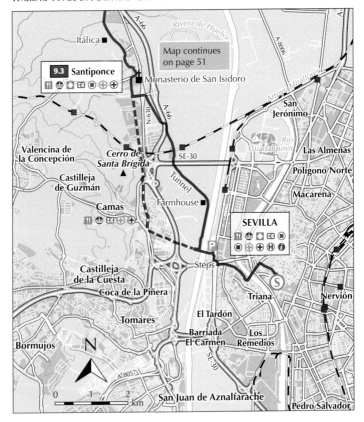

## Through Camas

Go straight ahead under the **A-66** and upon reaching the roundabout in town turn right onto Cl. José Payán. Keep straight on through **Camas**, passing café/bars, until you reach the junction with the N-630 and motorway exits. Go around the roundabout clockwise, taking the second exit towards a car garage followed by an industrial zone. Keep on for 2.2km to a roundabout in **Santiponce** to rejoin the main route.

## Direct route to Santiponce

Turn right down the path, going back towards the river. Take a left to a farmhouse, then right and through a **tunnel** (**2.6km**). Turn left to go under the **A-66** then right to a

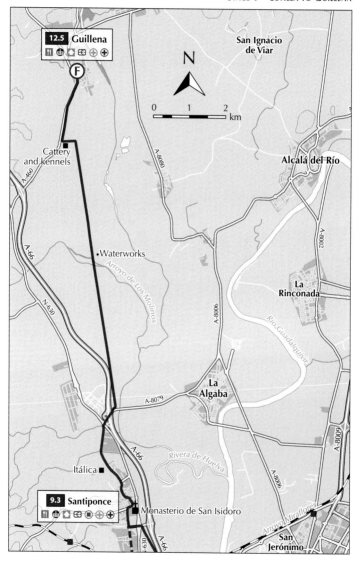

**12.5 Guillena**

San Ignacio de Viar

N

0   1   2 km

Cattery and kennels

Alcalá del Río

A-460

A-8090

A-66

N-630

•Waterworks

Arroyo de los Molinos

A-8006

La Rinconada

A-8002

Río Guadalquivir

La Algaba

A-8079

A-66

Rivera de Huelva

A-8006

A-8009

Itálica

**9.3 Santiponce**

Monasterio de San Isidoro

N-630

A-66

Arroyo Miraflores

San Jerónimo

51

roundabout (**2.1km**). Go left at this one (ignoring a confusing arrow pointing right) and then right at the next one, into **Santiponce**.

### 9.3KM SANTIPONCE (ELEV 12M, POP 8491) 🍴 ⊕ 🏠 🅲 ⊚ ⊕ ⊕ (986.0KM)

The splendid Gothic and Mudéjar-style **Monasterio de San Isidoro del Campo** was founded in 1301 and reformed by Cistercian and Jeronimo hermits in 1432. The first translation of the Bible into Spanish, known as the Biblia del Oso (Bible of the Bear), was made here.

🏠 Itálica Hostel 🅞 🅳🅾 🆁 🅺 3/26, €17, Plaza de la Constitución 10, tel 636 678 376.

**Main route**

With both options reunited, keep across the next roundabout and at the following one turn right behind the **Monasterio de San Isidoro**. Pass café/bars and head uphill to Itálica (**2.4km**).

Pilgrims start their 995km journey from the Catedral de Sevilla

The architectural site of **Itálica**, the first Roman city in Spain and birthplace of the emperors Trajan and Hadrian, is well worth a visit for its Roman walls, baths, theatre, amphitheatre, planetarium and arena. Open year-round, but check opening times to avoid disappointment (www.museosdeandalucia.es/web/conjuntoarqueologicodeitalica).

Keep to the same road towards the highway, cross over the roundabout and go under the **A-66** (**1.7km**). Turn left onto a wide dirt track and left again on to proceed on a very long straight stretch through wheatfields, passing **waterworks**.

Turn left towards a **cattery and kennels** (**7.7km**) then go right, alongside the **road**. The path steps down onto the road into **Guillena** and reaches the albergue on the left.

### 12.5KM GUILLENA (ELEV 24M, POP 13,054) 🍴 ⊕ 🏠 € ⊕ ⊕ (973.5KM)

Guillena is a bustling town with all services for pilgrims, showcasing the white-rendered yet colourfully decorated buildings that will become familiar in the towns to come. The **Iglesia Virgen de Granada** is in Mudéjar style, from the 15th and 16th centuries.

🏠 **Albergue Luz del Camino** Ⓞ Ⓓⓞ Ⓡ Ⓚ Ⓑⓡ Ⓦ Ⓢ 2/12, €14, Cl. Federico García Lorca 8, tel 955 785 262 or 667 727 380 or 665 068 222, pedroguillena@ hotmail.com.

# STAGE 2

## Guillena to
## Castilblanco de los Arroyos

| | |
|---|---|
| **Start** | Guillena |
| **Finish** | Castilblanco de los Arroyos |
| **Distance** | 18.2km |
| **Total ascent** | 445m |
| **Total descent** | 120m |
| **Difficulty** | Easy |
| **Duration** | 4¾hr |
| **Percentage paved** | 10% |
| **Albergues** | Castilblanco de los Arroyos 18.2km |

A serene landscape of gentle ups and downs between olive and cork oak trees dominates the day. The Camino winds through the Finca El Chaparral hunting estate and enters the territory of the Sierra Norte de Sevilla Natural Park. Grazing cattle and Iberian pigs may be present as well as local hunters and mountain bikers. Shade can be found, but prepare in advance since there are no provisions en route. Although a manual drinking water pump is signed after 10km, it is unreliable.

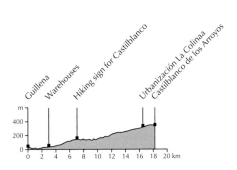

Leave the albergue and turn right onto Av. de los Príncipes towards the Parroquia Señora Nuestra de la Granada, after which go left onto Cl. Echegaral to reach the now closed *albergue municipal*. Turn right onto Cl. la Algaba to the river and a **ford** (**1.2km**).

Unless the river is easy to ford, turn left alongside it and then cross the river on the road bridge. If the river is fordable, turn right to cross it, then go left to meet the main route. Soon after crossing the road bridge, turn right onto a path, then turn left to arrive at a roundabout (**1.8km**). Alternatively, from the road bridge, keep to the road for 10min to join the main route at the roundabout.

From the roundabout, head towards the **warehouses** on the left, turn right and then promptly left onto a signed path among bamboo, which will lead through lovely *dehesas* almost all the way.

In 2002, these *dehesas* became part of the Sierra Morena's UNESCO Biosphere Reserve, and in 2015 the **Sierra Norte de Sevilla** gained its own UNESCO Global Geopark title. Its woodland has been cared for since the Neolithic period. The lush evergreen oaks make up an ideal landscape where Iberian pigs feed on acorns, cattle graze on nutritious grass and the trees themselves produce cork and charcoal.

Keep on past a **hiking sign for Castilblanco** (**4.7km**). Turn left and ramble down a narrow path to the left of the track. The Camino now flattens and becomes stonier and narrower before forking right to a **sign for (unreliable) drinking water** (**2.2km**) in a field on the right.

After 100 metres, make sure to **fork right**, as the waymark tends to be hidden among shrubs; 500 metres later, go right (the first arrow appears to point left) and over

Urbanización La Colina

N

0 1 2 km

Farmhouse

Fork right

unreliable

Sign for Castilblanco

*Embalse del Gergal*

*Rivera de Cala*

*Rivera de Huelva*

*Embalse de Castilblanco de los Arroyos*

Burguillos

A-460

San Ignacio de Viar

Road alternative Warehouses

N

0 1 2 km

Guillena

Ford

S

F

a cattle grid to reach a **farmhouse**. Eventually turn right onto a new track by a sign for Castilblanco (**3.3km**).

Reach a road (**0.9km**), cross over and follow the narrow path on its right-hand side past benches, coming parallel to the residential area of **Urbanización La Colina** (**2.3km**). Reach **Castilblanco de los Arroyos** by a road sign 1.1km later, and soon after pass a drinking fountain (**1.5km**). Arrive at a petrol station, after which immediately turn right following the sign for the albergue.

### 18.2KM CASTILBLANCO DE LOS ARROYOS (ELEV 324M, POP 5059) 🍴 ⊕ 🏠 (955.3KM)

With its whitewashed houses dazzling in the sun, Castilblanco offers all services to pilgrims in the town centre, down the road from the albergue. The well-stocked supermarket will help you prepare for the long day ahead tomorrow. The **Iglesia del Divino Salvador**, originally of Mudéjar construction and remodelled in the 16th and 17th centuries, displays the red and yellow contours common of the region, a unique trait of Spain's Moorish heritage.

🛏 Albergue de peregrinos de Castilblanco de los Arroyos 🅳🅾 🅺 🆂
 2/30, €Donation, Av. Antonio Machado s/n, tel 955 734 811,
 oficinaturismocastilblanco@gmail.com. Closed 1 Nov–27 Feb.

🛏 Casa Salvadora 🅾 🅿🆁 🆁 🆂 8/16, €-/17/30/-/-, Av. España 43, tel 615 500 963.

🛏 Hotel Castillo Blanco ** 🅾 🅿🆁 🆁 🅱🆁 🆂 17/34, €-/40/55/-/-, Ctra. Sevilla Cazalla de la Sierra km32, tel 955 734 523, info@hotelcastilloblanco.com, **https://hotel-castillo-blanco.negocio.site**.

*A drinking water pump lies through the gate, although it can be unreliable*

# STAGE 3

*Castilblanco de los Arroyos to
Almadén de la Plata*

| | |
|---|---|
| **Start** | Castilblanco de los Arroyos |
| **Finish** | Almadén de la Plata |
| **Distance** | 29.5km |
| **Total ascent** | 605m |
| **Total descent** | 480m |
| **Difficulty** | Very hard |
| **Duration** | 7½hr |
| **Percentage paved** | 62% |
| **Albergues** | Almadén de la Plata 29.5km |

This is a difficult stage, particularly in heat or rain, with nowhere to stock up and with two distinct halves. The first involves 15.5km of unavoidable stomping along a usually quiet road. The second is the reward of entering Finca El Berrocal, a gorgeous 70km² estate in the heart of Sierra Norte de Sevilla, where deer-spotting is a regular occurrence. A final swift 91m climb grants outstanding views atop the Cerro del Calvario before the steep descent into Almadén. Cautious of this stage's difficulties, some pilgrims cut the day in half by sharing a taxi to the entrance of the *finca*.

Go to the main road, turn right, and reach the **roundabout** at the bottom of town (**1.1km**). Turn left onto the **SE-505** following road signs for Almadén de la Plata. Commence the long road section that goes up and down with gorgeous *dehesas* and estates on either side, views that make up for the chore at hand. Pass an information board for the Sierra Norte de Sevilla Natural Park and rejoice at following the yellow arrow pointing right soon after. At long last, enter the **Finca El Berrocal** (**15.5km**), noting the park's unique stone waymarkers.

> In the **Finca El Berrocal**, the trail is part of the Sevilla network of transhumance roads, which total 30,000km in the province: the equivalent of going to Australia and back from Madrid.

Follow the winding track as it makes its way through the sumptuous *dehesa*, coming to an untreated (and unreliable) water fountain by the **Casa Forestal** (**1.5km**), the estate's main but vacant lodge; behind it, keep right. Proceed over a **bridge** (**3.2km**),

Pilgrims take a breather atop the Cerro del Calvario with views of Finca El Berrocal

then turn left over a ford (stepping blocks) towards ruins, a disused well and a **white lodge** (**1.2km**).

Keep left at the next fork and right 900 metres later. Go through the deer fence on the left via an unmissable big **gate** (with a humorous overload of yellow arrows) (**2.9km**). Start a **steep uphill climb** (**1.7km**), reaching a **viewpoint** at 559m altitude on the **Cerro del Calvario** to take in the immense scale of the estate.

The name **Cerro del Calvario** comes from the Latin *calvarium*, meaning a high place with no trees. At the top was a well which, through pipes, fed water into Almadén. The gum rockrose (*Cistus ladanifer*) grows on the slopes and its resin is used for artisan perfumes produced in Almadén and El Real de la Jara (Stage 4).

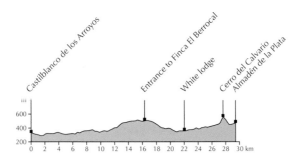

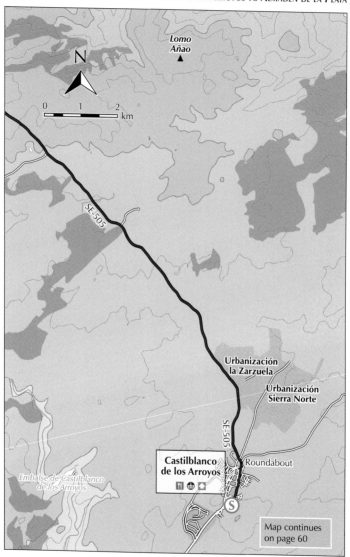

Map continues on page 60

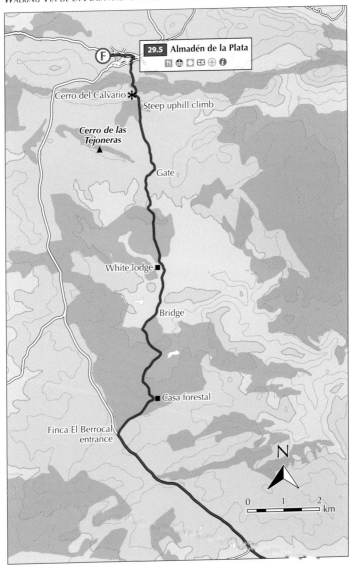

**29.5** Almadén de la Plata

Cerro del Calvario

Steep uphill climb

*Cerro de las Tejoneras* ▲

Gate

White lodge ■

Bridge

Casa forestal ■

Finca El Berrocal entrance

N

0    1    2 km

Cross straight over to descend steeply along the pavement by a cork oak *dehesa*, then pass farms as you draw nearer to Almadén. A swift detour behind boulders allows for a quiet moment of reflection by the Cruz de la Paz (Cross of Peace), revealing views of **Almadén** below.

> **Almadén** has a strong Catholic background, having been an enclave during King Fernando III's Reconquest. It was awarded the title of Loyal Town by Fernando and Isabela, the Catholic monarchs, after the 1492 fall of the Nasrid Kingdom of Granada, the last Muslim state in Western Europe, ending ten years of battle in the War of Granada.

Turn right onto Cl. Calvario then immediately left onto Cl. Olmo. Bend right onto Cl. Matadero then left (restaurant) onto Plaza del Pilar (tourist office and town hall), following signs for the *albergue municipal*. At the end of the square, veer left onto Plaza del Reloj with its red Torre del Reloj. Reach the end of the square, passing Plaza de la Palmera, then take Cl. Cervantes on the right-hand side to arrive at the *albergue municipal* 400 metres later.

### 29.5KM ALMADÉN DE LA PLATA (ELEV 458M, POP 1331) 🍴 ⊕ 🏠 🄴 ⊕ ❶ (925.8KM)

The town's name combines the Arabic word *Al-medin* (mine) and the Spanish word *plata* (silver). It originates from the mines here, which extracted silver as well as blue marble and copper. Almadén's vermilion-coloured **Torre del Reloj** is relatively recent (1905), although it maintains a Mudéjar air and creates an optical illusion when inspected attentively. The **Iglesia de Nuestra Señora de Gracia** dates from the late 16th century to the early 17th. Nearby, the **Cueva de los Covachos** limestone caves hold rock paintings and artefacts from the Neolithic period.

🏠 Albergue municipal de Almadén de la Plata 🄾 🄳o 🄺 🄶 🅂 4/72, €10, Cl. Cervantes s/n, tel 651 070 813, ayto.almaden@gmail.com. Discounts for under 30s and groups of 25 or more.

🏠 Albergue La Casa del Reloj 🄳o 🄺 🅆 🅂 2/10, €10, Plaza del Reloj 9, tel 692 552 659, luisevaristoml@gmail.com. Open all year except Christmas.

# STAGE 4

*Almadén de la Plata to
El Real de la Jara*

| | |
|---|---|
| **Start** | Almadén de la Plata |
| **Finish** | El Real de la Jara |
| **Distance** | 13.9km |
| **Total ascent** | 315m |
| **Total descent** | 300m |
| **Difficulty** | Easy |
| **Duration** | 3½hr |
| **Percentage paved** | <1% |
| **Albergues** | El Real de la Jara 13.9km |

On the last day of walking in Andalucía, the Camino follows the same path as the GR48 route, which is waymarked by red and white. At the beginning of the day, it skirts the Covachos hill and then goes through woods. Estates, hunting reserves and some climbs (although nothing too demanding) are the motif for most of the day, and sheep, goats, the Iberian pig and oak trees keep you company. There is nowhere to stock up, so plan ahead. Some pilgrims continue to Monesterio, resulting in a 35km day.

Turn left out of the albergue, going back the way you came. Take the second left and then right onto Cl. Coso to join the Camino, turning first left onto Barrio Nuestra Señora del Crucero. Soon it becomes a track leading to the **Plaza de Toros (0.5km)**.

The trail winds gently uphill past solar panels and goes through a gate. Then take a sharp left while ignoring the distracting tracks further to the left (**1km**). Soon fork left and go through a gate to a farm, now in green

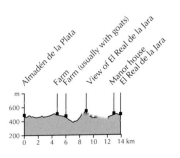

**13.9 El Real de la Jara**

Manor house on a hill

N

0   1   2 km

Track

View of
El Real de la Jara

Fenced off pond

Santa María
statue

Pond

Farm    Farm

Gate and track

Narrow path/GR48

Farmhouse

Plaza
de Toros

**S**

*Cerro Traviesa* ▲

**Almadén de la Plata**

*Cerro de las
Tejoneras* ▲

woodland. Pass a **farmhouse** and soon after cross over a stone bridge on the right (**0.8km**) and over a cattle grid. Some 100 metres later, be sure to go left onto a **narrow path** where the **GR48 route** is also signed.

> GR stands for **Gran Recorrido** (big trail), referring to long-distance multi-day hiking routes. The 550km GR48 spans the entire Sierra Morena mountain range to the town of Barrancos, just across the Portuguese border.

Keep on as the Camino meanders up and down and through a gate onto a very narrow path (a local road lies ahead). Go through another **gate** and turn left onto a **track** with pastures either side. Reach a **farm** (**2.3km**) and fork left through a gate to pass the **Santa María statue** (**1.2km**), another **farm** (usually with goats) and a house. By the statue, a plaque states '*Peregrino aquí está tu madre*' (Pilgrim, here is your mother).

Take the gate to the right, keep straight and fork right downhill towards a **pond**, after which turn left downhill (signage is less clear here). Go through another gate (**0.9km**) and soon keep right to cross a stream (often dry) and head straight uphill on a track.

Pass through a gate (where there is usually a poster giving distance information) for the steepest climb of the stage, reaching an altitude of 531m. Go slightly left uphill on the track and among trees to reach a **fenced-off pond** (**1.2km**). Follow the track, bending sharply left then right to go through a gate, and stay right near to the fence, going uphill again. Fork left at a waymark alongside the fence for your first **view of El Real de la Jara** ahead (**1km**).

Promptly turn sharp left and head downhill with the GR sign again and soon keep left above a pond to reach a gate. Turn right onto a wide comfortable **track** into town (**0.6km**), walking by a sheep farm and over a cattle grid (**2.5km**). Pass below a **manor house on a hill**, reaching the first road in **El Real de la Jara** 1.5km later.

The old *albergue municipal*, now a refuge shelter, is the first house on the left, yet another appears soon after on the right, and other accommodation options, including another albergue, host pilgrims in the town centre, at the end of today's stage. Continue down Cl. Picasso to the pilgrim drinking fountain. Turn right, first left, first right then first left to the supermarket and the Torre del Reloj on Cl. Real.

Passing farms on the way to El Real de la Jara, the last town in Andalucía

**13.9KM EL REAL DE LA JARA** (ELEV 476M, POP 1513) 🍴 ⊕ 🛆 🄲 ⊕ (911.9KM)

Overseen by its fantastic **14th-century castle**, the town of El Real lies in the southernmost area of the Sierra Morena range, one of the only habitats left for the endangered Iberian lynx. The eight-towered castle itself offers remarkable 360-degree panoramic views. Situated upon a hillock, its construction was strategically planned by King Sancho IV who, in 1293, insisted that nine castles be built in the area to protect the population from bandits as well as from invaders such as the Portuguese, Templars and the cavalry of the Order of Santiago. It was also used to control trade roads.

🏠 **Alojamiento del Peregrino** 🄾 🄳🄾 🄺 🅆 🅂 2/12, €10, Cl. Pablo Picasso 17, tel 654 862 553 or 675 306 121, atorresperegrino@hotmail.com.

🏠 **Alojamiento Molina** 🄾 🄳🄾 🄺 🅂 9/30, €12, Cl. Real 70, tel 954 733 053 or 610 026 132, conchitagilromero@gmail.com.

🏠 **Albergue municipal de peregrinos El Realejo** 🄾 🄳🄾 🅂 -/-, €-, Cl. Real, tel 954 733 007. The new albergue is due to open in late 2023.

# STAGE 5

*El Real de la Jara to Monesterio*

| | |
|---|---|
| **Start** | El Real de la Jara |
| **Finish** | Monesterio |
| **Distance** | 21.2km |
| **Total ascent** | 470m |
| **Total descent** | 195m |
| **Difficulty** | Easy |
| **Duration** | 5½hr |
| **Percentage paved** | 39% |
| **Albergues** | Hotel Complejo Leo 11.9km; Monesterio 21.2km |

The day begins among oak trees along drover's tracks as the Camino enters Extremadura. About halfway, it reaches the San Isidro chapel and collides with the N-630 and A-66 highways, where refreshments can be found at a local produce shop and then a big motorway services complex. A final ascent to the

Puerto de la Cruz pass (758m) brings you into the Tentudía region, named after the nearby 1112m peak, and then to Monesterio, home to the Museo del Jamón (ham museum).

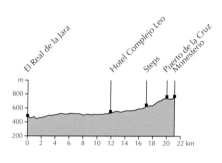

Keep straight on Cl. Real, passing the road that leads down to Iglesia San Bartolomé. Eventually leave the white buildings of El Real behind to go between walls along a dirt track, with views of the castle behind on the left. Cross the Arroyo de la Víbora stream and **enter Extremadura (1.2km)**, passing under the **ruins of Castillo de las Torres** soon after.

The architectural style of **Castillo de las Torres** points to the 15th or 16th century. It is thought to have been built with the dual purpose of controlling the Vía de la Plata as well as transhumance. It has now been included on Spain's Heritage Red List by the Hispania Nostra Association, with the aim of overturning its poor state of conservation.

Continue for a lengthy stretch on a **wide track** surrounded by *dehesas* and *fincas*, consistently heading gently uphill. At the next significant fork, **fork left (3.3km)** as the Camino proceeds to wind up and down through open countryside. Eventually bend left by the **Ermita San Isidro Labrador (6.7km)**, passing a

*The Iberian pig feeds off acorns in Extremadura's dehesas*

de Puerto
ncinilla ▲

Map continues
on page 68

N

Steps

0   1   2
—————————— km

A-66

Chapel ruins

**11.9** Hotel Complejo Leo

✝ Ermita San Isidro Labrador

N-630

N-630

A-66

Fork left

Wide track

Castillo de las
Torres ruins

Enter Extremadura

**El Real de la Jara**

S

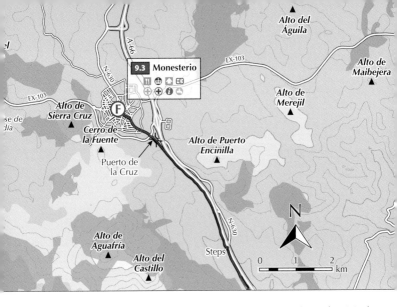

drinking fountain soon after (turn left for the Venta del Culebrín shop). Then join the **N-630** and walk along it to a roundabout and motorway services (**0.7km**).

### 11.9KM HOTEL COMPLEJO LEO (ELEV 534M) 🍴 🏠 (900.0KM)

🏠 Hotel Complejo Leo *** 🅾 Pf R Bf Cf W S Z 48/90, €-/45/62/90/-, A-66 km730, tel 924 517 048, complejoleo@grupoleo.es, **https://complejoleo.es**.

Follow the N-630 and take the exit for Monesterio, going under the A-66. Just after the **chapel ruins** on the right-hand side of the N-630, turn right onto a path (**1.2km**) by a waymarking cube, passing benches, and turn left following a sandy path between the N-630 and A-66.

After 500 metres, bend right uphill through eucalyptus trees and keep right. Keep on until you merge with the N-630 again by crossing it and turning right (**2km**). Take a track alongside the left of the N-630 to keep parallel to it. Turn left just before the motorway bridge and go down some **steps** (**1.9km**).

Turn right onto a lane that will now lead to the destination of the day. It heads uphill before a final steep push over the last 800 metres to a sheltered picnic spot at the hill pass of **Puerto de la Cruz** (**3.4km**), the highest point on the Camino so far

The Camino has now entered the Tentudía region, named after the mountain itself (15.6km away), where lies the splendid **Monasterio de Tentudía**. Founded in the 13th century under the Order of Santiago, and elevated to a monastery in the 16th, it contains a Mudéjar cloister and a main altarpiece made of beech tile. Its museum is open Tue–Sun 11:30–17:00, entrance fee €1.

The Camino drops down along a tree-lined lane, coming to a roundabout with a *jamón* (ham) statue. Go straight across and keep on past the Museo del Jamón (**0.9km**) into **Monesterio**, passing café/bars and hotels to a drinking fountain and information board. The *albergue parroquial* (church-run hostel) is a little further along the main road on the left, while the *albergue municipal* lies further on in town.

**9.3KM MONESTERIO (ELEV 753M, POP 4267)** 🍴 ⛲ 🏪 🏧 ➕ ⓘ **(890.7KM)**

The town of Monesterio dates back to Roman times. Its history is also linked to the Way of St James, as in the 13th century it was already under the jurisdiction of the Order of Santiago. The **Iglesia de San Pedro Apóstol**, constructed in the 15th century, was remodelled in the 17th and 18th centuries.

⌂ Albergue parroquial de Monesterio ⓞ 🅳🅾 🅺 🅱🅵 🆂 3/12, €10, Av. de Extremadura 218, tel 924 516 097.

⌂ Albergue Las Moreras ⓞ 🅳🅾 🅺 🅱🅵 🆆 🆂 🆉 7/50, €12.50, Ronda de Segura de León 3, tel 679 587 435, info@alberguemonesterio.es. Discounts for groups of 14 or more.

# STAGE 6

*Monesterio to
Calzadilla de los Barros*

| | |
|---|---|
| **Start** | Monesterio |
| **Finish** | Calzadilla de los Barros |
| **Distance** | 27.3km |
| **Total ascent** | 280m |
| **Total descent** | 465m |
| **Difficulty** | Moderate |
| **Duration** | 6¾hr |
| **Percentage paved** | 14% |
| **Albergues** | Fuente de Cantos 20.8km; Calzadilla de los Barros 27.3km |

The *dehesas* and hills are left behind, making way for bright yellows and greens through farmland, wheatfields, olive groves and vineyards. The Camino passes through the old town in Fuente de Cantos, so make a quick detour to the N-630 for refreshments. The way to Calzadilla de los Barros (little path of the mudlands/claylands) is appropriately named, as the path gets very muddy after rainfall and the Arroyo del Bodion Chico stream may be unpassable. Check with your hosts in the albergue, who will advise you about the level of water and recommend walking on the N-630 road instead, should there be concerns.

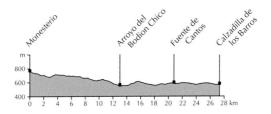

Leave Monesterio on Av. De Extremadura (N-630), and turn left after a **football pitch** (**1.2km**) along a walled lane to cross a **bridge** (**1.6km**). Keep right then go over a road (**2.7km**) onto a track that takes you past the **Dolmen de la Cabra**. The Dolmen de la Cabra, a megalithic burial ground dating from more than 5000 years ago, lies in a fenced-off field on the right.

Some 2.2km later, keep right then straight on to use a gate on the left (**3.2km**) and tackle **Arroyo del Bodion Chico** (**4.4km**). Head uphill and take the first left. At the next fork (**1.6km**), **keep left** to a long straight section that passes a **car scrapyard** (**4.3km**) and crosses the EX-202 into **Fuente de Cantos**. Turn left onto Cl. Martínez and fork left onto a cobblestone road to the Iglesia Nuestra Señora de la Granada on Plaza de la Constitución (drinking fountain). Services are on the N-630 to the right (east).

### 20.8KM FUENTE DE CANTOS (ELEV 589M, POP 4,684) 🏨 ⊖ 🏪 ⊕ ⊕ ❶ (869.9KM)

The town's tremendous claim to fame is that of being the birthplace of painter **Francisco de Zurbarán**, born in 1598. Influenced by the realism of Caravaggio, Zurbarán's distinctive and intense spiritual paintings made him the official painter of Sevilla between 1630 and 1650. Aided by his friend Velázquez, in 1634 he was also commissioned to paint mythological scenes for King Felipe IV's new

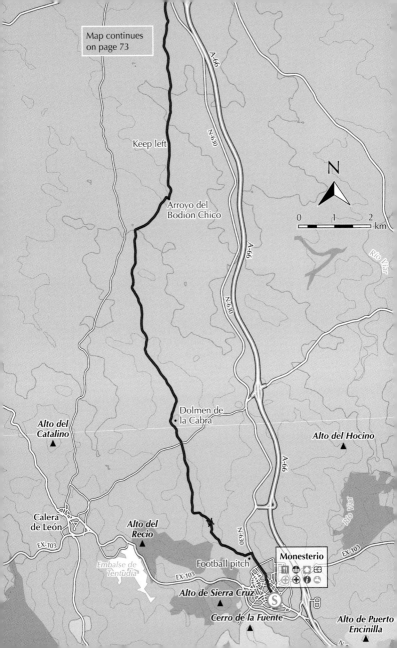

Map continues
on page 73

Keep left

Arroyo del
Bodion Chico

N

0 1 2 km

*Alto del
Catalino* ▲

*Alto del Hocino* ▲

Dolmen de
la Cabra

*Río Viar*

A-66

N-630

*Calera
de León*

EX-103

*Alto del
Recio* ▲

*Embalse de
Tentudía*

Football pitch

EX-103

N-630

**Monesterio**

*Alto de Sierra Cruz* ▲

S

*Cerro de la Fuente* ▲

*Río Viar*

EX-103

*Alto de Puerto
Encinilla* ▲

palace within the Buen Retiro park in Madrid. A museum dedicated to him is on Cl. Águilas.

The many religious buildings were deciding factors in the town's layout, in particular the **Iglesia Nuestra Señora de Granada**. Originally from the 15th century and dedicated to St Roch, it was remodelled in the 18th century with a Baroque design and a grand altarpiece from Spain's Golden Age. St Roch was born in France. As a young man, he sold all his possessions, gave the money to the poor and left on a pilgrimage to Rome. At this time, the plague was taking many lives across Europe and in Italy. St Roch fearlessly cared for the ill and buried those who died, unlike others who dared not approach. He contracted the disease in Piacenza and selflessly left the city, taking refuge in a forest, where a dog appeared with bread for him. Stealing more bread from his master, the dog returned daily, until one day the master followed his pet. Upon discovering St Roch, he took care of the saint until he was cured. St Roch returned to the city and continued to heal both people and animals.

🏠 Hotel Rural La Fábrica ⓞ Pr R Br Cr W S 11/22, €-/42/56/-/-, Cl. Real 117, tel 924 500 042, hotel@hrlafabrica.com, **www.hrlafabrica.com/ hrfuentecantos.htm**. Discounts for pilgrims, check prices directly.

🏠 Pensión Casa Vicenta ⓞ Pr R Br Cr S 10/15, €-/17/30/-/-, Cl. Real 33, tel 611 617 641.

Go to the right of the church, keep next left and then right onto Cl. Olmo, reaching Plaza Olmo. Keep right and go straight on to Cl. San Juan, then uphill to a football pitch (drinking fountain). Go right, immediately left on the BA-069, then turn right onto a **track** (**0.5km**). Tracing the exact route of the old Roman road, leave the town behind.

*Even during winter months in Fuente de Cantos, pilgrims can enjoy sunny days and a Mediterranean climate*

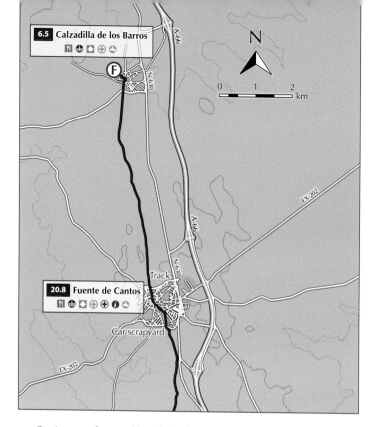

Continue past farms and keep left at the next fork (**2.7km**) into **Calzadilla de los Barros** (**2.7km**). Pass a bar, reaching a park with an iron cross and two options for the albergue, depending on whether you arrive before or after 15:00.

### Before 15:00

Turn right to the main square (drinking fountain) and town hall (keys for the albergue), then left on a promenade lined with orange trees. Ignore a confusing arrow on a lamp post; instead, ahead, follow a stone marker to turn left. Then be sure to continue straight, ignoring the waymarked right turn (tomorrow's route). Take the next uphill road on the right to the albergue.

### After 15:00

Go straight ahead on Cl. Manuel Galván. Turn right onto Cl. Ermita and reach the albergue.

### 6.5KM CALZADILLA DE LOS BARROS (ELEV 557M, POP 721) 🍴 ⊜ 🏠 ⊕
(863.4KM)

Calzadilla is a small agricultural town, where a traditional dish of *guarrito tapas* is very popular among locals. The nickname *guarrito* means 'little dirty one', an affectionate term for the Iberian pig. **Nuestra Señora de la Encarnación** is the patroness of Calzadilla de los Barros, and the chapel in her name was founded in the 16th century. In the **Iglesia del Divino Salvador**, look for Santiago within the Gothic–Mudéjar altarpiece.

🏠 **Albergue de peregrinos de Calzadilla de los Barros** Ⓞ D₀ Ⓦ Ⓢ Ⓩ 2/10, €8, Polígono Encarnación 3, tel 924 584 745. Keys from town hall before 15:00, otherwise phone numbers are on the door.


# STAGE 7
*Calzadilla de los Barros to Zafra*

| | |
|---|---|
| **Start** | Calzadilla de los Barros |
| **Finish** | Zafra |
| **Distance** | 18.3km |
| **Total ascent** | 155m |
| **Total descent** | 215m |
| **Difficulty** | Easy |
| **Duration** | 4¼hr |
| **Percentage paved** | 31% |
| **Albergues** | Puebla de Sancho Pérez 14.3km; Zafra 18.3km |

An effortless walk among olive groves and vineyards leads to the picturesque old town of Zafra, considered the capital of southern Extremadura. Declared an artistic and historic place of national interest, and with two good albergues, an afternoon of sightseeing is a must. In the old quarters, the lively Plaza Grande and its little neighbour, Plaza Chica, quench a pilgrim's appetite and thirst.

From the albergue, go back to Cl. Encarnación, turn left and then first left onto Cl. Zafra, following the arrow ignored yesterday and passing a pharmacy. Keep right after the big farm and left at the next fork (**1.2km**).

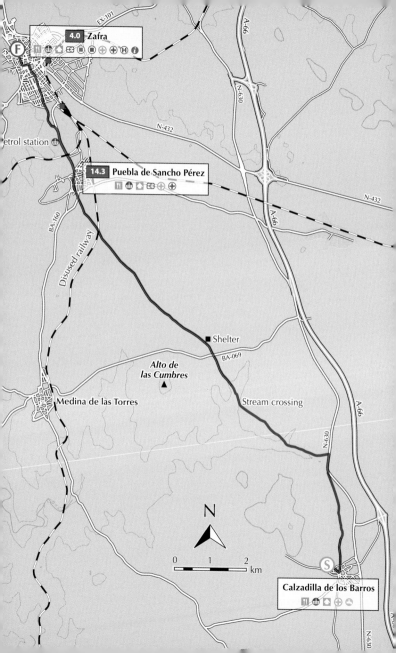

**F** ⬤

**4.0** Zafra

🏛️ ⛪ 🏠 📧 🔲 ⊕ ⊕ ⊕ **ℹ**

EX-107

A-66

N-432

N-630

etrol station ⊕

**14.3** Puebla de Sancho Pérez

🍴 ⛪ 🏠 🔲 ⊕ ⊕

BA-160

Disused railway

■ Shelter

BA-069

*Alto de las Cumbres*

▲

Medina de las Torres

Stream crossing

N-630

A-66

N

0  1  2

km

**S** ⬤

Calzadilla de los Barros

🍴 ⊕ 🏠 ⊕ ⊕

N-630

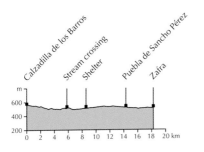

Fork right towards the **N-630** (**1.8km**) and walk along its left side briefly to then turn left away from it. From this point on, the Camino keeps consistently straight in a north-westerly direction, crossing a **stream** (muddy after rain). Cross the **BA-069** (**5km**) to continue straight on the track, coming to a **shelter** and information board.

Cross over a **disused railway** (**4.3km**) and the **BA-160** (**1.1km**). Go right and first left into **Puebla de Sancho Pérez**. Keep straight onto Cl. Nuestra Señora de Belén and then across all junctions to reach Plaza España.

### 14.3KM PUEBLA DE SANCHO PÉREZ (ELEV 526M, POP 2665) ▯ ⊕ ▱ ▱ ⊕ ⊕ (849.1KM)

Founded in 1498 and integrated into the jurisdiction of the Order of Santiago, Puebla de Sancho Pérez is the homeland of Celestino Coronado, artistic director of the Lindsay Kemp mime company. Its peculiar square-shaped **bullring** is thought to be one of the oldest in Spain, dated by some authors to the 14th century. The 16th-century **Parroquia de Santa Lucía** was constructed in Gothic style on Mudéjar foundations. The main entrance is of local marble. As they say, the best place to learn about local geology is in a town's church.

⌂ **Hostal El Monte** * ◙ ▯ ▯ ▯ ▢ 9/25, €-/22/36/50, Cl. San Antonio s/n, tel 924 575 581.

Cross to the opposite corner of the square to reach the Parroquia de Santa Lucía. Go right alongside the church and left onto Cl. Obispo Soto. Reach a wine bottle statue and arrive on the BA-160, also known as Avenida de Zafra. Turn left and walk on the pavement alongside it, taking a bridge over the **railway lines** and passing a petrol station.

Fork left onto a quiet road, the BAV-3012 (**1.4km**), and arrive at the first houses in **Zafra** 800 metres later. Keep straight until you merge with Av. de la Estación on the right (just after the museum) and pass the albergue Van Gogh (**1.8km**) on the right.

Cross the main road to the Parque de la Paz. You can go through the park and turn left after it to merge with the route, following signs for 'conjunto histórico' (historic town centre); or skirt around the park, going left and right past hotels, shops and restaurants. Reach the Plaza España park (tourist office) on the left, go up the steps into it

*Zafra's Plaza Grande bustles with life as locals soak up the sun over a lovely meal*

(or keep straight down the road and then left) and at the fountain turn right to leave the park. Cross to a pharmacy, turn left and then right onto Cl. Sevilla, which 200 metres later leads to Plaza Grande.

### 4.0KM ZAFRA (ELEV 514M, POP 16,786) 🚉 ⊕ 🏠 🅲 Ⓜ Ⓗ ⊕ ⊕ ❶ (845.1KM)

Zafra's name is thought to derive from the Arabic *Safra*, 'the yellow one'. It is sheltered by two hills: El Castellar, where a Moorish defensive fortress was seized by King Fernando III de Castilla in 1241 during the Reconquest, and San Cristóbal, on tomorrow's route.

King Enrique III de Castilla granted the city to Gómez I Suárez de Figueroa, albeit through much confusion. In fact, the donation was made to his father, Lorenzo I Suárez de Figueroa, 37th Maestre de la Orden de Santiago, who, within the agreement document, carefully specified that it go to his son so as to avoid possible claims from the Order of Santiago. A few years later, Gómez I Suárez de Figueroa ordered the construction of the city's defensive wall and of his place of residence, **El Alcázar**. This palace would be further expanded, in an Austrian style, and become known as the Palacio de los Duques de Feria, one of Spain's most noble families, with the first Duque de Feria being Gómez I's son, Lorenzo II Suárez de Figueroa. The palace is now a Parador hotel and museum. Gómez I also funded the Hospital de Santiago, built in 1438.

In the **Iglesia Colegiata de La Candelaria**, the altarpiece of the Virgen de los Remedios stands out, framing nine canvases painted by Zurbarán in 1644.

🏠 Albergue de peregrinos de Zafra (Vincent Van Gogh) 🄾 🔟 🆁 🆂 6/36, €10, Av. de la Estación 17, tel 924 969 123 or 617 846 551.

🏠 Albergue Convento San Francisco 🔟 🆁 🄱🄵 🆆 🆂 6/21, €12/-/30/-, Av. Fuente del Maestre 2, tel 680 663 806 or 924 036 245. Breakfast €2. Open all year except Christmas.

77

# STAGE 8
### *Zafra to Villafranca de los Barros*

| | |
|---|---|
| **Start** | Zafra |
| **Finish** | Villafranca de los Barros |
| **Distance** | 20.8km |
| **Total ascent** | 240m |
| **Total descent** | 340m |
| **Difficulty** | Easy |
| **Duration** | 5hr |
| **Percentage paved** | 35% |
| **Albergues** | Los Santos de Maimona 4.4km; La Almazara 13.3km; Villafranca de los Barros 20.8km |

The Camino quickly ascends the Sierra de San Cristóbal and drops into Los Santos de Maimona. The remainder of the walk is through sun-exposed olive groves and vineyards on red clay tracks. Following rainfall, many deep puddles appear. To avoid a dangerous bend on the N-630 and to enjoy a pit stop just over halfway, the recommended route goes via La Almazara albergue, adding only 800 metres. With the albergue in Villafranca closed for several months every year, an overnight in Almazara is the best inexpensive alternative, and for many pilgrims the number one choice regardless.

From Plaza Grande, take Cl. Tetuán. Turn right onto Cl. Conde de la Corte by the Iglesia de la Candelaria. At the end of the road, cross over, turn left and immediately right past the Albergue de San Francisco onto Cl. Ancha.

Take the crossing on the right to go over the roundabout and pass the 15th-century **Torre de San Francisco** (**1.1km**). Head uphill to reach the summit of **Alto de San Cristóbal**, with lovely views (**2.2km**). The Alto de San Cristóbal peak lies at 614m above sea level on the appropriately nicknamed Sierra los Olivos (hill of the olives).

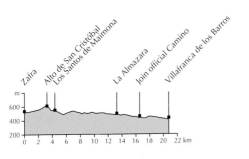

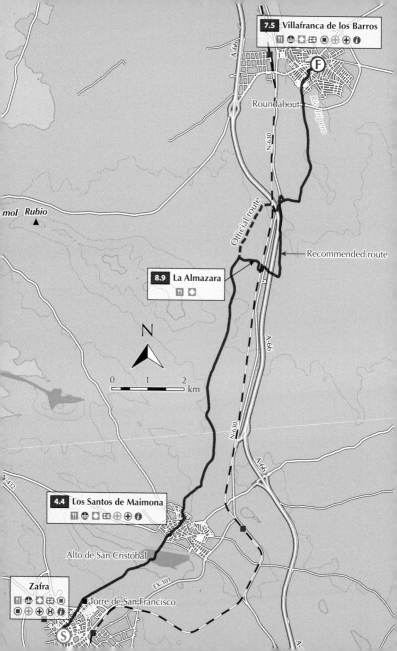

**7.5 Villafranca de los Barros**

F

Roundabout

Rubio

Recommended route

Official route

**8.9 La Almazara**

N

0    1    2
km

**4.4 Los Santos de Maimona**

Alto de San Cristóbal

**Zafra**

Torre de San Francisco

S

Descend on a steep paved section and proceed into **Los Santos de Maimona**, where waymarking is excellent. Reach Plaza España (tourist office) and the Iglesia Parroquial Nuestra Señora de los Ángeles.

### 4.4KM LOS SANTOS DE MAIMONA (ELEV 534M, POP 8064) 🏨 ⊕ 🛏 🄲 ⊕ ⊕ ⓘ (840.7KM)

With Zafra so close, pilgrims rush through Los Santos, yet the town boasts well-preserved Gothic and Renaissance architecture with its 16th-century **Iglesia de Nuestra Señora de los Ángeles**. At its entrance, at the **Puerta del Perdón**, admire the scallop shells on the coat of arms. The main square is lively and caters for all pilgrim requirements.

- 🛏 Albergue Vía de la Plata de Los Santos de Maimona ⓞ Do 🅂 2/12, €8, Cl. Maestrazgo s/n, tel 924 54 48 01 or 924 54 42 94, oficinadeturismo@lossantosdemaimona.org. Keys from tourist office or police station. The albergue is due to be open from August 2023 but check ahead.

Continue around the church and keep left to Cl. Ramón y Cajal. At its end, turn left and then first right. Cross the main road and take the second left by the *albergue municipal* (**0.6km**). Go right, fork left and turn right towards vineyards. Proceed downhill over a stream and on a tree-lined lane to fork right onto a track uphill, merging with a wider flat track (**1.8km**). Walk between fences (**2.9km**), ignore the first sign for La Almazara albergue, then find the **second sign by a tower ruin**, arriving at two options (**3.1km**).

### Recommended route (3.7km, unwaymarked)
Turn right, reaching **La Almazara** in 500 metres.

### 8.9KM LA ALMAZARA (ELEV 481M, POP 2) 🏨 🛏 (831.8KM)

The owner is a pilgrim, and a *menú del día* is available for €8. The historic building, resembling a castle, was originally an oil mill, now lovingly restored into a hotel/museum.

- 🛏 Albergue Turístico La Almazara ⓞ Pr Dr Do R Br 🄶 W S Z 7/28, €15/-/60/-/-, Ctra. N-630 km670.6 (Ctra. del Moro), tel 924 986 181 or 669 964 546, lejonari@hotmail.com, **www.albergueturisticolaalmazara.com**. Includes breakfast and summer swimming pool access.

Turn right out of the albergue and over **railway lines** 300 metres later, then cross the **N-630** and **A-66** (**0.8km**). Veer left, coming parallel with the N-630 (**2.3km**). At the next junction, turn right and join the official Camino 100 metres later.

*Scallop shells decorate the church's Puerta del Perdón in Los Santos de Maimona*

## Official route (2.9km)

Keep straight ahead on the Camino for another 1.6km and then turn right, going over **railway lines** to the **N-630**. Turn left and go under the **A-66**, passing a road sign for Villafranca. Soon, cross the **N-630** and turn right then left, connecting with the recommended route.

## Main route

When the two options rejoin, keep ahead then turn left after 500 metres. Keep straight to eventually go over the **roundabout (3.2km)** into **Villafranca de los Barros**. Fork left ('Ruta del Vino Ribero del Guardián' sign), passing the albergue, and step onto the colourful rainbow road. Turn right onto Cl. Zurbarán and straight onto Cl. Presidente Adolfo Suárez. Turn first left onto a pedestrian street, reaching Plaza Corazón de María (tourist office) and the Iglesia de Nuestra Señora del Valle. Turn left and reach Plaza España.

### 7.5KM VILLAFRANCA DE LOS BARROS (ELEV 417M, POP 12,534) 🏨 ⊕ 🛒 Ⓒ ⓜ ⊕ ⊕ ℹ (824.3KM)

Villafranca was repopulated during the second half of the 13th century, when the Maestres de la Orden de Santiago resided in the province; at the time, it was called Moncovil. In the middle of the 14th century, Maestre Don Fadrique, brother of the King, gave the place the title of 'city' and, soon after, its name changed to Villafranca. Its 16th-century **Parroquia de Nuestra Señora del Valle** combines a Gothic portal and Renaissance architecture as well as Baroque features incorporated during restoration works. The music-themed streets honour the town's nickname: the **City of Music**. For generations, it has been the custom among locals to congregate and play live music.

🛏 **Albergue Extrenatura** Do Pr R Br K W S 2/10 & 4/8, €14/25/45/-/-, Cl. Carvajales 2, tel 924 986 181 or 669 964 546. Unpredictable closures at variable times of the year, so call ahead and look out for updates.

🛏 **Hostal Rural Casa Perín** ** Pr R Br Ci W S 5/10, €-/28–30/45/65/78, Cl. Carrillo Arenas 40, tel 646 179 914. Closed at Christmas.

# STAGE 9

*Villafranca de los Barros to Torremejía*

| | |
|---|---|
| **Start** | Villafranca de los Barros |
| **Finish** | Torremejía |
| **Distance** | 27.3km |
| **Total ascent** | 105m |
| **Total descent** | 220m |
| **Difficulty** | Moderate |
| **Duration** | 6¼hr |
| **Percentage paved** | <1% |
| **Albergues** | Torremejía 27.3km |

The monotony of today's long, flat stage on the peneplain will be compensated tomorrow upon arrival in Mérida. Including 15.4km on the same track, the longest of the Vía, there is no getting around it: to enjoy the vineyard greens means walking in the scorching heat of summer, whereas during more pleasant weather the vines tend to wither. There is full exposure to the elements and no services unless you take an unrecommended 8km detour to Almendralejo.

Facing the town hall on Plaza España, go left and right up Cl. Santa Joaquina de Vedruna. Upon reaching Plaza Corazón de Jesús, turn immediately left onto Cl. Calvario, then fork right to reach Plaza de la Coronada and go left in front of the Iglesia de Nuestra Señora de la Coronada on Cl. San Ignacio. Keep straight ahead and leave town (**0.9km**).

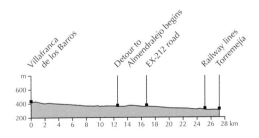

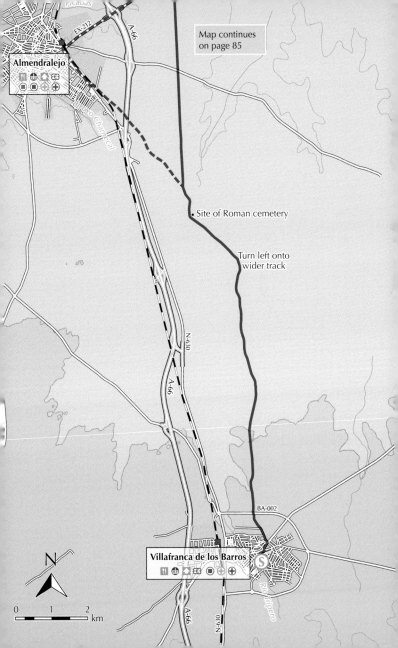

Map continues
on page 85

Almendralejo

EX-212

A-66

Picudas

Arroyo Charascal

Site of Roman cemetery

Turn left onto
wider track

N-630

A-66

BA-002

Villafranca de los Barros

S

A-66

N-630

Rio Tripero

N

0    1    2
km

Keep right at the fork and cross straight over the **BA-002** (**0.5km**). Keep straight ahead ignoring all narrower tracks until you take a track on the left (**3.5km**). Eventually, **turn left onto a wider track** (**3.5km**), then at the end of that track, and in line with the electricity pylons, turn right (**1.8km**). Although no longer visible, a Roman cemetery was once located to the right here.

Soon, take a narrower track on the right again and continue straight (north). Ignore the first track on the left. At the second (**2.3km**), continue straight ahead if you are following the direct route to Torremejía, or turn left if taking the detour to Almendralejo.

### Detour to Almendralejo
Almendralejo is 15.4km from Villafranca de los Barros. The detour totals 8km. Turn left and 1.7km later go over the **A-66**. After another 1.2km, reach the N-630 in **Almendralejo** ( ⓘ ⊕ 🏠 Ⓒ ◉ ◉ ⊕ ⊕). Turn right onto it, pass warehouses, café/bars and supermarkets. After 1.3km, just before a roundabout, follow a road sign on the right for Alange and the motorway to Sevilla, and turn right onto the **EX-212**. Go over railway lines and the **A-66** and return to the Camino 3.8km later, going left on the track and following the electricity pylons.

### Direct route to Torremejía
Continue straight ahead, pass houses, then cross a road (**1.7km**) to keep straight again. Pass a farm and water tanks, then cross straight over the **EX-212** (**2.4km**), following the electricity pylons. The detour to Almendralejo rejoins the direct route here.

*The long day to Torremejía passes seemingly endless vineyards*

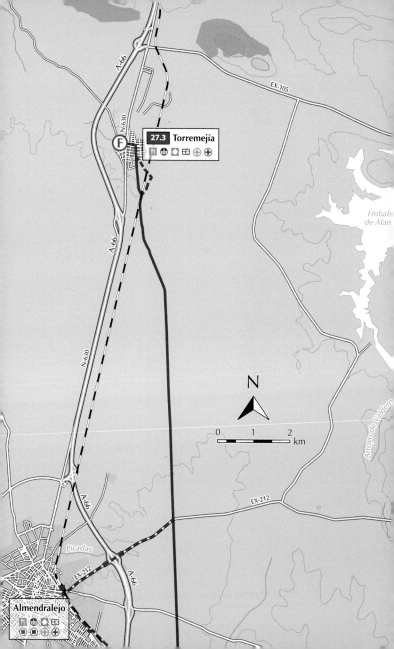

A-66

N-630

A-66

EX-105

Embals
de Alan

F **27.3** Torremejía

N

0 1 2 km

N-630

A-66

Arroyo de Valdem

EX-212

EX-212

A-66

Picadas

Almendralejo

Torremejía comes into view, although it is still a very long way to go. Eventually, draw parallel with **railway lines (8.5km)**. You now have two options: either go under the railway and keep straight following a dried-up stream for 200 metres, before veering to the right in a north-westerly direction away from the railway lines; alternatively, you can keep to the track, follow it to the right and turn left over the railway instead.

Come to the first buildings in **Torremejía (0.8km)** and keep straight, passing a sports complex. Cross the road onto Cl. Calzada Romana, pass a school and a sign for the albergue, directing you straight ahead. Turn left onto Cl. Camilo José Cela a few streets down and find the albergue across the N-630.

### 27.3KM TORREMEJÍA (ELEV 306M, POP 2249) 🏨 ⊕ 🏧 🅒 ⊕ ⊕ (797.0KM)

First belonging to the Order of Santiago, the town was later founded in 1370 by Don Gonzalo Mejía of the command of Mérida as part of his estate, hence the name. In 1808 it was burnt down by the French, and the old town was rebuilt around the **16th-century church** and **15th-century palace**, which is adorned with scallop shells on its facade. The town is known for being the birthplace of the protagonist of *La familia de Pascual Duarte* by the 1989 winner of the Nobel Prize in Literature, Camilo José Cela.

🏠 **Albergue Rojo Plata** 🅞 🕮 🅡 🅚 🅢 4/22, €14, Cl. José de Espronceda 23, tel 658 854 372, reservas@albergue-rojo-plata.com, **http://albergue-rojo-plata. com**.

# STAGE 10
*Torremejía to Mérida*

| | |
|---|---|
| **Start** | Torremejía |
| **Finish** | Mérida |
| **Distance** | 16.4km |
| **Total ascent** | 85m |
| **Total descent** | 180m |
| **Difficulty** | Easy |
| **Duration** | 3¾hr |
| **Percentage paved** | 29% |
| **Albergues** | Mérida 16.4km |

A simple and flat stage leads to memorable Mérida, the Roman Emerita Augusta. Pass through farmlands with great views towards La Moneda hill (500m) before indulging in an afternoon of exploration in this charming city, which gained its UNESCO World Heritage status in 1993. To avoid any muddy sections after heavy rainfall, and with no difference in distance, some pilgrims prefer to keep to the N-630.

Leaving Torremejía, you have two options.

### Shortcut via the N-630
Turn left out of the albergue and keep to the right-hand side of the **N-630** for 670 metres. Opposite a cemetery on the other side of the road, find a Camino sign that takes you right, to a track among olive trees.

### Main route
From the albergue, go back to Cl. Calzada Romana, turn left after the information board, keep straight as the lane becomes a track, then fork left to go diagonally towards the **N-630**, joining the shortcut (**1.5km**). Cross the **EX-105** (**2.3km**), hike along the right-hand pavement of the N-630, then take a wide lane on the right to leave the highway.

Go over **railway tracks** (**1.1km**), merge back onto the N-630 near the motorway, then take a right-hand path at the **waymarking cube** behind the highway's barriers (**2.2km**). Come to a road near **timber warehouses**, turn left, cross over a link road to the highways onto a track, and keep right at the next fork (**2.9km**) then straight. Some 300 metres later, keep right by an electricity pylon, away from a **farm building** (**1.1km**). Ignore a gate on the right, then turn right past electricity pylons and a quarry, reaching **warehouses** (**2.6km**) at the entrance to **Mérida**. Turn left onto a road, head along a track under the N-630, turn left alongside Río Guadiana and cross the **Puente Romano** (**0.9km**). Across the bridge, arrive at Plaza Roma by the **Alcazaba de Mérida** on a roundabout. If you are heading directly to the centre, you can keep straight up Cl. del Puente to Plaza de España and the Catedral de Santa María la Mayor.

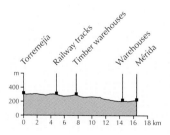

The **Puente Romano**, considered to be the world's longest remaining Roman bridge, was built at the end of the 1st century AD. It is 790 metres long, 12 metres high and consists of 60 arches.

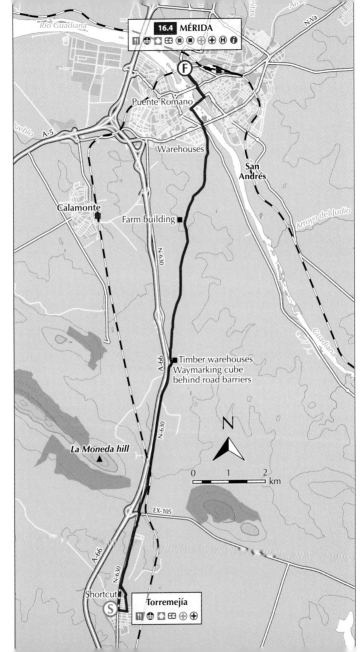

**16.4 MÉRIDA**

**F**

Río Guadiana

Puente Romano

A-5
Pueblo

Warehouses

San Andrés

Calamonte

Farm building

Arroyo del Judío

N-630

A-66

Guadiana

Timber warehouses
Waymarking cube
behind road barriers

N

0    1    2 km

N-630

La Moneda hill

EX-105

A-66

N-630

Shortcut

**Torremejía**

**S**

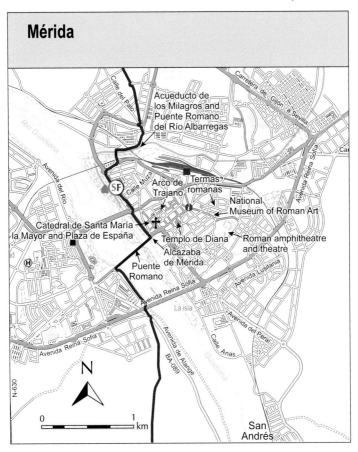

# Mérida

Following the mandate of the emir Abd el Rahman II, son of Al Hakem I, the **Alcazaba** was completed in 835 to defend the bridge, using stonework from its Roman foundation.

Turn left following arrows and signs for the albergue. Cross the next roundabout on palm-tree-lined Av. José Fernández López and 400 metres later go down steps by a red brick wall to the albergue.

*Pilgrims enter Mérida on the Puente Romano, the world's longest remaining Roman bridge*

**16.4KM MÉRIDA** (ELEV 224M, POP 59,424) 🏨 ⊕ 🏠 🄲 ◉ Ⓗ ⊕ ⊕ 🅸 (780.6KM)

With Roman ruins sprinkled across the city, it is no wonder that Mérida is unlike anywhere else in Spain. The Emperor Augustus selected this land to home the victorious veterans of his legion. Founded in 25BC, the town of **Emerita Augusta** prospered, thanks to its strategic position by Río Guadiana, and became the capital of Lusitania. A wall was raised, consisting of four gates, as was typical in the Roman urban layout.

At least one rest day is recommended to fully discover the city's many sites. Absolutely unmissable is a guided night tour of the spectacularly illuminated **Roman amphitheatre and theatre**. The theatre was inaugurated in 8BC and entertained with shows of gladiators fighting either with each other or against animals brought from Asia and Africa. For information and tickets, visit the office or see https://consorciomerida.sacatuentrada.es/en. Other must-see Roman remains are the **Circo Romano**, **Templo de Diana**, **Pórtico del Foro**, **Arco de Trajano**, and the **National Museum of Roman Art**, located just by the amphitheatre.

There is abundant evidence of the **Roman Mérida** of Octavio Augusto as well as facets of the city's many other influences, including: the **Muslim Mérida** conquered in 1230 by King Alfonso, who then transformed it into the seat of the Priory of San Marcos de León and the Order of Santiago; the **Christian Mérida**

protected by the Catholic monarchs; the Mérida that suffered during the War of Independence, losing parts of her heritage; and modern busy Mérida, bustling capital city of Extremadura, with delicious restaurants scattered along her pedestrian streets.

Among the religious gems, allow time to visit the following. The **Catedral de Santa María** is located on top of a Visigothic construction that had a baptistery and an adjoining episcopal palace. It was abandoned due to the Muslim invasion and recovered in the 13th century, undergoing multiple reforms lasting until 1579. The presbytery holds the tombs of the Knight of the Order of Santiago, Don Diego de Vera y Mendoza, and his wife, Doña Marina Gómez de Figueroa. The **Basílica de Santa Eulalia**, built on Christian foundations from the mid 5th century, was reconstructed in the 13th century. Next to the church is a chapel built in 1612 using the remains of a Roman temple consecrated to Mars. The **Xenodoquio**, founded by Bishop Mausona in the second half of the 6th century, was a monastery for monks and nuns as well as a hospital for the poor and a hostel for pilgrims. Prior to that, the area was a Christian necropolis. The **Convento de San Andrés** (1571) is notable for its Roman mosaics, the remains of a Visigothic church, and a Muslim cemetery and wall discovered following archaeological excavations. On Plaza Santiago, the **Parador hotel** was a former Convent Hospital of Jesús Nazareño, founded in 1724. The **Hospital de San Juan**

**de Dios**, now the seat of the Regional Assembly of Extremadura, has a remarkable octagonal floor plan and dome roof from the 17th century, and its 18th-century classical cloister has interesting double arches. Founded in 1602, the **Iglesia de Santa Clara** exhibits a collection of Visigoth art.

🏠 Albergue de peregrinos Molino de Pancaliente ◨◨ ⑤ 1/16, €10, Av. José Fernández López s/n, tel 682 514 366, amigoscaminodesantiagomerida@hotmail.com. Closed 21 Dec–9 Jan. Sells the *credencial*.

*One of Mérida's countless preserved Roman treasures, the Temple of Diana is fabulously lit up at night (Stage 10)*

# SECTION 2: MÉRIDA TO GRANJA DE MORERUELA

*The sparkling Alcántara reservoir conceals remains of the Roman road and mansio Turmulus (Stage 15)*

The Vía de la Plata officially commences in Mérida, and there is no shortage of reminders of the Roman presence along it. It passes a Roman dam at the Proserpina reservoir before heading through *dehesas*, areas of pastureland dotted with oak woodlands, into Aljucén. It continues on flat tracks to beautiful Cáceres and its mouthwatering restaurants, then ventures on more uneven terrain to the Embalse de Alcántara before encountering pine forests, more *dehesas* and farms en route to the Arco de Cáparra (Stage 18).

To enter the region of Castilla y León, the Camino climbs to the Pass of Béjar in a landscape of high mountains and sublime deciduous forests. Making its way through woods, farms and more *dehesas*, it lands on the vast Meseta plateau of the Zamora province, first visiting Salamanca followed by Zamora three stages later.

Another couple of days' walking brings pilgrims to Granja de Moreruela, a town that itself does not seem to be anything out of the ordinary. Yet it is the last stop on the Vía for pilgrims taking the Camino Sanabrés option towards Santiago, while those heading for Astorga realize they are only three to four days away from the Camino Francés.

## PLANNING

1   Watch for updates to this guide as (writing in 2023) there is still hope that the albergue at the Embalse de Alcántara on Stage 15 will reopen.

2   There are several options provided to tackle the long distance between Carcaboso and Aldeanueva del Camino on Stages 18 and 19.

3   Sections between towns can be long, with no provisions, so check each one carefully.

## WHAT NOT TO MISS

An endless list of memorable moments includes but is not limited to: counting mile markers, including one (on Stage 13) that served as a Roman postbox; relaxing at the thermal baths in Aljucén (Stage 11); treating yourself to lunch in Aldea del Cano (Stage 13); visiting the many sites in Cáceres, particularly the Museo de Cáceres (Stage 14); gazing at the beauty of the Embalse de Alcántara (Stage 15); taking an iconic photo under the Arch of Cáparra (Stage 18); enjoying communal dinners with the wonderful hosts of albergues in Puerto de Béjar and Fuenterroble de Salvatierra (Stages 19 and 20); people-watching on Salamanca's Plaza Mayor (Stage 22); having a glass of wine at the Castillo del Buen Amor, and trying local produce on a Sunday in El Cubo de Tierra del Vino's central bar (Stage 24); aiming to see as many Romanesque churches as possible in Zamora (Stage 25); and being spoilt at the fabulous *albergue donativo* in Fontanillas de Castro (Stage 27).

# STAGE 11
*Mérida to Aljucén*

| | |
|---|---|
| **Start** | Mérida |
| **Finish** | Aljucén |
| **Distance** | 16.3km |
| **Total ascent** | 240m |
| **Total descent** | 185m |
| **Difficulty** | Easy |
| **Duration** | 4hr |
| **Percentage paved** | 69% |
| **Albergues** | El Carrascalejo 13.7km; Aljucén 16.3km |

Welcome to the official Vía de la Plata route from Mérida to Astorga. After Mérida, the Vía's Roman history is hidden in mile markers lying in fields a little away from the Camino, but it comes to life at the Roman dam of Proserpina. After a section alongside a road to the dam, the Camino returns to tranquil *dehesas*. Reliable refreshments can be obtained at the start (the bars at the dam have seasonal opening times and the café/bar in El Carrascalejo is not always open). Camino Mozárabe pilgrims, coming from the south-east corner of Spain, connect to the Vía in Mérida.

From the albergue, turn left on Cl. José Fernández López. Turn right at the roundabout onto Cl. del Ferrocarril (first exit), then left onto Cl. César Lozano under **railway lines**. Just after crossing Río Albarregas, turn left onto Av. Vía de la Plata with a fantastic view of the **Acueducto de los Milagros** (Aqueduct of Miracles) and **Puente Romano** (**0.8km**).

Keep straight across the next two roundabouts, taking Av. del Lago at the second one, as signalled by the yellow arrow on the lamp post. Keep ahead past warehouses and straight over two further roundabouts, after the second of which the Camino hitches along with the **cycle path** on the right and crosses over the **A-5 motorway** (**2.1km**).

The cycle path bears right, passing a bar/restaurant (**0.4km**), returning

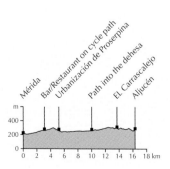

95

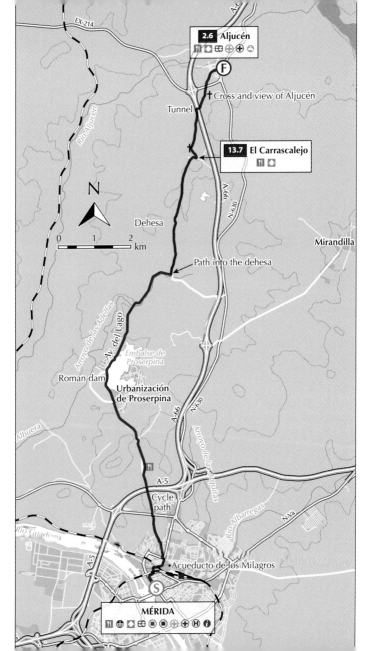

**2.6 Aljucén**

† Cross and view of Aljucén

Tunnel

**13.7 El Carrascalejo**

Mirandilla

N

0   1   2 km

Dehesa

Path into the dehesa

Arroyo de las Adelfas

Av. del Lago

*Embalse de Proserpina*

Roman dam

Urbanización de Proserpina

Arroyo de las Tripuitas

A-66

N-630

A-66

A-5

Albuera

Cycle path

Rio Guadiana

A-5

Rio Albarregas

N-Va

Acueducto de los Milagros

S

**MÉRIDA**

to the road and detouring briefly once more to the right, to arrive at houses in the **Urbanización de Proserpina** and a roundabout. Head directly across to the **Embalse de Proserpina** reservoir and dam (**2.8km**). Built in the time of Augustus, the reservoir collected water to supply the city of Augusta Emerita via the Aqueduct of Miracles.

Turn left onto a path along the reservoir's shores until you return to **Av. del Lago**. Take a right onto it for a lengthy stretch and finally, after the road bends sharp right, look out for markers indicating a left turn onto a **path into the** *dehesa* (**4km**).

The Camino heads straight north following waymarkers through the *dehesas* of Toril and Carrascalejo, where cattle often graze lazily away. Keep straight on the lane to arrive at Cl. Extremadura in **El Carrascalejo** (**3.2km**); turn right and after the Iglesia de la Consolación turn left downhill, keeping left at the roundabout and finding the albergue on the right opposite a café/bar (irregular opening times).

### 13.7KM EL CARRASCALEJO (ELEV 302M, POP 225) 🍴 🛏 (766.9KM)

The village lies 2km from the Roman road itself, but the Camino passes through here to provide accommodation and provisions for pilgrims. The **Iglesia de la Consolación** was built in the 14th and 15th centuries, with restoration work carried out in 1999.

🏠 **Albergue El Carrascalejo** Ⓞ Ⓓ Ⓡ Ⓦ Ⓢ Ⓩ 3/24, €12, Paraje La Cuesta s/n, tel 618 979 583, albergue.elcarrascalejo@gmail.com.

Continue downhill to arrive at a junction of tracks with a **cross** and take the waymarked track on the right, heading north. After 900 metres, cross over a road and head under the **A-66** through a Camino-themed **tunnel**. Head uphill to a **cross** for a view of the village before the Camino winds downwards and reaches Cl. Real in **Aljucén** at a crossroads (drinking fountain to the left).

Fork right, turn right onto Cl. Santiago de Compostela then first left to Bar Kiosko el Parque opposite Iglesia de San Andrés (drinking fountain). Register for the albergue at Bar Kiosko, then turn right out of the bar and walk up the road to reach the albergue on your left.

### 2.6KM ALJUCÉN (ELEV 270M, POP 250) 🍴 🛏 Ⓒ ✛ ⊕ (764.3KM)

Aljucén, as its name suggests, has Muslim antecedents (what may be an Arab cistern was located on Cl. Castillo), yet there are Roman remains also, including a necropolis excavated over the winter of 1999–2000. The church of the town's patron saint, **San Andrés Apóstol**, spectacularly framed by huge palm trees, has a 16th-century Renaissance facade built by the Order of Santiago. An inscription of a prayer to St Andrew is visible on the contour of the portal, and there are engravings of San Andrés and Santiago in the stonework over the entrance. Some

*Santiago's cross and an albergue advert before the descent into Aljucén*

soaking and pampering is in order at the **Roman baths** in town, with a pilgrim price of €10/hr. Booking is recommended (tel 924 145 623, **www.aqualibera. com**).

🔺 Albergue San Andrés Ⓞ Ⓓⓞ Ⓡ Ⓚ Ⓖⓡ Ⓦ Ⓢ Ⓩ 6/24, €12, Cl. San Andrés 21, tel 691 231 248. Keys at Bar Kiosko.

*Aljucén's Iglesia de la Consolación is spectacularly framed by gigantic palm trees*

# STAGE 12

*Aljucén to Alcuéscar*

| | |
|---|---|
| **Start** | Aljucén |
| **Finish** | Alcuéscar |
| **Distance** | 19.3km |
| **Total ascent** | 285m |
| **Total descent** | 110m |
| **Difficulty** | Easy |
| **Duration** | 4¾hr |
| **Percentage paved** | 12% |
| **Albergues** | Alcuéscar 19.3km |

This is a light day, where the Camino heads north through the quiet of the Parque Natural de Cornalvo amid sumptuous *dehesas* and enters the province of Cáceres. Remain prudent and carry provisions for the whole day. The walk offers such tranquillity that absent-mindedness might cause a possible wrong turn. The Camino follows an accessible route, whereas the original Roman Vía itself is mostly through fenced-off private farmland. Towards the stage end, however, the Camino and Vía reunite at the split for the Herrerías option before the march down to Alcuéscar.

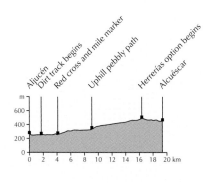

Retrace your steps to Bar Kiosko to return the keys. Turn left out of the bar and veer right at the fork, following this road until it combines with the **N-630** (**1.4km**). Turn left, and then 400 metres later, just after an intersection of roads and before a disused petrol station, head right on a **dirt track** towards trees and an abandoned building, now within the Parque Natural de Cornalvo.

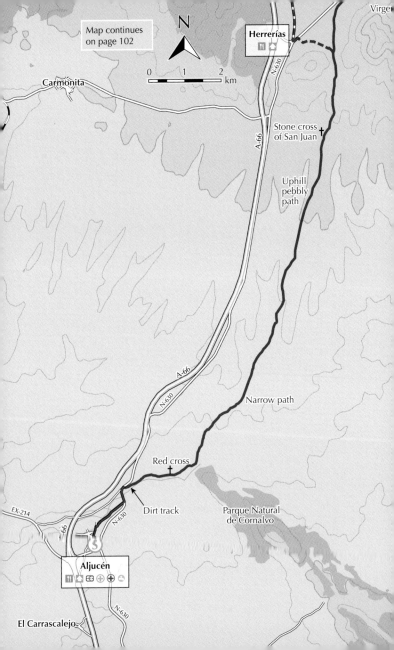

Map continues
on page 102

N

0    1    2
km

Virge

**Herrerías**

N-630

Stone cross
of San Juan †

A-66

Uphill
pebbly
path

Carmonita

A-66

N-630

Narrow path

Red cross
†

Dirt track

Parque Natural
de Cornalvo

EX-214

-66

N-630

**Aljucén**

N-630

El Carrascalejo

In 1989, just a few years before the regional government of Extremadura named this area the **Parque Natural de Cornalvo** in early 1993, the European Union declared it an Important Bird Area. Fascinatingly, the park is also home to the mongoose (*Herpestes ichneumon*), one of the only locations of its kind in Europe.

The biggest Roman remain in the area, 22km away from Aljucén, is the **Cornalvo dam**, designated a national monument in 1912. The dam's drainage tower in the middle of the Cornalvo reservoir was the starting point for the aqueduct that supplied water to Mérida.

*After rain, the sandy tracks and puddles through the dehesas can be somewhat bothersome*

Keep ahead at the **red cross** with a Roman mile marker (**2.8km**). At the next fork, keep left following waymarks (**2.4km**). Continue along and take a **narrow path** on the right, ignoring the wider dirt track straight ahead (**2.4km**).

The Camino is now a narrower **uphill pebbly path**, with higher bushes surrounding it as it gradually climbs and reaches the **stone cross of San Juan** (**5.3km**). Turn left onto a wide track, as per the waymark cube, and keep gently uphill past farms until you arrive at a significant fork in the track where signs offer two options (**2.1km**).

### Herrerías option (unwaymarked)
A left turn leads down to a hotel/restaurant (⌂ **Hostal/Restaurante Los Olivos** * 🅾 🅿🆁 🆁 🅱🆁 🅶🆁 🆆 🆂 11/17, €-/15/30, Ctra. N-630 km591, tel 661 256 990) and service station on the N-630, off the Camino. After the services, head along the **N-630** for a 4.3km stretch to reconnect with the Camino (Stage 13), without having to go into Alcuéscar. It is neither waymarked nor recommended, even though it cuts off 1.5km overall.

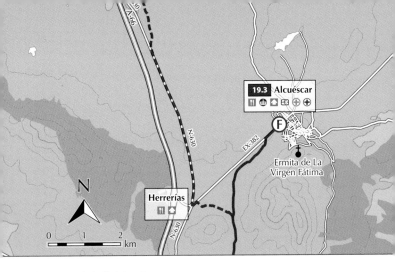

## Recommended official route

Fork right to keep to the Camino, turning right 1.7km later as Alcuéscar comes into view. Then fork left to reach the **EX-382 (2.6km)**, where a right turn leads to **Alcuéscar** and the albergue 500 metres later.

### 19.3KM ALCUÉSCAR (ELEV 486M, POP 2486) ⓘ ⊕ ⌂ Ⓒ ⊕ ⊕ (745.0KM)

The centre of town is up the road, but fortunately the café/restaurant opposite the albergue tends to open early. The **Iglesia de Nuestra Señora de la Asunción** is a 15th-century construction, with the main altarpiece dating from the 1940s. The circular **Ermita de la Virgen Fátima**, with a facade built in 1952, stands on the hill of Calvario, named after the priest who placed the cross. The view from here is superb, although it is 1.7km from the albergue, with 150m of ascent.

⌂ Casa de Acogida de los Esclavos de María y de los Pobres Ⓞ Ⓓ Ⓢ 4/12, €Donation, Av. de Extremadura 2, tel 651 323 466. Run by a Christian congregation and volunteers.

# STAGE 13
### Alcuéscar to Valdesalor

| | |
|---|---|
| **Start** | Alcuéscar |
| **Finish** | Valdesalor |
| **Distance** | 26.5km |
| **Total ascent** | 150m |
| **Total descent** | 210m |
| **Difficulty** | Moderate |
| **Duration** | 6¼hr |
| **Percentage paved** | <1% |
| **Albergues** | Aldea del Cano 15.3km; Valdesalor 26.5km |

This is a lovely historic day on drover's tracks, where Camino, Vía and Cañada Real harmonize, and with the presence of the Romans along the route much more evident than previously. After rainfall, two fords in the first 4km may involve crossing barefoot, and in bad weather albergues might advise taking the N-630 instead, words which should be heeded. Aldea del Cano can be skipped, if necessary, despite a good albergue and a fabulous lunch menu at the local restaurant by the town hall. The 11km remaining distance to Valdesalor is straightforward, providing an excellent opportunity to digest your meal.

From the albergue, turn left onto the EX-382 and first left onto Av. de la Constitución. Keep straight at the first fork, then fork right at the second and, finally, left at the

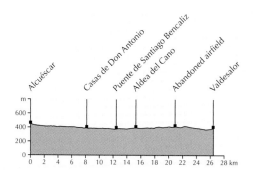

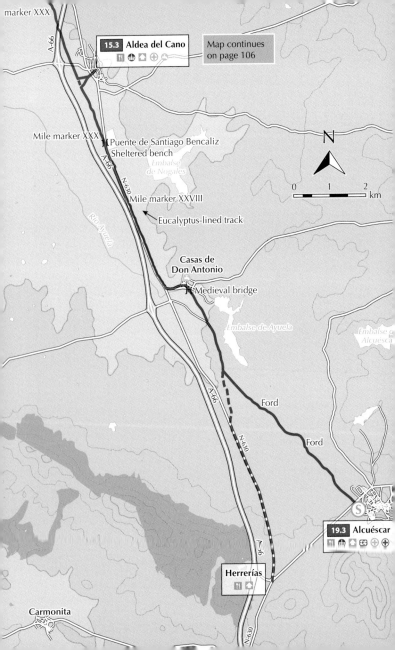

marker XXX

A-66

**15.3** Aldea del Cano

Map continues
on page 106

Mile marker XXX · Puente de Santiago Bencaliz
Sheltered bench

*Embalse
de Nogales*

N-630

Mile marker XXVIII

Eucalyptus-lined track

*Río Ayuela*

N

0    1    2
km

Casas de
Don Antonio

Medieval bridge

*Embalse de Ayuela*

*Embalse de
Alcuesca*

A-66

Ford

N-630

Ford

**19.3** Alcuéscar

Herrerías

A-66

N-630

Carmonita

*The minuscule village of Casas de Don Antonio has a blue-and-white-themed square lined with orange trees*

third fork (**1km**). Cross the first **ford** (**1.1km**) and the second **ford** (**1.8km**). The Herrerías option (see Stage 12) rejoins soon after the second ford. Eventually, go right among trees (**3.1km**). Join a minor road ahead and almost immediately take the first track on the right to leave it. Cross the **medieval bridge** (**1km**) and cross the main road into **Casas de Don Antonio** (no services). Arrive at Plaza de José Antonio (**0.2km**), with its stone cross, where a café/bar sporadically opens.

The 17th-century **stone cross** (*rollo jurisdiccional*) on Plaza España was once a symbol of the town's independence. The stone used is thought to be from a former Roman bridge.

Keep left on Av. Virgen del Pilar to reach the Ermita de Nuestra Señora del Pilar (drinking fountain). Look through the gates to see the shield of Casas de Don Antonio, representing the cobblestones of the Roman way and the cross of Santiago. Veer right, following the CC-147. Just before the N-630, take the dirt track on the right. Soon, pass a **eucalyptus-lined track** on your right. This leads to the Santiago Bencaliz estate with its 17th/18th-century mansion, as well as 15th/16th-century chapel ruins and preserved 17th-century murals.

Reach **mile marker XXVIII** (**3km**), which was used as a 'postbox' by the Romans, and arrive at a **sheltered bench** and the medieval **Puente de Santiago Bencaliz** of Roman origin (**1.3km**). Soon, cross over the N-630 to turn right on the track alongside it and pass **mile marker XXX** (**1.7km**).

Although the first track on your right leads to **Aldea del Cano**, take the second, more direct right-hand track (**0.6km**) for the albergue and facilities (if not heading into the town, keep straight). Turn right and reach the albergue opposite a restaurant. Cross

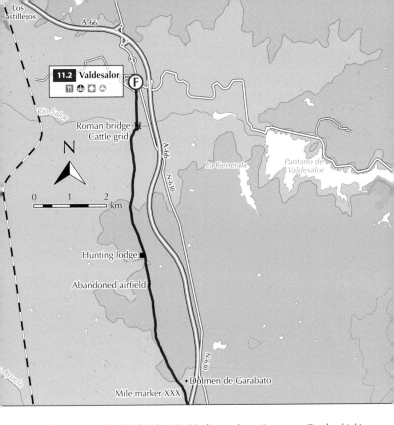

over the N-630 and take Cl. Sebastián Sánchez to the main square. (For the drinking fountain, head up to Cl. Real past the church to reach a small square.)

### 15.3KM ALDEA DEL CANO (ELEV 394M, POP 610) 🍴 ⊕ ⌂ ✛ (729.7KM)

Aldea del Cano is a small, interesting town, where the 15th-century **Iglesia de San Martín** stands opposite the 1905 **town hall**, behind which is situated the town's favourite hearty lunch spot at the local restaurant. The drinking fountain is a rebuilt, ornate well on Cl. Canchalillo. The old bishops' residence, **Casas del Cura** (18th century), has a unique chimney and tiny windows.

⌂ **Albergue municipal Miliario del Verdinal** Ⓞ Ⓓⓞ Ⓚ Ⓦ Ⓢ 3/12, €6, Ctra. N-630 s/n, tel 927 38 30 02 or 927 38 30 04. Keys from Bar Las Vegas.

Retrace your steps past the albergue and fork right onto the track. Turn right onto the next track (**0.6km**) and go under the **A-66** (**1.3km**), after which turn right (no waymark) and pass **mile marker XXX**. The Dolmen de Garabato sits on a knoll in the field on the right (access is difficult), where remains of mile markers are also scattered.

Continue to an **abandoned airfield** (**3.7km**) and follow a waymark leading towards the metallic warehouses. Pass a **hunting lodge** (**0.9km**), and at the **cattle grid** (**3.3km**) follow the track to the right, downhill (no waymark). Turn left onto the eight-arched **Roman bridge**, cross the road, and arrive at the albergue (drinking fountain in a small park on the corner between Cl. Cristóbal Colón and Cl. Cabeza de Vaca).

### 11.2KM VALDESALOR (ELEV 388M, POP 553) ▯ ⊕ ▯ (718.5KM)

Valdesalor is a prime architectural example of the rural development of Spain under the Franco dictatorship. In 1963, the 60 original settlers received six hectares for growing crops, using the Salor reservoir for irrigation. The **eight-arched bridge** into town is of Roman origin; it has been rebuilt numerous times since the Middle Ages, but retains some Roman ashlars. Today, within the inner patio of the Bar Salor on Cl. Cristóbal Colón, the Vía is colourfully depicted by a delightful mural of a pilgrim making his way across a bridge.

🏠 **Albergue de peregrinos de Valdesalor** Ⓞ Ⓓ Ⓦ Ⓢ Ⓩ 1/14, €6, Valdesalor s/n, tel 927 129 711 or 927 129 859. Keys from the bar/shop La Despensa del Salor (Mon–Sun 07:00–11:00) or the town hall (mornings only).

# STAGE 14

*Valdesalor to
Casar de Cáceres*

| | |
|---|---|
| **Start** | Valdesalor |
| **Finish** | Casar de Cáceres |
| **Distance** | 23.3km |
| **Total ascent** | 245m |
| **Total descent** | 260m |
| **Difficulty** | Easy |
| **Duration** | 5½hr |
| **Percentage paved** | 45% |
| **Albergues** | Cáceres 12.0km; Casar de Cáceres 23.3km |

The closure of the albergue at the Alcántara reservoir entails some forward planning for the next two to three days. An alternative option to the one provided would be to split the walk by staying in Cáceres, followed by Casar de Cáceres the next day, then Cañaveral on the third day. Otherwise, from Cáceres it is a 44.5km walk to Cañaveral. For many, a lunchtime visit of Cáceres may be enough; but, if not in a rush, and to enjoy Cáceres fully, including its nightlife of *tapas* bar crawling, a good idea is to split this stage into two easy walking days.

Turn left out of the albergue, take first right, first left and first right over the N-630, keeping left alongside it. Pass a petrol station/restaurant opposite, then cross the **A-66** (**1.1km**). Turn left at the road (**2.2km**) and soon cross the **N-630**. Promptly turn right to a first view of Cáceres on the **Puerto de las Camellas** hill pass (**1.6km**). Cross the N-630, keep straight and fork right towards Cáceres.

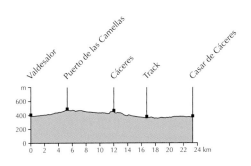

Come to **Cl. Océano Atlántico** (**3.9km**), now in **Cáceres**. Cross to the petrol station and turn left, then fork right onto Ronda de San Francisco behind the supermarket. Keep straight until you reach **Plaza de San Francisco** with an 18th-century bridge on the roundabout (**2.4km**). From here, there are two route options.

## Official route
Go anticlockwise and take Cl. Mira al Río. Take the walkway on the left into the Jewish quarter. Turn left onto Cl. Fuente Consejo through the Arco del Cristo then go immediately right through Puerta de Coria onto Plazuela del Socorro. Traverse diagonally onto Cl. Zapartería, fork right onto Cl. Godoy and arrive at the **Iglesia de Santiago el Mayor**. A Camino sign shows you the options. Turn left onto Cl. Camberos, straight onto Cl. Moreras and left on Cl. Nidos. Reach Cl. de Sancti Spíritus and turn right onto it to rejoin the main route.

## Recommended route through the old town
Go around clockwise and take Cl. Damas. Turn left onto Cl. Hornos and follow it as it bends right to turn left onto Cl. Postigo then first right onto Plaza de San Juan. Walk

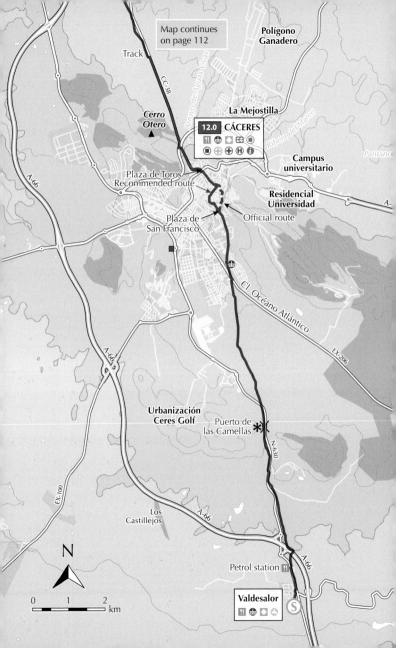

Map continues
on page 112

Track

CC-38

Polígono
Ganadero

La Mejostilla

*Cerro
Otero* ▲

**12.0** CÁCERES

Campus
universitario

Ribera del Marco

Pantanc

Plaza de Toros
Recommended route

Residencial
Universidad

Official route

Plaza de
San Francisco

A-66

Cl. Océano Atlántico

EX-206

A-

A-66

Urbanización
Ceres Golf

Puerto de
las Camellas ✳

N-630

EX-100

Los
Castillejos

A-66

A-66

N

Petrol station

**Valdesalor** Ⓢ

0    1    2
━━━━━━━━ km

*A medley of Roman, Islamic, Jewish, Gothic and Renaissance styles is preserved in an otherwise modern bustling Cáceres*

downhill with the park on your left and follow the Gran Vía at the fork. Reach **Plaza Mayor** and the **tourist office**, behind which the charms of the historic monuments lie. Across Plaza Mayor, take Cl. Gabriel y Galán then turn left onto Cl. de Sancti Spíritus.

### 12.0KM CÁCERES (ELEV 388M, POP 95,418) 🍴 ⊕ ⌂ 🄴 ⊙ ⊙ Ⓗ ⊕ ⊕ 🛈 (706.5KM)

Declared a UNESCO World Heritage site on 26 November 1986, Cáceres is well known for its extraordinary history and refined *tapas* culture. Human settlement dates back to the upper Palaeolithic period. In 139BC, during the Roman conquest of the North, Quinto Servilio Cepión set up camp nearby, and the second official *mansio* of the Vía, **Castra Caecilia**, is cited to be here. Cáceres was then founded in 25BC.

After the 6th-century Roman collapse and post-Visigoth occupation, the **Almohads** built the many palaces and towers seen today. One of the world's best-preserved Hispano-Muslim cisterns (*aljibe*) is in the fantastic **Museo de Cáceres** (http://museodecaceres.juntaex.es).

In 1229, during the **Reconquest**, King Alfonso IX of León gained the territory, and people from León, Galicia and Asturias, joined by monks and nobles, settled here and transformed Cáceres into a prosperous place. The ruined and restored towers are a result of internal struggles whereby Isabela la Católica imposed her authority in 1447, destroying noble palaces. After a period of stability, Cáceres gained a bourgeois population, and commercial and political importance thus reached its apogee. Amusingly, after King Alfonso XII accidentally named the town of Cáceres a 'city', he had to keep his word and proclaim it as such in 1882. Wandering through the narrow twisting cobbled streets of the old town, before an evening of eating on beautifully lit Plaza Mayor and its neighbouring side streets, is well worth a day off.

🏠 **Albergue Turístico Las Veletas** Ⓞ 𝐏𝐫 𝐃𝐨 𝐑 𝐂𝐟 𝐖 𝐒 11/40 & 2/4, €16/20/40/- /-, Cl. General Margallo 36, tel 681 258 701 or 927 211 210, info@ alberguelasveletas.com, **www.alberguelasveletas.es**.

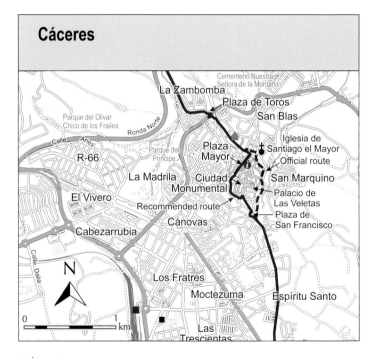

**Main route**

With both options reunited, keep down Cl. de Sancti Spíritus to the end then cross to the **Plaza de Toros**. One of Spain's oldest bullrings, the Plaza de Toros was declared a national heritage site in 1992.

Follow the road sign left for Casar de Cáceres, descend the palm-tree-lined avenue, cross at the lights on the next big roundabout and turn right alongside the

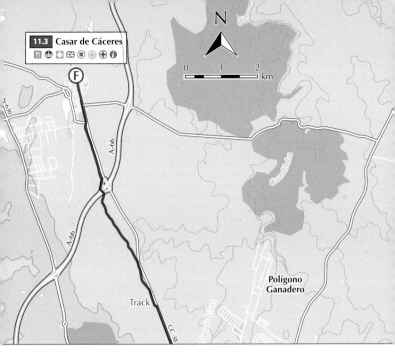

CC-38 (1.9km). Keep on the road and then turn left onto a **track** (2.7km). Veer right and under the **A-66 motorway** (3.5km). Cross the road and into a park in **Casar de Cáceres** (2.1km). Keep ahead, passing bars and shops, to the albergue on Plaza España.

### 11.3KM CASAR DE CÁCERES (ELEV 368M, POP 4516) 🍴 ⊕ 🏠 🔲 ⊙ ⊕ ⊕ ⓘ (695.2KM)

The **Roman road** set the tone for the rectilinear appearance of a town that is accustomed to travellers passing through. The **Parroquia de Nuestra Señora de la Asunción** (15th–16th century) has been declared an Asset of Cultural Interest, while the **modern bus station** is one of the most unique constructions in an otherwise very traditional Extremadura. For the hungry pilgrim, the **Cheese Museum** will not disappoint, and the Torta del Casar strong creamy cheese is an utter delicacy.

🛏 Albergue de peregrinos de Casar de Cáceres ⏹ 🅿 Ⓚ Ⓦ Ⓢ 2/22, €6, Plaza de España s/n, tel 669 961 887. Keys from tourist office (10:00–14:00 and 17:00–19:00, except Sunday afternoons), town hall (Mon–Fri 08:00–15:00), El Siglo bar or Majuca restaurant.

# STAGE 15

*Casar de Cáceres to Cañaveral*

| | |
|---|---|
| **Start** | Casar de Cáceres |
| **Finish** | Cañaveral |
| **Distance** | 33.2km |
| **Total ascent** | 425m |
| **Total descent** | 440m |
| **Difficulty** | Very hard |
| **Duration** | 8¼hr |
| **Percentage paved** | 22% |
| **Albergues** | Cañaveral 33.2km |

Although the stage is inevitably long, it is filled with magnificent walking. Preparing ahead is essential as there are absolutely no provisions on the way and very little shade. Perhaps the albergue at the Embalse de Alcántara will reopen in the future, allowing for a shorter day and a more manageable 23km from Casar de Cáceres. A beautiful stage in terms of both history and nature, it presents no difficulties, and the N-630 section graces the walker with marvellous views of the sparkling Alcántara reservoir.

Leave the albergue north to the **Ermita de Santiago**, where two original Roman mile markers are located. Follow the cube and VP (standing for *Vía pecuaria*: cattle road) markers by farms as the Camino sets off on a wide track and passes an **information board** (**1.9km**).

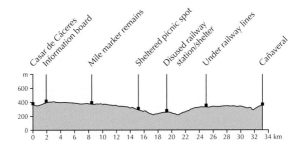

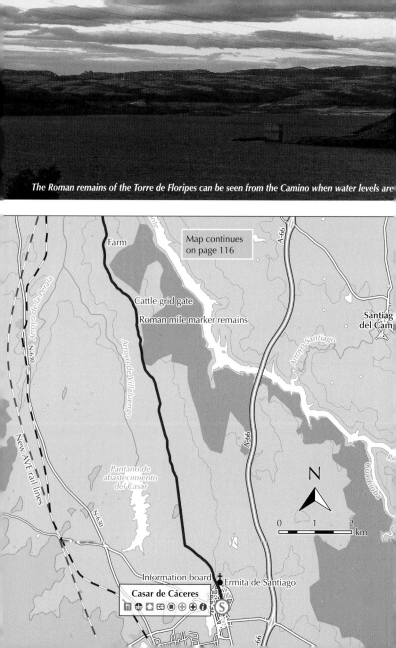

*The Roman remains of the Torre de Floripes can be seen from the Camino when water levels are*

Farm

Map continues on page 116

A-66

Cattle grid gate

Roman mile marker remains

Santiag
del Cam

Arroyo Santiago

Arroyo de la Perala

N-630

Arroyo de Villaluengo

New AVE rail lines

A-66

Guadiloba

Pantano de
abastecimiento
del Casar

N-630

N

0    1    2
km

Information board    ✝ Ermita de Santiago

**Casar de Cáceres**

🍴 🏨 🏠 💱 🏤 ➕ ❶    Ⓢ

A-66

Start a long straight section with fantastic views to the countryside on either side, passing the odd farm, to reach a field of broken **Roman mile markers** (**6.6km**). The Camino then goes through a **cattle grid gate**, keeps straight, winds down to the left through another gate and reaches a **farm** (**2.1km**), after which it continues straight then goes right at a gate (and not through the gate). Some 200 metres later, ignore a track on the left and go through a gate and then another gate between drystone walls (**1km**) to reach the **AVE rail lines** (**2.3km**). AVE workers waymark any diversions to assist pilgrims when construction affects the Camino.

Head right then left to cross over the lines, and go left straight after onto a narrow path (**0.7km**), sharing the route now with the signed and waymarked **GR113 Camino Natural del Tajo** long-distance route (which leaves the Vía after Cañaveral). Turn right onto the path as the N-630 runs below you. Soon pass a **sheltered picnic spot** above the Alcántara reservoir.

At the time it was built in 1969, the **Embalse de Alcántara** (from the Arabic word for 'the bridge') was the second longest reservoir in Europe and today is the second largest in Spain. Hidden under its waters are parts of the Roman road and *mansio* Turmulus, 66 Roman miles from Mérida.

The **Torre de Floripes** still stands as part of the fallen castle and can often be seen from the Camino when water levels are low. Initially used by the Romans for surveillance of the Vía, it maintained its importance as a defensive tower for the Arabs and later the Templars during the Reconquest. From the tower, the Romans also strategically oversaw the Alconétar bridge which spanned the Río Tajo. Researchers date it back to the 2nd century AD. The impressive granite ashlars of the remains of the bridge were moved during the reservoir construction and to see them would involve heading further along the N-630. This is possible as the highway also hits Cañaveral 9.6km later.

Join the **N-630** (**2.2km**) and turn right along it, cross the bridge (**0.5km**) over **Río Almonte** and pass a **disused railway station** (**2km**, shelter), then head over **Río Tajo**

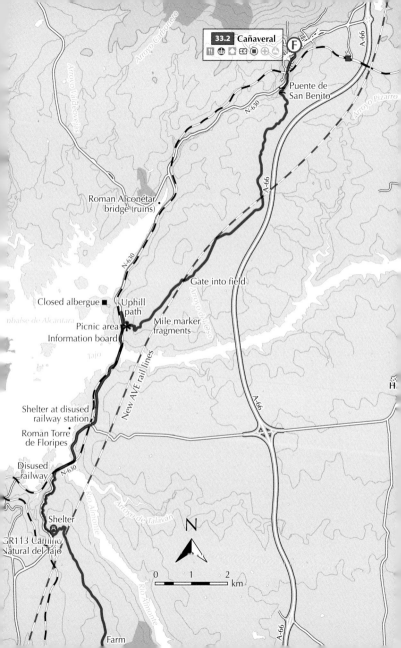

33.2 Cañaveral

Cañaveral

Puente de
San Benito

Arroyo Carbonero

Arroyo Valdeovejas

N-630

A-66

Arroyo Pizarro

Roman Alconétar
bridge (ruins)

N-630

Gate into field

Arroyo del Lloso

Closed albergue  Uphill
path

Picnic area
Information board

Mile marker
fragments

nbalse de Alcantara

Tajo

New AVE rail lines

A-66

Shelter at disused
railway station

Roman Torre
de Floripes

A-66

Disused
railway

N-630

Shelter

Río Almonte

Arroyo de Talaván

GR113 Camino
Natural del Tajo

N

0        1        2
━━━━━━━━━━━ km

Farm

Río Almonte

A-66

(**1.6km**) to reach an **information board** (**1.2km**). Ignore arrows pointing left towards the now closed albergue. Cross the N-630 and take the path uphill on the right to another **picnic spot** with more fabulous views.

Pass **fragments of mile markers** and walk alongside the **railway tracks** to then pass under them (**2.9km**) and go through a **gate into a field** just opposite. Turn left and walk through the field to pass over the **railway lines** (**3.5km**) and a cattle grid. Views of Cañaveral and the Sierra del Arco mountains form as the Camino leads past farms and hills, then down through the valley to cross the medieval **Puente de San Benito** (**3.5km**).

Keep to the path alongside the N-630 before joining it to go right into **Cañaveral**. Soon, arrive at the albergue. A drinking fountain is on Cl. San Juan.

### 33.2KM CAÑAVERAL (ELEV 363M, POP 1024) 🏨 ⊕ 🛒 € ◉ ⊕ (662.0KM)

The Vía and Cañada Real drover's track did not pass through the town but rather went via the site of today's railway station (2.7km away) which, when built in 1880, used to be a lively hotspot for trading of limes and chocolate. Religious buildings in and around town include the **church of Santa Marina** (14th–15th century), the **chapel of San Cristóbal** (1980s) and four *ermitas*: **San Roque** (16th–17th century), **Cristo del Humilladero** (17th century), **San José** (contemporary) and **Nuestra Señora del Cabezón** (17th–19th century, with the Virgin of the Child carving dating from the 13th century).

🛏 Hostel Cañaveral 🄾 🄿🅁 🄳🄾 🅁 🄱🅁 🄶🅁 🅆 🅂 🆉 4/23, €15/30/45/60, Av. Doctor Luis Boticario 12, tel 669 402 446 or 655 351 976, info@hostelcanaveral. com, **www.hostelcanaveral.com**.

# STAGE 16
*Cañaveral to Galisteo*

| | |
|---|---|
| **Start** | Cañaveral |
| **Finish** | Galisteo |
| **Distance** | 28.7km |
| **Total ascent** | 440m |
| **Total descent** | 510m |
| **Difficulty** | Hard |
| **Duration** | 7hr |
| **Percentage paved** | 19% |
| **Albergues** | Grimaldo 8.5km; Galisteo 28.7km |

The Camino rambles through beautiful *dehesas* to fortified Galisteo. Sharing the trail with the GR113 at the start, watch for Camino waymarking. For provisions, take a swift detour to Grimaldo or, 16.5km into the stage, a longer detour to Riolobos. Just before Galisteo, there is an option to follow the original Roman Vía by leaving the Camino. This route goes through San Gil (no accommodation) and reconnects with the Camino at the end of Stage 17, in Carcaboso. The distance being the same, the recommended option is the Camino route through the much more interesting towns of Galisteo and Aldehuela del Jerte.

Turn right out of the albergue, pass the petrol station and turn left uphill (**1.2km**), keeping straight 200 metres later (no waymark). Ignore the left track, turn right and immediately fork left. Keep straight uphill, ignoring a confusing waymark

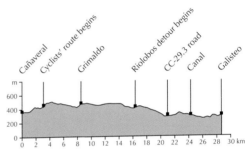

and parting with the GR113. Soon turn left uphill and keep ahead on a **steep uphill** (**2km**). Cyclists should take a left turn here. Walk through the **pine forest** and drop down across the EX-109 (**1.6km**) towards the **El Puerto nightclub** (strip club). Skirt behind it into a *dehesa*.

The Camino heads right, briefly away from the fence, then keeps to the left side of the field closer to the fence and under **electricity lines** downhill. The fence line itself traces the original Roman road with rigorous precision.

Come to a sign for **Grimaldo** to the right (**3km**). To avoid Grimaldo, keep straight ahead on the Camino. For the village, follow the sign, passing under the A-66 and heading uphill to a restaurant on the N-630. Cross and head left, passing the albergue on the right (bar).

### 0.5KM GRIMALDO (ELEV 475M, POP 82) 🍴 ⌂ (653.5KM)

The **15th-century castle** conserves milestones from the Roman road.

⌂ **Albergue de peregrinos de Grimaldo** Ⓞ Ⓓ Ⓦ Ⓢ 3/12, €Donation, Ctra. N-630 s/n, tel 650 848 181. Keys from the bar next door.

Valdencín

Holguera

Map continues
on page 121

Canal

Riolobos detour

Dehesa

Dehesa

Cerro
Cabildo ▲

Dehesas

N-630

Dehesas

A-66

Road to
Holguera

Avoiding
Grimaldo

Track

Electricity lines

N-630

**8.5** Grimaldo

mbalse de
rrejoncillo

EX-109

Dehesas

Pedroso
de Acim

Pre

Casas de
Millán

El Puerto nightclub

Pine forest

Cyclists' route

Steep
uphill

N-630

Petrol station

**S**

Cañaveral

N

0          1          2
╞════╪════╪════╪════╡ km

A-66

Arroyo Pizarroso

Rivera del Castaño

**Waymarking shows options for pilgrims on foot and those on wheels**

Pass a drinking fountain, leave town and take a road on the left for Holguera, (**0.6km**) taking the first track on the right downhill (no waymark) under the **A-66**. Follow the lane to turn first left onto a narrow path. Turn right onto another path to join the Camino (**1.3km**) through the sumptuous Dehesa de Grimaldo, reaching a fork and signpost for the detour to Riolobos (**6.1km**).

**Riolobos detour (4.3km to Riolobos, 9.3km from Riolobos to Galisteo)**
For Riolobos, fork left on the track and follow it for 3.3km, crossing a **canal** and reaching the **CC-29.3**. A right turn here takes you back to rejoin the Camino 2.7km later at the Embalse del Boquerón. Go left onto the road into town. (◻ ⊕ ◻ ◻ ⊕ drinking fountain. ♠ Casa Rural Abuela Maxi ◻ ◻ ◻ ◻ ◻ ◻ 6/12, €-/25/50/70/70, Cl. Egido 6, tel 670 733 093, **https://abuelamaxi.com**. Includes breakfast. Whole house available. ▲ Camping Las Catalinas ◻ ◻ ◻ 6/32, €-/15/30/45/50, Ctra. de Plasencia s/n, tel 927 451 150, info@campinglascatalinas.es, **www.campinglascatalinas.es**. Bungalows for pilgrims. Closed in Jan.)

After the last houses, turn right towards a petrol station. At the end of the road, turn right then cross a bridge. Some 1.1km later, reach the **Ermita de Nuestra Señora de la Argamasa** and turn right onto a road. After 2.7km go over the Arroyo de las Monjas and 2.4km later reach a roundabout in **Galisteo**. Cross onto Cl. Luis Chamizo and turn right up Av. del Puente Romano along the Almohad walls to the Puerta del Rey.

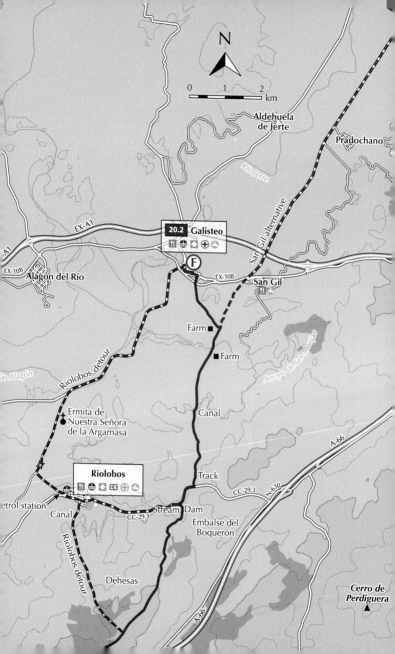

*On the approach to fortified Galisteo*

## Main route

Keep right at the fork, towards the **Embalse del Boquerón**. Head downhill past the **dam** and cross the **stream** (**4.1km**). Go up the bank to turn right onto the **CC-29.3**, where another connection with Riolobos is possible. Keep to the CC-29.3 until waymarking takes you left onto a **track** (**1.4km**). Fork right at the next junction to a **canal** (**2.2km**). Cross and take a diagonal track on the right, passing a **farm** to turn left over Arroyo de las Monjas (**1.8km**). Soon, near another **farm**, come to an information board and sign for Galisteo. The San Gil alternative starts here.

## San Gil alternative to Carcaboso (1.5km to San Gil, 12km from San Gil to Carcaboso)

At the information board, keep straight on to **San Gil** (café/bars and drinking fountain) and the **EX-108**. Turning left here leads to Galisteo, 1.5km away. Cross the road, turn right and immediately left following road signs towards Pradochano (no services). Pass an information board 4.3km later then another with a stone arch at a turn-off to **Pradochano**. Keep straight and after 3.9km turn left by a sign for an **acequia** (water channel), towards buildings. Turn left at the next fork, and 1.2km later turn left onto the road into **Carcaboso** (see end of Stage 17).

## Main route

For Galisteo, turn left at the information board, then first right, and keep straight over the junction to drop down into **Galisteo** (**2.1km**). Cross, turn right on Ctra. Alagón and left onto Ctra. de Plasencia where a right leads to the albergue. Pass a drinking fountain by the Almohad walls and go through the Puerta del Rey.

**20.2KM GALISTEO** (ELEV 305M, POP 902) ▯ ⊕ ▯ ⊕ (633.3KM)

With views across the Jerte valley and to the Sierra de Ambroz, Galisteo evokes centuries of history within its **Almohad walls**: a medieval layout, whitewashed houses and stone arcades. The 3-metre-thick by 11-metre-high fortified walls were built and restored between the 9th and 14th centuries with earth, limestone and pebbles. **La Picota tower** is the only remnant of the old castle and was rebuilt in the 15th century.

🛏 **Albergue Turístico de Galisteo** ▯ ▯ ▯ ▯ 1/8, €15, Cl. Viña de Egido s/n, tel 927 451 150 or 605 824 086, info@campinglascatalinas.es. Includes breakfast. The same hosts run the campsite in Riolobos and drive pilgrims there and back if there is no space in the albergue.

# STAGE 17
## *Galisteo to Carcaboso*

| | |
|---|---|
| **Start** | Galisteo |
| **Finish** | Carcaboso |
| **Distance** | 10.8km |
| **Total ascent** | 105m |
| **Total descent** | 125m |
| **Difficulty** | Easy |
| **Duration** | 2½hr |
| **Percentage paved** | 100% |
| **Albergues** | Carcaboso 10.8km |

This short stage provides the opportunity to rest prior to a longer stage the following day, which will involve the dilemma of accommodation between Carcaboso and Aldeanueva del Camino. Although Carcaboso might resemble a modest Extremadura town, it is a significant point of interest: it unifies the original Roman Vía and the Camino at the Iglesia de Santiago and the adjacent Parque de los Miliarios.

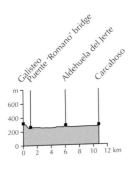

Go through Puerta del Rey into the old town. Turn left past a supermarket then first right onto Trav. del Rey to Plaza España (drinking fountain). Go straight through the first arcade and turn left onto Cl. Gabriel y Galán. Leave the old town through Puerta de la Villa, where swallows have made their home. Head right down Cl. Huerto de los Olivos. Turn right at the bottom to reach the medieval, so-called **Puente 'Romano'** (**1km**) over Río Jerte. The bridge, built with granite ashlar in 1546, has seven arches and a shrine with the image of St Paul.

Turn right onto the EX-108 and cross straight over the roundabout and under the **motorway** following signs for Aldehuela del Jerte (**0.7km**). A confusing arrow may make you take the exit on the right! At the second roundabout, go around anti-clockwise and take the second exit, following the sign for Carcaboso and continuing past **greenhouses** (**1.5km**).

After a left bend in the road, some houses appear (**2.3km**). Enter **Aldehuela del Jerte** (🏠 ✛) on a tree-lined road, reaching an information board. Keep straight, with the Iglesia Parroquial San Blas (dating from 1771) to the right. Pass a shop and then another opposite a drinking fountain by a **shelter** (**0.5km**).

*A mosaic of Santiago Matamoros near the entrance to Carcaboso's church recalls the legendary battle of Clavijo*

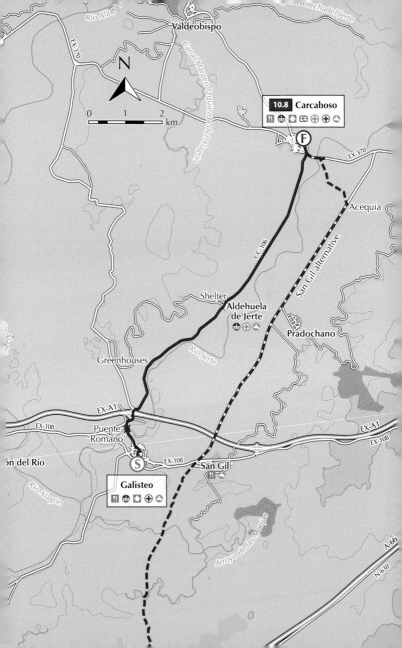

The landscape surrounding **Aldehuela del Jerte** offers a combination of agriculture and *dehesa*. In the nearby Patua estate, archaeological remains of Roman *tegulas* (overlapping roof tiles) and slate slabs have been found.

Pass near another drinking fountain and follow the **CC-106** until you land in **Carcaboso** (4.6km), where many helpful signs direct the route to accommodation and services.

To reach the stage end at the church, cross over and take the road heading slightly uphill by the Vía information board. Follow Cl. de la Iglesia and arrive at the Iglesia de Santiago Apóstol and Parque de los Miliarios. A drinking fountain can be found in a triangular park off the main street.

### 10.8KM CARCABOSO (ELEV 275M, POP 1080) ⊞ ⊕ ⌂ ⓒ ⊕ ⊕ (622.5KM)

The original Vía de la Plata passed 2km from the centre of Carcaboso, yet the town boasts six **original mile markers** bearing miles CII and CIII. Previously ruled by the Galisteo manor, Carcaboso became a municipality in 1837 and has seen continuous population growth.

The **Iglesia de Santiago Apóstol** was established on 25 March 1995 by the Bishop of Cáceres, Ciriaco Benavente Mateos, and holds a mosaic of Santiago Matamoros. As the tale goes, after the death of King Alfonso II of Asturias, his son, Ramiro I, dreamt of Santiago on the eve of the legendary battle of Clavijo against the Muslim army of Abd ar-Rahman II in the year 844. The next day, Santiago, bearing a white banner, appeared as a warrior on a white horse and came to the aid of the Christian King and his armies to win the battle. The **Order of Santiago** is said to have originated following this battle and lives on today. The monarchs of the Reconquest also recognized the apostle as the patron saint of Spain.

🏠 **Albergue Señora Elena** ⓞ 🅳🅾 🆁 🅺 🆆 🆂 4/12, €13, Ctra. de Plasencia 23–27, tel 927 402 075 or 659 774 580. Register at the bar next door.

🏠 **Hostal Ciudad de Cáparra** ⓞ 🅿🆃 🆁 🆂 5/10, €-/28/52, Ctra. de Plasencia 35, tel 927 402 032 or 927 402 444.

# STAGE 18

### Carcaboso to
### Hotels Asturias and Jarilla

| | |
|---|---|
| **Start** | Carcaboso |
| **Finish** | Hotels Asturias and Jarilla |
| **Distance** | 28.4km |
| **Total ascent** | 330m |
| **Total descent** | 200m |
| **Difficulty** | Hard |
| **Duration** | 7hr |
| **Percentage paved** | 21% |
| **Albergues** | Arco de Cáparra (transfer to Hotels Avión or Asturias) 18km; Hotels Asturias and Jarilla 28.4km |

This is one of the most symbolic days on the Vía, where the emblematic Arch of Cáparra finally comes to life. Today's four options are: walk to Aldeanueva del Camino on the official route, totalling 39.8km; walk 18km to the Arco de Cáparra and use the free shuttle service to Hotels Avión or Asturias; take a 13.1km detour to Oliva de Plasencia; or follow this book's proposed 28.4km stage, deviating off the Camino by 2.1km to finish at Hotels Asturias and Jarilla. Carry provisions for the whole day.

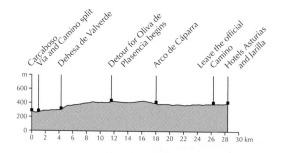

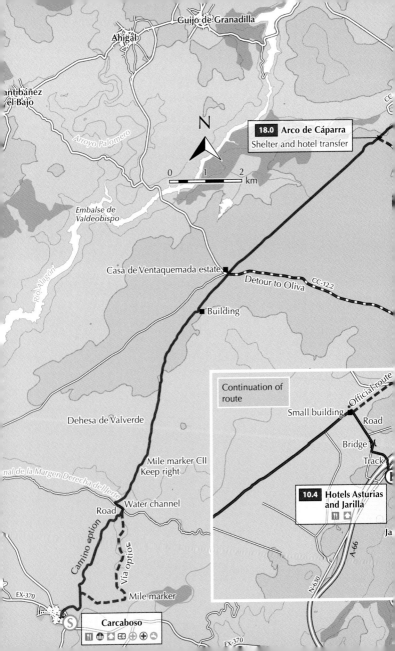

Guijo de Granadilla

Ahigal

antibañez
el Bajo

*Arroyo Palomero*

N

0  1  2
km

**18.0** **Arco de Cáparra**
Shelter and hotel transfer

*Embalse de
Valdeobispo*

*Río Alagón*

Casa de Ventaquemada estate

Detour to Oliva  CC-12.2

■ Building

*Dehesa de Valverde*

Continuation of
route

Small building

Official route

Road

Bridge

Track

Mile marker CII
Keep right

nal de la Margen Derecha del Jerte

Water channel

**10.4** **Hotels Asturias
and Jarilla**

Road

Camino option

Vía option

Mile marker

Ja

N-630

A-66

EX-370

**S**  **Carcaboso**

FX-370

Río Ambroz

See inset for continuation of route

Hotel/Restaurant Avión

Oliva de Plasencia

A-66

N-630

N-110

From the Iglesia de Santiago, go up Cl. de la Iglesia and turn left to Plaza España. Turn right onto Cl. Pozo and fork right by the cube marker, taking a sharp left onto a track (**0.9km**). Soon reach another cube, which indicates a choice between Vía or Camino. Both are straightforward but the Camino is shorter.

### Vía option (4km)

Follow the turquoise waymarking and go right. After 1.4km, turn left and left again past a **mile marker**. Go through a gate and keep left at the next significant fork to reach a **road**.

### Camino option (3km)

Following the yellow on the cube, go straight on to reach a **road**.

### Main route

Both options reunited, turn left onto the **road** by a **water channel**. Cross over both and go through a gate uphill into the **Dehesa de Valverde**. Turn right onto a narrower path (**4.9km**) among denser oak trees, passing the base of **mile marker CII** *in situ* (**1.3km**). Stroll through gorgeous *dehesas* separated by drystone walls, passing more remains of mile markers.

Eventually, go right and left around a **building** (**3.3km**), then reach the CC-12.2 road at the **Casa de Ventaquemada estate** (**1.4km**), where there is an option to detour to Oliva de Plasencia instead of continuing direct to the Arco de Cáparra on the official Camino.

### Oliva de Plasencia (13.1km detour)

Oliva to Aldeanueva del Camino totals 17.4km. Turn right onto the **CC-12.2** to reach **Oliva de Plasencia** after 6.7km (🍴 ⛲ 🏧). Arrive at a square where a sign indicates a left turn for the albergue. (🛏 **Albergue Turístico San Blas** 🅾 Pr Do R K S 4/16, €20/35/50/-/-, Cl. Real 2, tel 647 563 450, pichon24@hotmail.com.)

Reach another square (drinking fountain). Go across and take the road on the left, passing a shop.

*Pilgrims take in the magnitude of the Arco de Cáparra, the Vía's emblem par excellence (photo: Marta Bossa José)*

Cross the CC-12.2 and follow a sign ahead for Cáparra to reach a **track**. Some 6km later, at the end of the track, turn right to the **Arco de Cáparra** and ruins of old Cáparra city (shelter).

**Official Camino (direct route)**

From the Casa de Ventaquemada estate, the Camino crosses the road and takes a track on the right alongside a stone wall, with views towards the Sierra de Gredos. Pass a big farmhouse (**5.6km**) and arrive at the **Arco de Cáparra** (shelter).

### 18.0KM ARCO DE CÁPARRA (ELEV 401M) (NO SERVICES EXCEPT HOTEL TRANSFER) (604.5KM)

The fifth *mansio* from Mérida, the **Roman ruins of Cáparra** are the clearest depiction of what the Vía de la Plata would have been. It is no wonder that the monumental 9m quadrifrontal arch (*tetrapylum*) of the **Arco de Cáparra** has become the most represented icon of the route. Abandoned during the Middle Ages during the Muslim invasion and subsequently left to ruin during the *Reconquista*, current remains include the CX milestone with a tribute to the Emperor Nero, the forum, amphitheatre, baths and gates of the wall, as well as cobblestone paving. Excavations have discovered abundant sculptures, ceramics and glasswork.

🏠 Hostal/Restaurante El Avión 🄾 🄿 🆁 🆂 8/16, €-/35/50/-/-, Ctra. N-630 km455, tel 652 779 448 or 927 489 287. Located 6.1km off the Camino. Call the day before to book the transfer.

Reach the **CC-11.2** road, cross it onto the lane ahead and immediately fork right onto a track. There are four fords on this section, with stepping stones, which may be tricky after heavy rainfall. Eventually, merge left onto a **road** (**5.4km**) instead of continuing along the track, which is often overgrown and muddy; this avoids a possibly impassable stream.

By a **small building**, reach a junction with a **road** coming in from the right (**2.9km**). Leave the official Camino and turn right onto it, towards mountains. If proceeding direct to Aldeanueva del Camino on the official route, don't turn right but keep straight on to reach the CC-15.2 (see Stage 19). After 1.1km, cross a **bridge** then take the next **track** on the left (**1.3km**). Keep straight over the roundabout, go under the **A-66** and straight over the next roundabout to reach the N-630, with **Hotel Asturias** on the right and **Hotel Jarilla** across the road to the left.

### 10.4KM HOTELS ASTURIAS AND JARILLA (ELEV 401M) ⛰ ⛺ (594.1KM)

🏠 Hostal/Restaurante Asturias 🅟🆁 🆁 🅱🆁 🅖🅡 🆆 🆂 11/16, €-/20/40/-/-, Ctra. N-630 km448, tel 927 477 057, hostalasturias@hotmail.com, **www.hostalasturias. es**. Located 2.1km off the Camino. Call the day before to book a transfer from Cáparra. Closed 23–24 Dec and 31 Dec–1 Jan.

🏠 Hotel/Restaurante Jarilla * 🅟🆁 🆁 🅱🆁 🅖🅡 🆂 10/20, €-/30/60/-/-, Ctra. N-630 km448.5, tel 927 477 040, hotel@hoteljarilla.com, **www.hoteljarilla. com**. Located 2.1km off the Camino. Might come to collect you in Cáparra depending on how busy they are. Closed on Sundays. Closed 23–24 Dec and 31 Dec–1 Jan.

# STAGE 19
*Hotels Asturias and Jarilla to
Puerto de Béjar (Colonia la Estación)*

| | |
|---|---|
| **Start** | Hotels Asturias and Jarilla |
| **Finish** | Puerto de Béjar (Colonia la Estación) |
| **Distance** | 24.2km |
| **Total ascent** | 570m |
| **Total descent** | 105m |
| **Difficulty** | Moderate |
| **Duration** | 6¼hr |
| **Percentage paved** | 29% |
| **Albergues** | Aldeanueva del Camino 11.4km; Baños de Montemayor 21.0km; Puerto de Béjar (Colonia la Estación) 24.2km |

Having taken a short detour off the Camino on the previous stage, the day ahead offers three options to re-join it. Out of the three, the Vía Verde is recommended as the most pleasurable. The Camino hikes uphill into mountainous terrain through deciduous forests, bidding farewell to Extremadura and greeting Castilla y León, the biggest autonomous region of Spain, which will now accompany you until Galicia (Stage 34). Provisions are available in Aldeanueva and Baños, dividing the stage nicely.

### N-630 option (10.2km)
Take the N-630 to **Aldeanueva del Camino**.

### Official Camino to Aldeanueva del Camino (12.8km)
Diligently retrace your steps to the junction where you turned off the official Camino on Stage 18, turn right to reach the **CC-15.2** and fork left onto a road. Go under the **motorway** and turn left along the **N-630**. Promptly turn right, under the **motorway** again, then left and right twice onto a track. Use stepping stones over a stream and reach a junction. Turn right here to link to the Vía Verde. Turn right to a farmhouse, left under the **motorway**, right onto the N-630 and left into **Aldeanueva del Camino**.

### Vía Verde option (recommended) (10.8km)
Go through the car park of Hotel Asturias and turn left onto the **Vía Verde**. Go under a road (**3.8km**) and pass the **old Casas del Monte railway station**. At a junction by a **ruin** (**3.6km**), you can join the official Camino route by turning left for 350 metres then first right. Otherwise, continue on the Vía Verde, which goes straight ahead to the old Aldeanueva railway station (**2.7km**). Turn left off the Vía here onto the road, cross over the motorway and enter **Aldeanueva del Camino**.

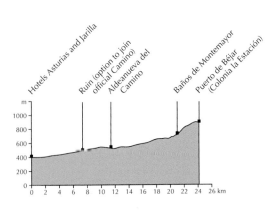

### Main route
All three routes now converge on Cl. las Olivas in Aldeanueva to reach Plaza

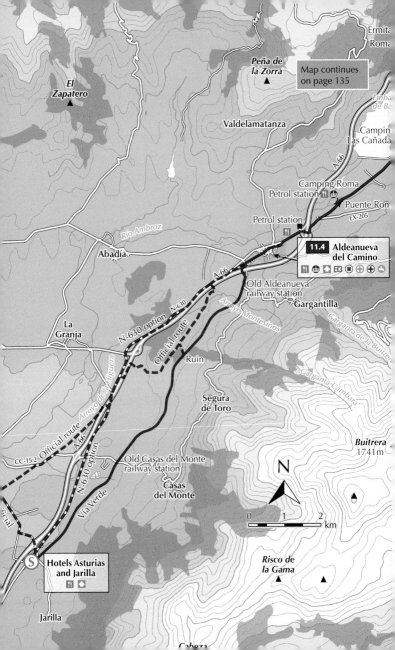

Map continues
on page 135

*El
Zapatero*
▲

*Peña de
la Zorra*
▲

Valdelamatanza

Ermita
Roma

Embal
de Ba

Campin
Las Cañada

A-66

Camping Roma
Petrol station

Puente Ron

EX-205

Petrol station

**11.4** **Aldeanueva
del Camino**

*Río Ambroz*

Abadía

A-66

Old Aldeanueva
railway station

Gargantilla

*Arroyo Montesinos*

*Garganta de la Bu*

N-630 option

N-630

Official route

Ruin

*Garganta Cambara*

La
Granja

*Arroyo de la Figuera*

Segura
de Toro

*Buitrera*
1741m

Official route

A-66

N-630 option

Old Casas del Monte
railway station

Casas
del Monte

CC-15-2

**N**

0        1        2

━━━━━━━ km

*Vía Verde*

**S**

**Hotels Asturias
and Jarilla**

*Risco de
la Gama*
▲        ▲

Jarilla

Cabeza

del Mercado (turn left for a drinking fountain) and the stone bridge over Garganta de la Buitrera.

### 11.4KM ALDEANUEVA DEL CAMINO (ELEV 528M, POP 729) (582.7KM)

The Vía de la Plata would have crossed the town exactly as the official Camino now does. Aldeanueva was founded by the Romans, as evidenced by the **Romanillos bridge**. Its famous paprika, traditionally smoke-dried over oak for exceptional quality, is used in the local *migas extremeñas* (breadcrumbs fried with pork, peppers and garlic) and in meats such as *chorizo* or black pudding.

**Albergue de peregrinos de Aldeanueva del Camino** O Do W S Z 2/10, €Donation, Cl. las Olivas 52, tel 637 580 772.

**Albergue La Casa de Mi Abuela** O Do R Br W S 5/26, €13, Cl. Alcázar 4, tel 630 410 740, 692 531 587 or 927 479 314, lacasademiabuela@arhrestauracion.com, **www.lacasademiabuela-albergue.com**. Breakfast €2.

Cross the town hall square, pass the Parroquia de San Servando and take a left to then go right onto the N-630 (**0.6km**). Pass a restaurant and at a roundabout (café at **petrol station**) take the exit for Baños de Montemayor over the **motorway**. At the next roundabout, turn left. Pass **Puente Romanillos**, then a **petrol station** (shop) and **Camping Roma** (restaurant) (**1.5km**). Continue past **Camping Las Cañadas** (**3.1km**).

The Camino skirts around the N-630 twice: first on the right (**1.8km**), then on the left, where a few steps off the Camino lead to a **Roman bridge**. Back on the N-630, pass the **Ermita del Humilladero** on the outskirts of **Baños de Montemayor**. Turn right off the N-630 (**2.2km**) and fork left past a church. Cross a square and pass a restaurant, arriving at the town hall (drinking fountain) to follow signs for the albergue.

### 9.6KM BAÑOS DE MONTEMAYOR (ELEV 708M, POP 749) (573.1KM)

The albergue has a fantastic **Vía de la Plata Museum**, and the town enjoys its Roman history at the **thermal baths**, built in 1AD (**www.balneariomontemayor.com**, closed in winter). The spa was declared an Asset of Cultural Interest in 1992. The chalet-style architecture on display in town is popular throughout the Béjar mountain range.

**Albergue Turístico Vía de la Plata** O Do R Br W S 3/12, €13, Cl. Castañar 40, tel 655 620 515, sagrariocastelani@yahoo.es. Breakfast €2.

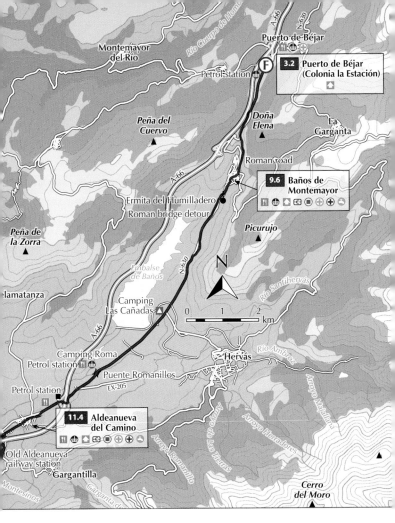

Keep straight then left onto Cl. Castillejo, then veer right, uphill, and turn left onto the CC-16.2. Reach the N-630, turn right and immediately take the restored original **Roman road** uphill, looking back at the Embalse de Baños, before landing back on the N-630 (**1.5km**). Turn right, cross over and take a path on the left, entering Castilla y León. Return to the N-630 and turn left to a petrol station. Soon, the Camino goes to the left (**1.6km**), but cross the N-630 for the albergue on the next road on the right.

*Pilgrims cross the Béjar Pass on the preserved original Roman road before entering Castilla y León*

### 3.2KM PUERTO DE BÉJAR (COLONIA LA ESTACIÓN) (ELEV 882M, POP 370 IN TOWN) 🛏 (569.9KM)

The actual village of Puerto de Béjar (🚌 ⊕ ⊕) is located 1.3km away on the N-630. Some sources place the sixth *mansio* from Mérida, Caelionicco, in the vicinity.

🛖 Albergue de Peregrinos de Puerto de Béjar 🄳🄾 🅁 🄺 🄱🅁 🅆 🅂 🆉 3/12, €Donation, Colonia de la Estación 1, tel 683 610 660 or 652 506 189, peregrinospuertodebejar@gmail.com. Open 1 Mar–31 Oct. Sells the *credencial*.

# STAGE 20

*Puerto de Béjar (Colonia la Estación) to Fuenterroble de Salvatierra*

| | |
|---|---|
| **Start** | Puerto de Béjar (Colonia la Estación) |
| **Finish** | Fuenterroble de Salvatierra |
| **Distance** | 29.8km |
| **Total ascent** | 460m |
| **Total descent** | 400m |
| **Difficulty** | Hard |
| **Duration** | 7½hr |
| **Percentage paved** | 29% |
| **Albergues** | Albergue Puente Malena 3.5km; La Calzada de Béjar 9.3km; Valverde de Valdelacasa 17.9km; Fuenterroble de Salvatierra 29.8km |

Bountiful original *miliarios* mark the Roman miles perfectly, and dense forests where colours change with the seasons make for a divine stage indeed along the Camino Real de la Plata, through the valley between the Sierra de Béjar on the right and Sierra de Francia to the left. Cube waymarkers are replaced by wooden posts with yellow arrows, unique to the Salamanca province.

Return to the N-630 and cross to the lane ahead, promptly taking a right-hand track. Go under the **motorway**, pass the Fuente del Peregrino (drinking water) and **picnic spot** (**0.7km**), then cross a road. Pass **mile markers**: after passing the first one, descend through the forest, passing another one (**1.5km**), to reach the welcoming **Albergue Puente de la Malena** and a café sign (in winter, check in advance for services).

### 3.5KM ALBERGUE PUENTE DE LA MALENA (ELEV 677M, POP 2) ⬆ (566.4KM)

🏠 **Albergue Puente de la Malena** 🄳🄳 🄺 🄱🄵 🅂 2/8, €Donation, wilfried. siegen@rubertus.de, **www.rubertus.casa**. Open all year, but in Jan and Feb it is essential to check in advance.

Go over the **Puente de la Malena** and pass a *miliario*. Concealed behind a fence nearby, several mile markers were found as recently as the late 1980s. Turn right on a track parallel to the road, passing an estate that houses another *miliario* in its courtyard and, soon after, the base of another *miliario* by another farm. The Camino reaches **Ermita de San Francisco** (**2.8km**) and then turns right onto another road, leaving it soon on an **uphill path** on the left (**1.1km**).

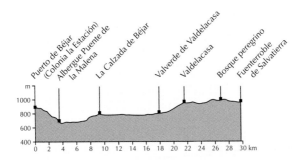

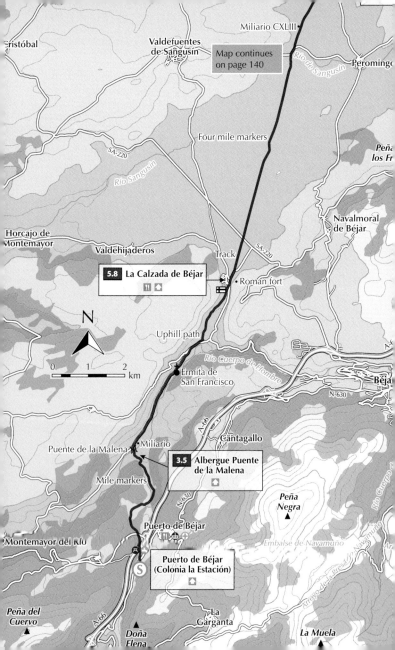

Miliario CXLIII

Valdefuentes
de Sangusín

Map continues
on page 140

Peromingo

Río de Sangusín

ristóbal

Peña
los Fr

Four mile markers

SA-220

Río Sangusín

Navalmoral
de Béjar

Horcajo de
Montemayor

Valdehijaderos

Track

SA-220

**5.8**  La Calzada de Béjar

Roman fort

N

Uphill path

Río Cuerpo de Hombre

Béja

0    1    2
km

Ermita de
San Francisco

N-630

A-66

Cantagallo

Puente de la Malena    Miliario

**3.5**  Albergue Puente
de la Malena

Peña
Negra

Mile markers

N-630

Embalse de Navamuño

Puerto de Béjar

Montemayor del Río

**S**  Puerto de Béjar
(Colonia la Estación)

Peña del
Cuervo

A-66

La
Garganta

La Muela

Doña
Elena

Pass farms and a **cemetery** by the Ermita del Humilladero to enter **La Calzada de Béjar**. Pass the albergue (**1.7km**) and take Cl. Calzada Romana, reaching the 1553 Iglesia Parroquial Nuestra Señora de la Asunción (bar behind the church).

### 5.8KM LA CALZADA DE BÉJAR (ELEV 795M, POP 91) 🏨 ⬜ (560.6KM)

The name of the town alludes to the **Roman road** that coincides with its main street. A **Roman fort** from the early imperial era is situated only 500 metres away.

🏠 **Albergue Alba-Soraya** 🇩🇷 🇩🇴 🇧🇷 🇸 4/28, €12, Camino Real de la Plata, tel 923 416 505 or 646 410 643 or 606 958 145, info@alojamientosalbasoraya.com, **http://alojamientosalbasoraya.com**. Open all year but call ahead in winter.

Pass a shelter and pilgrim statue, going straight ahead to leave town. As the road bends right, take the **track** opposite then cross the **SA-220** (**1.3km**), keeping to the track past farm buildings and *miliario* CXXXIX, the first of **four mile markers**.

The next three mile markers are neatly in order, leading to the **Río de Sangusín** (**4.9km**). Turn right onto the road to head left uphill on a track, passing *miliario* **CXLIII** (**1.5km**). Use the **ford** (reused Roman culvert) to reach the 18th-century Iglesia Románica Santiago Apóstol and stone cross in **Valverde de Valdelacasa**. For the albergue, turn immediately left.

### 8.6KM VALVERDE DE VALDELACASA (ELEV 804M, POP 66) 🏨 ⬜ ⊕ (552.0KM)

The *mansio* Ad Lippos is said to have been located here, as well as an old and modest pilgrim hospital within the house of 'Tío Martín', although construction work has made it unrecognizable as such.

🏠 **Albergue Santiago Apóstol** 🅾 🇩🇴 🇷 🇰 🇧🇷 🇸 7/22, €12–17, Cl. Real 25, tel 696 368 046 or 923 165 050, vicky.casquero@gmail.com.

Proceed to a drinking fountain, bar/restaurant and rest spot with a *miliario*. Turn right out of town on a road, reaching another mile marker before arriving at the first houses in **Valdelacasa** (**3.5km**). For services (🏨 ⊕), turn right and then left onto Cl. La Atalaya, pass the town hall and fork left. Return to the Camino by turning left at the bottom of the road onto the SA-214 at the mini-roundabout.

If not in need of Valdelacasa's services, turn left, then fork right and over the **SA-214** to take a road to a junction (**2.5km**) with views towards a **quarry**. Turn left to head along the widest track. The old route kept closer to the road but it is no longer waymarked and access is unadvisable.

Pass a wooded area called the **Bosque Peregrino**, with another mile marker base (**3.3km**), and come parallel to the road, soon turning left onto it (**1.7km**). Reach

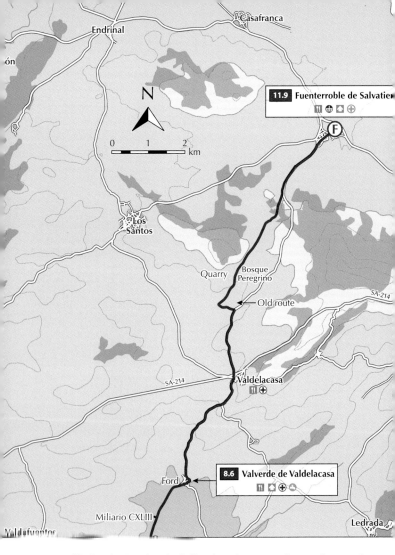

Endrinal

Casafranca

**11.9** Fuenterroble de Salvatier

Los Santos

Quarry

Bosque Peregrino

Old route

SA-214

SA-214

Valdelacasa

Ford

**8.6** Valverde de Valdelacasa

Miliario CXLIII

Ledrada

Valdefuentes

**Fuenterroble de Salvatierra** by a football pitch (**0.8km**), proceeding on Cl. Larga (shop on the parallel street) past the Ermita del Cristo del Socorro, pharmacy, bar/restaurants and town hall to the albergue.

Volunteers at the albergue in Fuenterroble take pilgrims on a guided tour of the church before a communal dinner

**11.9KM FUENTERROBLE DE SALVATIERRA (ELEV 954M, POP 264)** 🍴 🚻 🏠 ⊕
**(540.1KM)**

The albergue is run by Father Blas, the town's parish priest, and volunteers take pilgrims on a tour of the beautifully restored 15th-century **Iglesia de Santa María la Blanca**. The visit highlights an exquisite, carefully designed light-and-shadow effect behind the altar. The town's traditional architecture uses slate, differentiating it from the granite seen thus far en route.

🏠 Albergue parroquial Santa María **Dr Do Br S** 7/70, €Donation, Cl. de la Iglesia 3, tel 923 151 083, alberguefuenterroble@gmail.com, **https:// alberguedefuenterroble.wordpress.com**.

# STAGE 21

*Fuenterroble de Salvatierra to*
*San Pedro de Rozados*

| | |
|---|---|
| **Start** | Fuenterroble de Salvatierra |
| **Finish** | San Pedro de Rozados |
| **Distance** | 27.8km |
| **Total ascent** | 420m |
| **Total descent** | 400m |
| **Difficulty** | Hard |
| **Duration** | 6¾hr |
| **Percentage paved** | 13% |
| **Albergues** | San Pedro de Rozados 27.8km |

The view of Salamanca's *dehesas* from the top of the Pico de las Dueñas in the Sierra de Frades is lovely, and at 1170m altitude it is the highest point on the Vía so far. Prior to this, the route passes through a landscape of meadows and farmland on tracks and grassy paths. Once again, there are no provisions, so plan ahead. San Pedro de Rozados can be skipped by taking a more direct route to Morille through Pedrosillo de los Aires, which is 2.1km shorter overall although it adds 1.5km to this stage and involves more road-walking. A further option involves sleeping in Pedrosillo, which results in a lighter 17.8km day. After extremely heavy rainfall, albergues may advise taking longer road alternatives as the Camino could be flooded.

Turn right out of the albergue. Follow the road as it bends left then right, heading to Linares, and leave town. The road merges with the **SA-212**, which the Camino then leaves on a right-hand **dirt track** (**1.3km**). Be sure to keep straight on the drover's road (**1.5km**), passing **two mile markers**, and eventually turn right and left (**3.8km**). Turn right 200 metres later and then first left. Keep straight across the next three junctions and then fork right and left. Keep to the same track until you reach the two choices for the day (**4.9km**).

**Main route via Pico de las Dueñas**
Veer left uphill on a **stony path** into trees and climb towards the **wind turbines**, reaching the Santiago Cross of the Pilgrim (**3.3km**) on the **Pico de las Dueñas**.

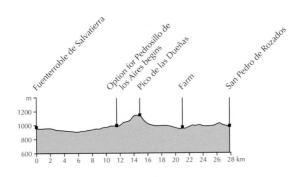

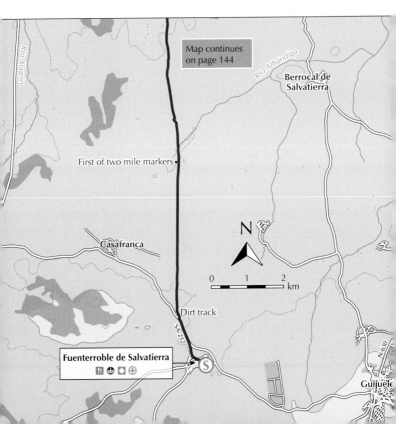

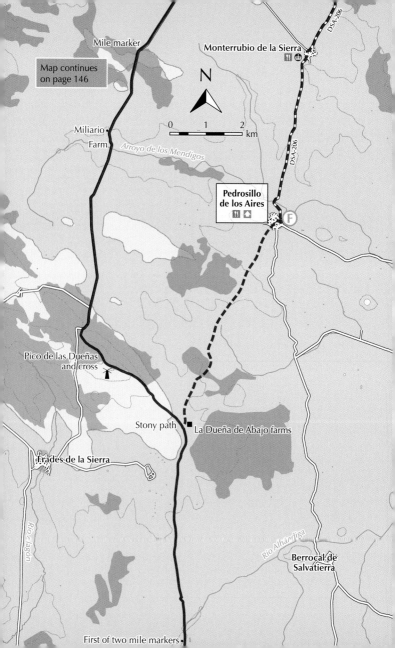

Mile marker

Map continues
on page 146

Monterrubio de la Sierra

DSA-206

N

0    1    2
km

Miliario
Farm

*Arroyo de los Mendigos*

Pedrosillo
de los Aires

F

DSA-206

Pico de las Dueñas
and cross

Stony path

La Dueña de Abajo farms

Frades de la Sierra

*Río Vagon*

*Río Alhandiga*

Berrocal de
Salvatierra

First of two mile markers

A miliario in situ *sits upon a plain which can be flooded after persistent heavy rain*

Part of the Sierra de los Herreros mountain range in the centre of the province of Salamanca, the **Pico de las Dueñas** accommodates a long chain of wind turbines. Nearby Pedrosillo de los Aires gets its name from the wind that passes through this landscape of hills and valleys. The name of the peak refers to the two beautiful cattle *fincas* below it: la Dueña de Abajo and la Dueña de Arriba.

The Camino starts dropping through woods to reach the road (**0.9km**), where it turns right along it and then onto a track on the left, running parallel to the road. Cross over the **Arroyo de los Mendigos** stream, and pass a **farm** of the same name (**5.4km**) and a ***miliario*** (**1.4km**). Spot another mile marker to the left in a field (**1.5km**).

Eventually, turn left onto a **grassy track** towards San Pedro (**1.4km**). Arrows direct you to keep straight ahead if you don't need the services at San Pedro. Soon the town can be seen below, and after another 1.8km turn left by a play park onto the local road into **San Pedro de Rozados**. Turn second left onto Cl. Oriente and reach the albergue on the left. A drinking fountain is at the top of the road.

### 27.8KM SAN PEDRO DE ROZADOS (ELEV 975M, POP 276) 🍴 ⊕ 🛏 (512.3KM)

The Vía ran barely 1km away from the town, which is modest as exemplified by its small houses and the 17th-century Iglesia de Santa María.

🛏 **Albergue Mari Carmen** 🅾 ⊡ 🆂 1/14, €10, Cl. Oriente 8, tel 923 344 075.
The albergue has been known to close at short notice, so check ahead.

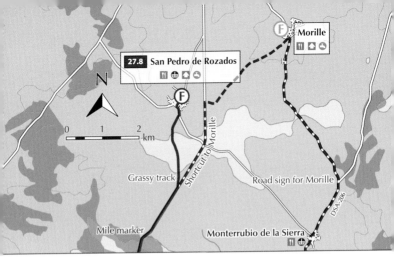

**Pedrosillo de los Aires variant (6.3km to Pedrosillo and a further 11.5km to Morille)**
Go directly up and down through **cattle farms at La Dueña de Abajo**. Sentice, the eighth *mansio* since Mérida, was probably located here. Cross one ford (**2.3km**) and then another (**1.2km**) to arrive in **Pedrosillo de los Aires** (🍴🏠) by a bar on the left. Turn left then right, coming to Iglesia de San Benito. For the albergue, turn second right, pass the town hall and head behind it. (🏠 **Refugio de peregrinos de Pedrosillo de los Aires** Ⓞ Ⓓ Ⓚ Ⓢ 1/10, €Donation, Cl. San Benito s/n, tel 629 129 647 or 609 107 381. Keys from the yellow house by the town hall.)

At the church, turn right along the wall onto Cl. Aurora, with a view of the countryside. Keep to the end and turn right downhill, cross the road and continue straight on Cl. Escuelas. Fork right and reach the DSA-206 road out of town. Turn left onto it, keep on over the **Arroyo de los Mendigos** stream and follow the **DSA-206** for 5km to **Monterrubio de la Sierra** (🍴🍷). Pass the Iglesia de San Miguel Arcángel and leave on the same road. Turn left at a **road sign for Morille** and join the San Pedro option in **Morille** (Stage 22).

# STAGE 22

*San Pedro de Rozados to Salamanca*

| | |
|---|---|
| **Start** | San Pedro de Rozados |
| **Finish** | Salamanca |
| **Distance** | 25.3km |
| **Total ascent** | 260m |
| **Total descent** | 430m |
| **Difficulty** | Easy |
| **Duration** | 6hr |
| **Percentage paved** | 28% |
| **Albergues** | Morille 4.1km; Salamanca 25.3km |

The Camino passes through a landscape that differs considerably in colour depending on the season. After Morille, the path heads through a final Salamancan *dehesa* and sets foots onto the immensity that is the Meseta. These vast multicoloured agricultural plots will now be the theme for the upcoming week or so. After a swift hike up to the Cruz del Peregrino for scenic views towards the old Salmantice and a jaunt under the city's ring roads, the itinerary into the centre is very pleasant, avoiding the infamous industrial zones and instead meandering through a local park.

Turn left out of the albergue, turn right by the drinking fountain, and leave town on a **dirt track**. Cross straight over a road and ensure you head left at the next fork (**1.1km**). Eventually fork right towards **Morille** (**2.3km**) and arrive at a drinking fountain behind a play park. Cross a stream and turn left by a mile marker, passing the town hall and Monumento a la Maestra (dedicated to female teachers) with the albergue behind.

### 4.1KM MORILLE (ELEV 930M, POP 227) 🏠 🛏 (508.2KM)

In tiny Morille it is fascinating to discover a unique museum, just 600 metres away from the town hall, called **El Cementerio de Arte** (www.morille.es/cementerio-de-arte). Within the 50,000m² plot allocated in 2005 to its founding artists, Domingo Sánchez Blanco and Javier Utray, recognized and valued avant-garde and contemporary art pieces are 'buried'. The works are thus preserved in this 'Museum–Mausoleum'.

🏠 **Albergue de peregrinos de Morille** Ⓞ 🛏 🅂 1/24, €6, Cl. Mayor s/n, tel 659 928 010. Keys from Bar Marcos.

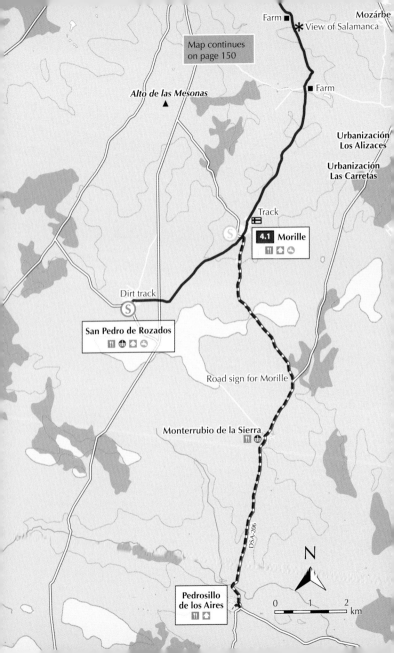

Mozárbe

Farm ■ ✳ View of Salamanca

Map continues
on page 150

Farm ■

**Alto de las Mesonas**
▲

Urbanización
Los Alizaces

Urbanización
Las Carretas

Track
⊞

Ⓢ  **4.1** Morille

Dirt track

Ⓢ

**San Pedro de Rozados**

Road sign for Morille

Monterrubio de la Sierra

**Pedrosillo
de los Aires**

DSA-206

N

0        1        2
km

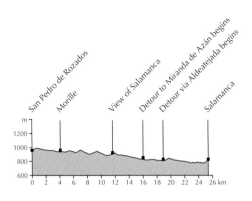

Keep straight on Cl. Mayor across a stream and go uphill. Cross the road and take the **track** ahead to leave Morille, passing solar panels and then the **cemetery**. The Camino keeps straight at a junction by a **farm** (**4.3km**), then goes through a gate, taking a path between two walls.

Follow the track as it bends left by the wall (**2.5km**) and then heads off diagonally away from the wall uphill to reach another wall on the left. Go through a gate, with a **view of Salamanca** to the north. Turn left towards a **farm** and upon reaching it turn right (**1.9km**). Keep to the wide track, passing the ruins of the **Ermita de Valbuena** (**1.8km**) and a **farm**. You are now about halfway to Santiago (if you choose the Camino Sanabrés option from Granja de Moreruela).

Arrive at an optional detour into **Miranda de Azán** (**1.4km**, 🏠 ⊕), 400 metres off the Camino. Either take the detour (rejoining the main route slightly further on) or keep ahead to reach a junction with a road (**2.4km**), by a sign for the detour via Aldeatejada.

### Alternative through Aldeatejada (adding 700 metres)

Go left on the road to reach **Aldeatejada** (🏠 ⊕ 🏠 🄲 ⊕ ⊕) after 1.6km. Turn right then left at the end of the road to reach the Iglesia de Santiago then the CL-152. Turn right onto it and follow a **cycle path** to reach a roundabout in Salamanca 5km later. A right turn (yellow arrow) takes you to a petrol station.

### Direct recommended route

Keep straight on at the junction, heading uphill and across rocks to the yellow **Cruz del Peregrino** cross at 837m altitude. Turn right under the **A-66** (**2.3km**) then the **SA-20** (**1.3km**). Cross a roundabout (drinking fountain in the **park** on the left) and turn right along a park path through birch trees to cross **railway lines** (**1.4km**) and reach a petrol station.

### Main route

With both options united, turn right, pass the Iglesia Vieja del Arrabal and cross the N-630 as the magnificent university city appears across the 15-arched **Puente Romano**. At the end of the bridge, reach the Iglesia de Santiago (**1.2km**) behind the Toro

149

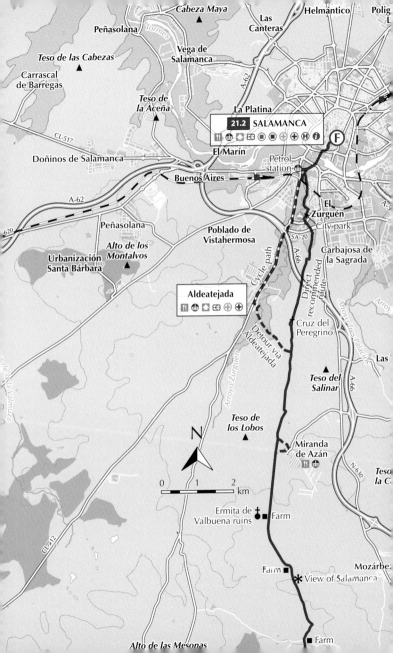

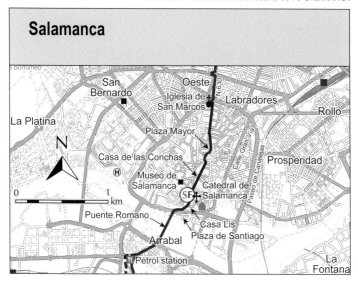

Verraco Ibérico statue. Turn right, then head up the walkway behind the Cruz de los Ajusticiados/Cruz de Cristo cross.

For the albergue, follow the golden shells on the ground, turning right onto Cl. Gibraltar behind the **Catedral de Salamanca** and then right onto Cl. Arcediano.

For the centre, turn left onto Cl. Tentenicio following signs for tourist information. Reach Plaza Juan XXII and turn right to the **Catedral de Salamanca**.

*At nightfall, lights illuminate what is considered by many to be the most beautiful Plaza Mayor in Spain*

## 21.2KM SALAMANCA (ELEV 804M, POP 143,269) ⊞ ⊕ ⊡ ⊂ ⊙ ⊙ ⊕ ⊕ ⊕ ⊙
(487.0KM)

Entering the ninth Roman *mansio* over the **Puente Romano** is awe-inspiring, and this very bridge is one of the few Roman remains in grandiose Salamanca. Before the Romans, Salamanca was, according to Ptolemy, a city of the Vettones, and its prominence began in 220BC when it was attacked by Hannibal. Those glorious years began to deteriorate around the 4th century BC. In the High Middle Ages, it was conquered by the Muslims then recovered by King Alfonso VI in 1102. Yet it was only a century later, in 1218, that King Alfonso IX created the General Study, which would sow the seed for King Alfonso X's university and mark a turning point for the city. As one of the oldest universities in Europe, the splendour of the **University of Salamanca** truly emerged at the end of the 15th century, and it is still one of the most popular choices for students in Spain. The marvellous Gothic, Renaissance and Baroque architecture preserved in its monumental university heritage determined the UNESCO World Heritage accolade in 1988. Alumni include ex-President Adolfo Suárez (1932–2014), writer Miguel de Unamuno (1864–1936), the friar and playwright Fray Luis de León (1527–1591) and religious philosopher Francisco de Vitoria (1483–1546).

To fully discover the city's jewels, golden sandstone buildings and magical night-time illuminations, at least two days of sightseeing are recommended. A sunset visit to the rooftops and bell tower of the **Old and New Cathedral** complex (12–13th century and 16th/18th century respectively) is a favourite activity. Thematically, the **Casa de las Conchas**, now the public library, also catches the eye, with more than 300 decorative scallop shells. At the request of Rodrigo Maldonado de Talavera, Knight of the Order of Santiago, Rector Professor of Law at the University and member of the Royal Council of Castilla, construction of the Casa de las Conchas began in 1493 and was completed in 1517.

Arguably, the most fun to be had is to go in search of Salamanca's famous **skull and frog** on the facade of the university building. Seeing the frog, a symbol of Salamanca, is said to have brought good luck to students in their exams, whereas if they didn't manage to find it, they would fail, hence the threat from the skull.

⌂ Albergue de peregrinos Casa la Calera ⊙ ⊡ ⊠ 2/16, €Donation, Cl. Arcediano 14, tel 652 921 185. Sells the *credencial*.

# STAGE 23
*Salamanca to Calzada de Valdunciel*

| | |
|---|---|
| **Start** | Salamanca |
| **Finish** | Calzada de Valdunciel |
| **Distance** | 16.7km |
| **Total ascent** | 160m |
| **Total descent** | 165m |
| **Difficulty** | Easy |
| **Duration** | 4hr |
| **Percentage paved** | 44% |
| **Albergues** | Castellanos de Villiquera 12.4km; Calzada de Valdunciel 16.7km |

The Meseta continues as the Camino weaves its way, parallel to the highways, across the plateau's massive expanses of land, where small towns are dotted across the plains and slopes. The tracks make for easy walking but can be muddy and slippery after rain, when some pilgrims opt to stick to the N-630 instead. The winds can be strong and the sun extremely fiery, but fortunately refreshments are available after 5km, then 7km later and at stage end.

With your back to the cathedral and Plaza de Anaya on your right, keep straight down Rúa Mayor, cross the road and veer left, passing the Iglesia de San Martín, to arrive at **Plaza Mayor**.

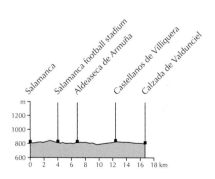

Construction of the Baroque square of **Plaza Mayor**, considered one of the most beautiful plazas in Spain, began in 1729 after three fires had destroyed the first building. King Fernando III, named 'el Santo' after he was canonized

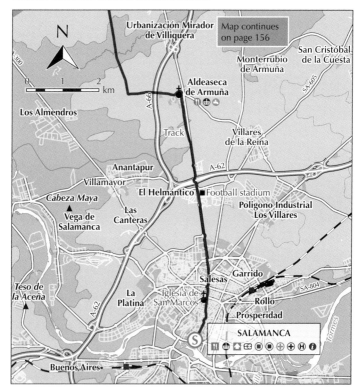

Map continues
on page 156

in 1671 by Pope Clement X, is at the centre of the Royal Pavilion to the east, with more Spanish monarchs on either side. The Southern Pavilion houses effigies of soldiers and conquerors, and the medallions on the west represent cultural figures.

Cross the square under the town hall through Puerta de Zamora onto Cl. Zamora. Keep straight with the park on your left and reach a roundabout just after the circular 13th-century **Iglesia de San Marcos** (**1km**). Cross straight over, following the N-630 (road sign for Zamora), and stay on the left-hand side.

Continue over all roundabouts, taking a pedestrian crossing to use the cycle lane, thus leaving the city (**1.8km**). Pass the **Salamanca football stadium** (**1.2km**). For safety and ease, cross back over the N-630 to go straight over the roundabout and keep to the left side of the N-630 under the **A-62**. Go straight over yet another roundabout and leave the N-630 onto a **track** on the left, uphill (**1.6km**).

Arrive in **Aldeaseca de Armuña** by a restaurant (**1.3km**). Keep straight to the next park (drinking fountain), pass a shop and turn left onto Cl. Campillo. Turn right before the **Iglesia de Santa Cruz** and left behind it.

Built in 1613, the **Iglesia de Santa Cruz** contains a coffered ceiling that continues through the nave, an octagonal chancel and a Baroque main altarpiece which includes an image of San Blas.

Ignore the first track, take the second one on the right under the **A-66** (**1km**) and at the next junction turn right. Pass a **football pitch** (**3.7km**) and veer left to take the road into **Castellanos de Villiquera**. Arrive by a fountain and go left onto Cl. del Pozo (for the bar, take the next road on the right and go up some steps). Turn left onto Cl. Medio and arrive at a play park (drinking fountain).

*Miliario fragments are located opposite Calzada's two albergues*

## 12.4KM CASTELLANOS DE VILLIQUERA (ELEV 829M, POP 653) 🏨 ⊕ 🛒 ⊕
**(474.6KM)**

The town's name stems from the Castilian settlers who founded it in 975. The 16th–17th-century **Iglesia de San Juan Bautista** is of Romanesque origin, while its Gothic façade, nave and bell tower are from the Gil de Hontañón school of architects. Within, the paintings and carvings at the main altarpiece are from the 16th century.

🛖 **Posada/Restaurante Real Vinarius** 🄾 Pr R Br Gr W S 2/6, €-/65/65/85/130, Cl. Calzada 8, tel 659 955 955. Prices are higher on Fri and Sat. Call ahead.

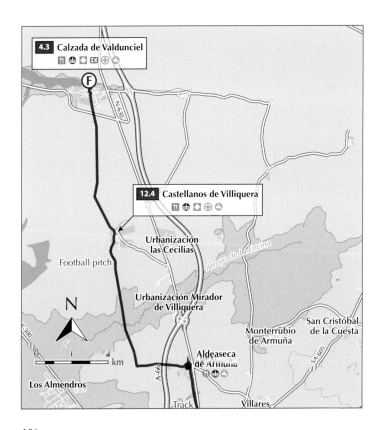

Keep the park on your left, cross the road and take the road slightly to the right, which becomes a track. Fork right (**1.2km**) and proceed across a road (**2.3km**) to **Calzada de Valdunciel**. Arrive at Plaza de la Constitución (drinking fountain), turn right and left across it to come to the town hall. Turn right to get to both albergues.

### 4.3KM CALZADA DE VALDUNCIEL (ELEV 800M, POP 698) 🍴 ⊕ 🏠 🄲 ⊕
(470.3KM)

This is another town name on the Vía providing evidence of the Roman road. There was a Roman citadel here, of which unfortunately there are no remains. However, the medieval **Fuente Buena** protects a **Roman tombstone** bearing the image of a woman. The fountain must have quenched the thirst of many a traveller to come through these parts. The **Iglesia de Santa Elena** dates from the 16th and 18th centuries, with some remnants from its 12th-century origin well preserved.

🏠 **Albergue de peregrinos de Calzada de Valdunciel** ⓄⒹ🄺🅂 1/8, €7, Cl. La Cilla 21, tel 717 706 637. Keys from the ACUM behind the albergue (Mon–Fri 11:30–13:00) or the library on Cl. Teresa Herrero behind the church (Mon–Fri 18:00–20:00), otherwise call them.

🏠 **Albergue La Casa del Molinero** ⓄⒹ🅁🄺🅱🅂🆉 1/7 & 2/4, €15/-/34/-/-, Cl. Ruta de la Plata 10, tel 689 008 562, mteresaehijos@gmail.com. Sells the *credencial*. Breakfast €3.

# STAGE 24

*Calzada de Valdunciel to
El Cubo de Tierra del Vino*

| | |
|---|---|
| **Start** | Calzada de Valdunciel |
| **Finish** | El Cubo de Tierra del Vino |
| **Distance** | 20.7km |
| **Total ascent** | 190m |
| **Total descent** | 150m |
| **Difficulty** | Easy |
| **Duration** | 5hr |
| **Percentage paved** | 11% |
| **Albergues** | El Cubo de Tierra del Vino 20.7km |

A day alongside highways is rewarded by El Cubo's hospitality. Although the 19th-century phylloxera plague destroyed vineyards across Spain and France with an irreparable impact on the region, some were spared around El Cubo and today the town pours its wine proudly. Carry all provisions; if the paths were muddy yesterday, today will be no different, so some pilgrims prefer to take the quiet N-630 with identical views. The route reaches the province of Zamora, where it will stay until Galicia. A recommended detour to the Castillo del Buen Amor hotel/museum is also described (5.2km return).

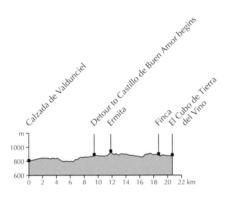

Head left out of the albergue to the *miliarios* and go right. Pass a **bird-watching viewpoint** and soon take a track on the right (**1.1km**).

The **bird-watching viewpoint** allows for inspection of the landscape of this region of La Armuña, while observing numerous steppe eagles and waterfowl that flock to the pond for food and rest.

*The Zamora province is crossed on the Meseta, which changes colour with the seasons*

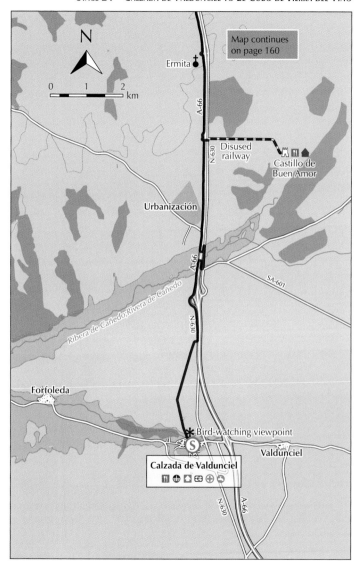

Map continues
on page 160

159

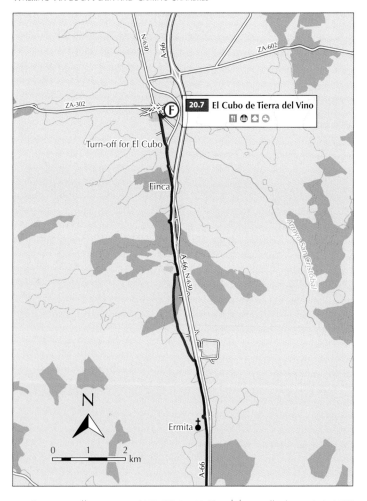

Keep on until you veer right to the **N-630**. Turn left to walk alongside first the N-630 (**1.8km**) and then the **A-66**, until a right turn takes you under the motorway (**2.3km**).

Return to the N-630, turn left and this time walk on its pavement. Turn left to the motorway, go under it and walk parallel to it again, passing an ***urbanización*** (**2.3km**).

There used to be an albergue here, which may reopen. Unless you are making a detour to the Castillo de Buen Amor, ignore the road on the right and follow the track as it bends left then keeps straight alongside the N-630 once again (**1.9km**).

### Detour to the Castillo de Buen Amor (2.6km one-way)

Take the road on the right that leads up over the **A-66** and under electricity lines. After the bridge, follow the road to the right and turn left over disused railway tracks. After 1.7km, press the bell at the gates of the castle grounds or take the track that winds its way to the **Castillo** (hotel, restaurant).

> Originally built as a military fortress in the 11th century, by the 15th century the **Castillo de Buen Amor** belonged to the Catholic kings. Its endearing name, the Castle of Good Love, flows from a love story. In 1478, Alonso de Fonseca y Quijada, Bishop of Ávila, acquired the castle and made it into a home to live in with his lover, Doña Teresa de las Cuevas, far away from village gossip. The castle is now a hotel and museum with its own vineyards (www.buenamor.net).

### Main route

Back on the Camino, notice an **ermita** to the left (**2.3km**). Keep straight ahead over all junctions as the Camino follows the motorway for a long stretch, until eventually, after a **finca** on the left (**7km**), it starts to head away from the motorway and instead turns right to the N-630.

Turn left onto the N-630 and take the turn-off for **El Cubo de Tierra del Vino** (**1.1km**), with views of houses swiftly reached. In town, for the albergue, turn right, first right and first left.

### 20.7KM EL CUBO DE TIERRA DEL VINO (ELEV 839M, POP 314) 🍴 ⊕ ☐ (449.6KM)

The tenth *mansio* from Mérida, Siberiam, is thought to be located in the neighbouring peaks of Monte del Cubo, as a halfway point between Salamanca and Zamora. In pre-Roman times, according to Ptolemy, the territory was occupied by the Vacceos, who may have been the forefathers of the region's viticulture. Sunday is *tapas* day in the bar on the square, and with every drink a traditional local bite is savoured, such as rooster comb.

🏠 **Albergue Torre de Sabre** Pr Dr Do R Br W S 3/10, €30/27/34/45/-, Tr. de la Ermita 1, tel 633 424 321, torredesabre@gmail.com. The dorm price of €30 includes a three-course dinner with drinks and plentiful breakfast. Open year-round but check ahead Nov–Jan.

# STAGE 25
### El Cubo de Tierra del Vino to Zamora

| | |
|---|---|
| **Start** | El Cubo de Tierra del Vino |
| **Finish** | Zamora |
| **Distance** | 31.9km |
| **Total ascent** | 170m |
| **Total descent** | 370m |
| **Difficulty** | Very hard |
| **Duration** | 7¼hr |
| **Percentage paved** | 14% |
| **Albergues** | Villanueva de Campeán 13.6km; Zamora 31.9km |

Today's route runs through the undulating terrain of the salvaged vineyards of Tierra del Vino (Land of Wine) to Zamora, or Ocelo Duri, the eleventh *mansio* from Mérida, located 225 Roman miles from Augusta Emerita. As on the previous two stages, it can be extremely muddy along the tracks. As with many café/bar/restaurants, the one in Villanueva is unreliable, so carry all provisions unless taking a detour through San Marcial.

From the albergue, return to Cl. Mayor and pass a park (shelter and drinking fountain) and Iglesia Santo Domingo de Guzmán, leaving town.

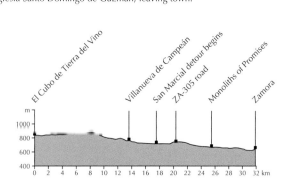

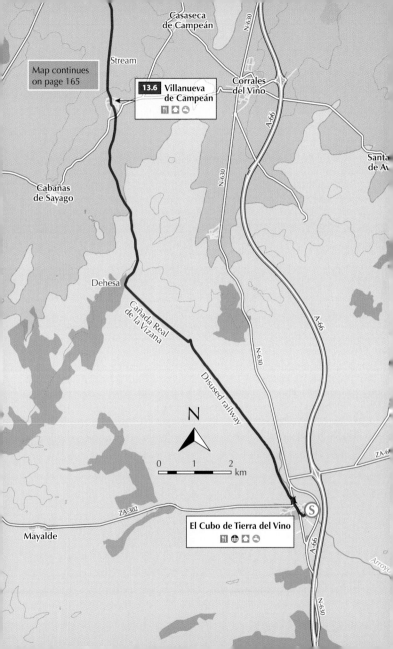

Casaseca
de Campeán

N-630

Stream

Map continues
on page 165

Corrales
del Vino

**13.6** Villanueva
de Campeán

A-66

Santa
de A

Cabañas
de Sayago

N-630

Dehesa

Cañada Real
de la Vizana

Disused railway

N-630

A-66

N

0   1   2
━━━━━━━━
km

ZA-6

ZA-302

El Cubo de Tierra del Vino

**S**

Mayalde

A-66

N-630

Arroyo

Cross a **bridge** (**1.2km**) and turn left onto a track alongside a **disused railway**. Turn left (**4.8km**), then first right through farmland on the **Cañada Real de la Vizana**. The track bends right into a small *dehesa* and forks right, downhill (**2.7km**). Reach **Villanueva de Campeán** on Cl. Calzada (**4.6km**) by the cemetery (turn next right onto Cl. Ote for two drinking fountains: one in a play park and another by the town hall), passing the albergue.

### 13.6KM VILLANUEVA DE CAMPEÁN (ELEV 760M, POP 116) 🍴 ⛲ (436.0KM)

On the border between Tierra del Vino and Sayago, Villanueva del Campeán is traversed by both the **Roman road** and the transhumance route of merino sheep herds along the **Cañada de la Vizana**. The **Iglesia de San Juan Bautista** has been rebuilt following a fire, with only the original belfry remaining. **El Monasterio de Nuestra Señora del Soto** was initially constructed in the 13th century and renovated by Franciscan monks in the 16th and 18th centuries.

🏠 Albergue privado Villanueva de Campeán ⓪ 🅳🅾 🆁 🆆 🆂 6/23, €12, Cl. Calzada 6, tel 630 980 967 or 980 560 365. Keys from Bar Vía de la Plata.

Proceed out of town, cross a road and take the dirt track ahead. At the fork, keep right, cross over a junction and ford a **stream** (**1.2km**) to reach an optional detour to San Marcial (**2.7km**).

### San Marcial detour (2.9km)
Keep straight ahead and after 1km turn right onto the ZA-305 into **San Marcial** (🍴 🚻). Stay on the **ZA-305** to reunite with the main route 1.9km later.

### Direct route (3.2km)
If not detouring to San Marcial, go right and take the second track on the left. At the next junction, take the track ahead (**1.9km**), turn left and then right onto the **ZA-305** (**1.3km**), where the San Marcial detour rejoins from the left.

### Main route
Both options reunited, proceed along the **ZA-305** and take the third track on the left (**1.1km**). Cross a road, and at the end of the track turn left (**2.4km**) then turn right on the next track, sharing the route with the GR14 to the **Monoliths of Promises** (**1.3km**). Inscriptions on the Monoliths explain that this is a peaceful crossroads of paths, cultures and beliefs.

Take the option on the right to a mini-roundabout and **industrial estate** (**1.9km**). At the end of the track, turn right past houses and then right (**1.3km**) towards buildings. Cross the main road (**1.5km**) and enter **Zamora**.

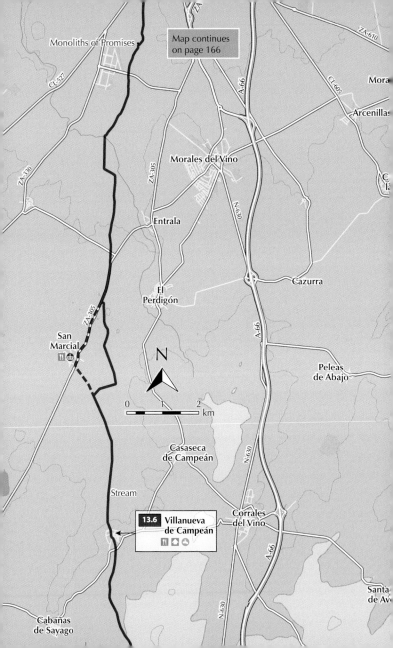

Map continues
on page 166

Monoliths of Promises

CL-527

ZA-610

Mora

Arcenillas

ZA-305

Morales del Viño

A-66

CL-405

ZA-330

N-630

Entrala

Cazurra

El
Perdigón

A-66

ZA-305

San
Marcial

Peleas
de Abajo

N

0    1    2
━━━ km

Casaseca
de Campeán

N-630

Stream

Corrales
del Vino

**13.6**   Villanueva
de Campeán

A-66

Santa
de Av

N-630

Cabañas
de Sayago

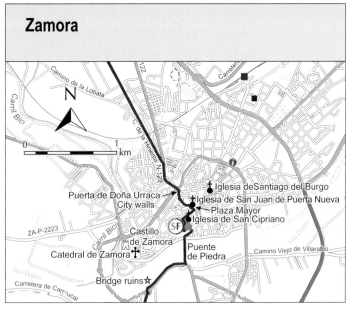

## Zamora

Turn left towards a roundabout (bar) but keep to the road on the right, passing the Iglesia de San Frontis. Cross over the roundabout and go right, hugging the park by the **Río Duero**. Pass a drinking fountain and cross the **Puente de Piedra** (1.2km) to follow signs for the albergue and tourist office. Pass by the Museo Provincial de Bellas Artes then the Iglesia de Santa María, behind which turn left. Keep left uphill then turn right up Cuesta San Cipriano to the albergue.

**18.3KM ZAMORA (ELEV 656M, POP 60,297)** 🍴 ♿ 🏧 🏧 🅿 💊 🅗 ✚ ⊕ ❶
**(417.7KM)**

The marvels of the city of Zamora boast 23 **Romanesque churches**, the most in any one city in the world. Human presence in the area dates to the late Bronze Age. Almost every historic building and monument has been declared a national treasure, so perhaps it is only a matter of time before the city's Roman, Visigoth, Muslim, Catholic and Jewish wonders gain UNESCO World Heritage recognition. Most of the sites are in the small old town, making for relaxed sightseeing delimited by the remains of **wall fortifications** built from the 11th to 14th centuries. The 8m-high walls include two gates that have survived: the **Treason Gate** and the **Doña Urraca Gate**, named after King Fernando I's daughter, who he chose to inherit the city.

Church foundations from 1151 gradually expanded to the current magnitude of the **Catedral de Zamora**. Within, it features a presbytery with a neoclassical altarpiece, seven chapels, a sacristy, a choir and after-choir. This is topped with a magnificent dome and an entrance through Puerta del Obispo combining Romanesque and Mozarabic styles.

Most curious is the **monument to the black-robed Merlú** on Plaza Mayor. It represents the two brothers who, during Semana Santa (Holy Week), are responsible for gathering the rest of the Brotherhood of Jesús Nazareno and the extended hooded congregation to commence the processional parade, known to be one of the most elaborate in all of Spain.

🏠 **Albergue de peregrinos de Zamora** 🅞 🅓🅞 🅑🅡 🅚 🅢 6/32, €Donation, Cl. Cuesta de San Cipriano s/n, tel 980 534 097. Sells the *credencial*.

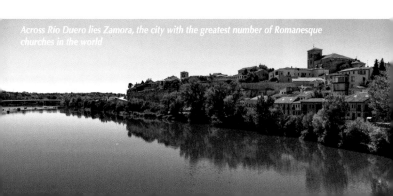

*Across Río Duero lies Zamora, the city with the greatest number of Romanesque churches in the world*

# STAGE 26
## Zamora to Montamarta

| | |
|---|---|
| **Start** | Zamora |
| **Finish** | Montamarta |
| **Distance** | 19.6km |
| **Total ascent** | 170m |
| **Total descent** | 120m |
| **Difficulty** | Easy |
| **Duration** | 4½hr |
| **Percentage paved** | 23% |
| **Albergues** | Montamarta 19.6km |

After sightseeing, a speedy 1km exit from the city to rejoin the open stretches of the Meseta brings back the calm of the Camino, easing walkers back onto a northbound route along lengthy flat dirt tracks, constantly accompanied by extensive hayfields and, in the spring and summer months, many storks. The small town of Roales del Pan, 7km after Zamora, is the only location along the stage to top up on provisions. Apart from the usual observation skills required when leaving the city, the Camino is well signed, giving the pilgrim plenty of opportunities for daydreaming.

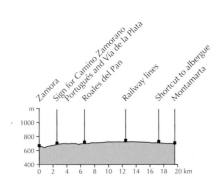

Turn right out of the albergue and follow the wall waymarks up the road as it bends through an alleyway behind **Iglesia de San Cipriano**, after which turn left through the square, passing the library. Turn right opposite the park with the Emperor Viriato statue, noting the golden shell waymarkers on the ground.

**Viriato** was a Lusitanian warrior, born in the Zamora province. The provincial flag is made up of nine strips: a green one awarded to the city by the Catholic monarchs, and eight red ones, each representing a Roman legion defeated by Viriato.

Soon, arrive at the **Plaza Mayor**, where waymarkers are harder to spot. Turn immediately left to head to the back of the **Iglesia de San Juan de Puerta Nueva**.

Turn left up Cl. Reina at the back of the church, then down Cuesta San Bartolomé and through the **Puerta de Doña Urraca**. Turn left onto Cl. Feria, cross straight over a roundabout (pedestrian crossings on the left) onto Cl. Puebla de Sanabría (with clearer signage). At the next fork, take a left on **Cl. de la Hiniesta**, leaving Zamora.

Continue ahead for 1.4km to cross over the next roundabout and find a **sign for the Camino Zamorano Portugués** (heading left) **and the Vía de la Plata** (right) (**2.4km**). Take a small path on the right-hand side of the N-630 then go right onto a gravel dirt track before crossing over the **A11**, twisting immediately right after the bridge to walk briefly by the motorway.

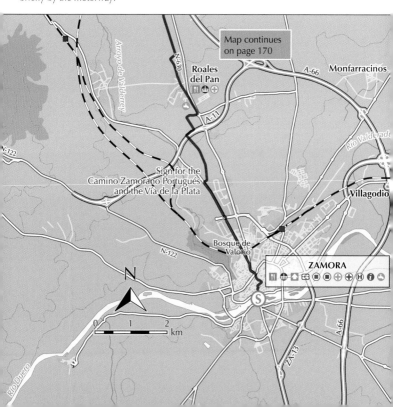

Map continues on page 170

Follow some short stretches of dirt track as they turn left then right towards the **N-630**. Turn left when you reach it to follow a paved path, eventually veering away into **Roales del Pan** (**4.2km**, 🍴 ⊜ ⊕). An agricultural town, Roales del Pan dates back to 1248, while its Iglesia de Nuestra Señora de Asunción is from the 15th century.

Keep to Cl. General Franco to pass a drinking fountain in the play park on the left, where a mural maps the Vía de la Plata route through the Zamora province, and benches and trees provide a shaded picnic spot. Then continue straight through the village, passing its services, until you reach a dirt track. Head along the track, turning

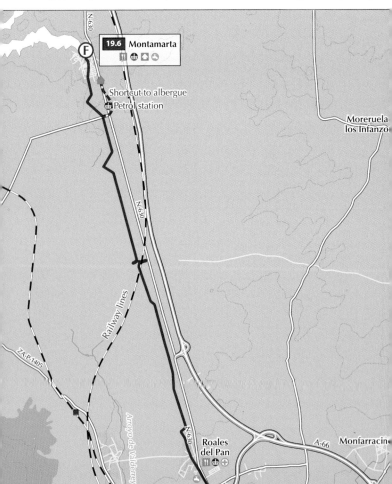

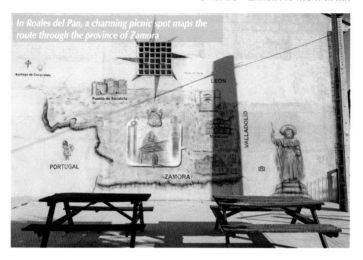

In Roales del Pan, a charming picnic spot maps the route through the province of Zamora

first right and then next left. This second part of the day meanders northwards again along long tracks with excellent waymarking, parallel to the N-630. Keep straight for 4.7km, then turn right, then left following the Camino over **railway lines** and then right again (**6km**).

Continue for a further 2.7km then fork right to cross a minor road onto a dirt track opposite. For the albergue, shortcut here by turning right on the road then left onto the N-630 opposite a **petrol station**, to reach the albergue. At the next fork, take the right-hand track, coming to a farm (**6km**), and soon after reach a road into **Montamarta**. Head along Cl. Majada and then onto Cl. Morales to arrive at the main square and Iglesia San Miguel (drinking fountain).

### 19.6KM MONTAMARTA (ELEV 694M, POP 559) 🍴 ⊕ 🏠 (398.1KM)

Both the **Cañada Real de la Vizana** and the **Roman road** passed through Montamarta, which lies on the banks of the **Ricobayo reservoir**, an area of scenic interest. Work on the **Iglesia de San Miguel Arcángel** began in the 16th century, conserving Renaissance elements.

🏠 **Albergue de Peregrinos de Montamarta** ⊙ Ⓓⓞ Ⓚ Ⓢ 1/50, €5, Ctra. N-630 s/n, tel 685 070 072 or 980 550 112.

# STAGE 27
*Montamarta to Granja de Moreruela*

| | |
|---|---|
| **Start** | Montamarta |
| **Finish** | Granja de Moreruela |
| **Distance** | 22.3km |
| **Total ascent** | 225m |
| **Total descent** | 210m |
| **Difficulty** | Easy |
| **Duration** | 5¼hr |
| **Percentage paved** | 11% |
| **Albergues** | Fontanillas de Castro 11.8km; Granja de Moreruela 22.3km |

Today's criss-crossing over the AVE railway lines, N-630 and A-66 brings pilgrims to the long-awaited Astorga/Ourense split in Granja de Moreruela, where it's decision time! The ruins of Castrotorafe are a true highlight. With no shade to speak of and with unreliable café/bars in Riego del Camino, plan ahead unless you want to make a detour just before Fontanillas de Castro. Otherwise, there is a restaurant just before Granja itself. Fortunately, there are drinking fountains in Fontanillas de Castro, Riego del Camino and Granja de Moreruela.

Facing the Iglesia San Miguel, go left along Cl. de la Ermita and turn first right into the fields ahead. Turn left onto a track (**0.6km**) and follow it towards the 16th-century

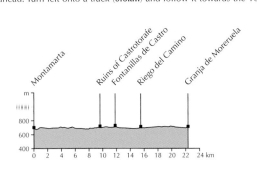

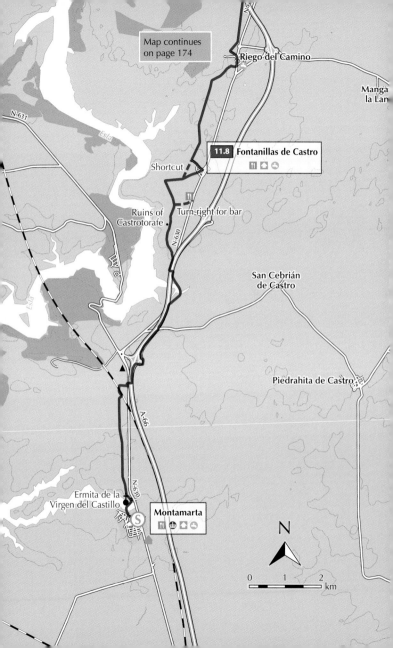

Map continues
on page 174

Riego del Camino

Manga
la Lan

N-631

Esla

**11.8** Fontanillas de Castro

Shortcut

N-630

Turn right for bar

Ruins of
Castrotorafe

San Cebrián
de Castro

Esla

Piedrahita de Castro

A-66

N-630

Ermita de la
Virgen del Castillo

**S** **Montamarta**

N

0        1        2
km

hilltop **Ermita de la Virgen del Castillo**. After extreme rainfall you may be diverted onto the road due to flooding. Skirt behind the church to go left, uphill, then parallel to the **N-630** and right over **railway tracks** (**2.9km**). Turn left, then fork right immediately away from them.

Ignore the arrows on the locked gate in front of you (the old Camino route) and turn right, downhill, towards the highways. Cross over them (**0.9km**) and turn left alongside the **A-66**. Veer right away from the roads but eventually cross back over them

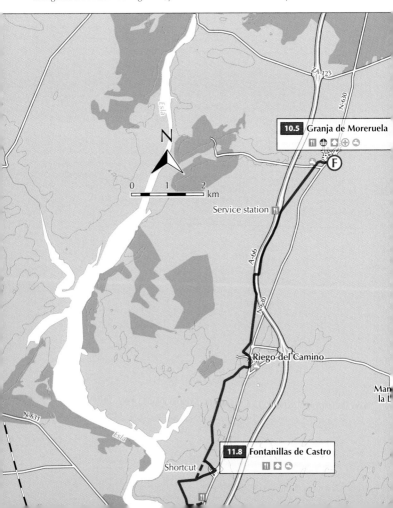

on the left (**3.9km**). Then turn right, away from the N-630, and reach the **ruins of Castrotorafe** (**1.3km**).

Between the 12th and 18th centuries, the town of **Castrotorafe** overlooked the Esla River from its hilly position. Built strategically, its military order lasted until the end of the 15th century, when the bridge collapsed, after which the town began a slow decline. The ruins include the castle (fortress), church, bridge and abandoned town.

*In summer, temperatures can be extremely hot and drought impedes agriculture*

Keep straight at the next crossroads of tracks, passing a sign on the right for a bar. The bar is located on the N-630 and the Camino can later be picked up in Fontanillas. Unless heading for the bar, continue to the next junction of paths and turn right towards Fontanillas. After 500 metres, go straight on to the village (or turn left to skip it, the difference being a mere 200 metres), entering **Fontanillas de Castro** on Cl. Río to reach Cl. Barca. The drinking fountain can be found on the N-630.

### 11.8KM FONTANILLAS DE CASTRO (ELEV 715M, POP 84) 🛉 ⌂ (386.3KM)

Both Fontanillas and Castrotorafe were under the jurisdiction of the Order of Santiago, yet only the former survived. The **Parroquia de la Inmaculada** dates from the 18th century.

🛖 Albergue de peregrinos de Fontanillas de Castro Ⓞ Ⓓⓡ Ⓓⓞ Ⓚ Ⓑⓡ Ⓢ 1/12, €Donation, Cl. Barca 5, tel 676 151 949 or 980 555 507. Angela and Paco along with their wonderful dog, Diva, receive pilgrims with true Camino spirit.

Follow Cl. Barca to return to fields and leave the village (**0.6km**). Turn right, continue for 2km and go right at the fork towards Riego del Camino (no services). After 1km, turn right to reach **Riego del Camino** and the N-630 (**3.2km**). The drinking fountain is by the Parroquia de San Cristóbal (16th–17th century) on Cl. Pozo.

Turn left, passing a bar (unreliable times), then take the third road on the left, which becomes a track. Turn right onto the next track to cross the **A-66** (**2.9km**). Turn left after the bridge and continue near the A-66 to a service station (**2km**), with Granja de Moreruela directly ahead. Use the gate for restaurants at the service station, if needed.

Cross over the road by a mile marker and drinking fountain into **Granja de Moreruela**. Follow the track heading right, reach the N-630 and Bar Tele-Club (café/bar) to register for the albergue (drinking fountain behind the bar).

### 10.5KM GRANJA DE MORERUELA (ELEV 708M, POP 265) 🏨 ⊕ 🛏 ⊕
(375.8KM)

Granja de Moreruela owes its existence to the **Monastery of Santa María de Moreruela**. The monastery, now in ruins (its church and two cloisters have been relatively spared), lies 3.5km away from town. It was declared a national monument in 1931. Initially a Benedictine monastery under the patronage of Santiago Apóstol in the 9th century, in 1158 it passed over to the Cistercian order and its cloister is the oldest in Spain. In town, artwork from the monastery is kept in the **Iglesia de San Juan Evangelista** (19th century), which also reused stone from the monastery for its construction. Behind the church is the Vía de la Plata and Camino Sanabrés crossroad.

🏠 **Albergue de peregrinos de Granja de Moreruela** ◎ 🗐 🆂 2/20, €6, Av. Ángel de la Vega s/n, tel 980 587 005. Keys from Bar Tele-Club.

# SECTION 3: EXTENSION TO ASTORGA

VIA DE LA PLATA

*The Roman road linked Augusta Emerita (Mérida) with Asturica Augusta (Astorga)*

*The Vía Verde, a disused railway, is the preferred option for pilgrims before and after Benavente*

The short distance of almost 100km to Astorga continues to explore the Meseta along wide flat tracks near highways, with few climbs, descents or changes in scenery. As before, pilgrims are often accompanied by immense golden grainfields and intensive agriculture, combined with scenic forests, rivers and *dehesas*. The Camino's easy route through historic towns of varying sizes unravels Spain's profound history further. Lively Benavente and La Bañeza are invitations to wine, dine and discover.

The Vía Verde, a straight path along a disused railway either side of Benavente, was inaugurated in 2020 and provides an enjoyable and well-waymarked section, following burgundy signs marked 'Caminos naturales'.

## PLANNING

1    Most pilgrims divide the route into four stages with overnights in Benavente, Alija del Infantado, La Bañeza and Astorga.

2    Unlike some previous difficult stages of the Vía de la Plata, the route to Astorga is well serviced for provisions.

3    Less popular than the Camino Sanabrés option, the walk and albergues may feel and be quite empty.

## WHAT NOT TO MISS

Walking highlights include the Vía Verde sections and the *dehesa*-style landscape after Palacios de la Valduerna. Find time to visit the historical centres of Benavente and La Bañeza to delight in their architecture and gastronomy. Astorga is a most tempting city for a rest day before taking on the Camino Francés. Home to a multitude of museums, bars and restaurants, its old town prospers with joyful pilgrims, making for a nice change from the solitary Vía.

# EXTENSION

*Granja de Moreruela to*
*Astorga and the Camino Francés*

| | |
|---|---|
| **Start** | Granja de Moreruela |
| **Finish** | Astorga |
| **Distance** | 94.6km |
| **Total ascent** | 705m |
| **Total descent** | 545m |
| **Difficulty** | Easy |
| **Duration** | 22¼hr |
| **Percentage paved** | 39% |
| **Albergues** | Barcial del Barco 18.0km; Benavente 27.1km; Alija del Infantado 48.2km; La Bañeza 69.8km; Palacios de la Valduerna 75.8km; Estación de Valderrey 87.4km; Celada 90.6km; Astorga 94.6km |

Following flat, solitary dirt tracks and roads continuously north, this stage makes for easy-going walking with many pit stops en route, although with full exposure to the elements. The Vía Verde options, as well as several shortcuts, are recommended. Few original mile markers and only some Roman remains are encountered, yet the impact of the Napoleonic Wars is more noticeable, along with the now-familiar Mudéjar, Romanesque, Renaissance and Gothic buildings.

Pass the albergue and turn first left behind the church to the Camino split. Pilgrims heading for Ourense on the Camino Sanabrés will go left here. Go right following the

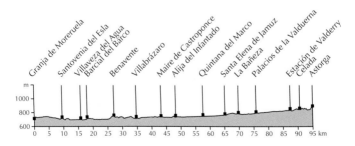

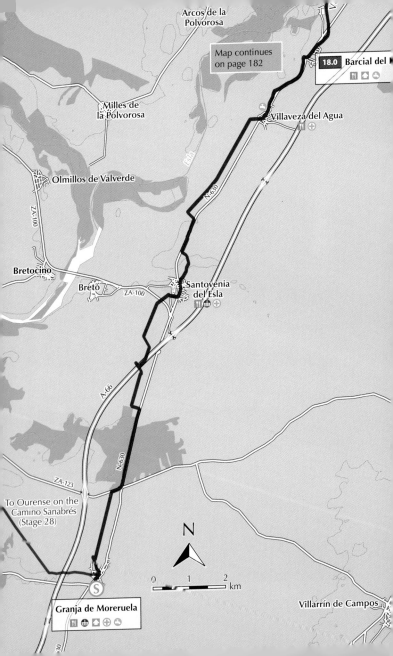

Map continues
on page 182

Arcos de la
Polvorosa

Milles de
la Polvorosa

**18.0** Barcial del

Villaveza del Agua

Olmillos de Valverde

N-630

ZA-100

Bretocino

Bretó

ZA-100

Santovenia
del Esla

A-66

N-630

ZA-123

To Ourense on the
Camino Sanabrés
(Stage 28)

N

0    1    2
km

**S**

Granja de Moreruela

Villarrín de Campos

arrow to Astorga, and take the second on the left into fields, where you turn first right, then right and left to cross a road (**2.8km**). Go right onto a path alongside the **N-630**. Soon, turn left (**2.5km**), first right and left over the **A-66** (**1.4km**).

Turn right then left following electricity lines by the motorway, then turn first left and first right over the **ZA-100** (**2.4km**) to take the first left into **Santovenia del Esla** (**0.6km**, ⛺ ⊕ ⊕).

Turn left, passing the 18th-century Iglesia de Nuestra Señora de Tovar. After the church, ignore a Camino sign that seems to lead down a road and instead take the next road on the right by a stone marker, reaching a fountain. Turn right behind it, and promptly fork left then turn right on a path near the **N-630** (**1.4km**). Cross the N-630 to walk on its left side, turn left at the end of the track and then first right over a stream (**1.3km**). Reach the end of the track and turn right into **Villaveza del Agua** (**3.6km**, ⛺ ⊕).

> Remains from the Lower Palaeolithic era were found in the surrounding meadows of **Villaveza del Agua**. The Iglesia de San Salvador, originating from 1571, is said to be jinxed, having first flooded in 1825 and then been struck by lightning in 1920.

Reach the **N-630**, turn left onto it (drinking fountain) and head left onto a track behind a restaurant. At the end of the track, turn left then immediately right uphill (**2km**) to fork right into **Barcial del Barco**. Turn left (drinking fountain) to Bar Borox. Another drinking fountain is behind the bar.

### 18.0KM BARCIAL DEL BARCO (ELEV 716M, POP 247) ⛺ ◻ (337.4KM)

Barcial is yet another town on the Vía that is accustomed to travellers, seeing that the **Cañada de la Vizana** and the railway both passed through it. Its **Iglesia de Santa Marina**, built in 1773, has a square tower that is startlingly finished in an octagonal shape. Within, there are tables and a carving of Santiago Apóstol from the 16th century.

　🏠 **Albergue Las Eras** Ⓞ Ⓓ◦ Ⓡ Ⓚ Ⓑⓡ Ⓦ Ⓢ Ⓩ 1/14, €10, Cl. las Eras 2, tel 980 640　073 or 675 550 051, barborox@hotmail.com. Register at Bar Borox. Breakfast　€2.

Keep to the right-hand side of the **N-630** then turn left underneath it onto the **Vía Verde** (**0.7km**). Hugging Río Esla, head through the forest to cross an **iron bridge** (**3km**) and arrive at a choice.

### Official Camino

Turn immediately right, turn left opposite a water channel then turn left into **Villanueva de Azoague**. Pass a drinking fountain and turn right directly towards Benavente. Pass a

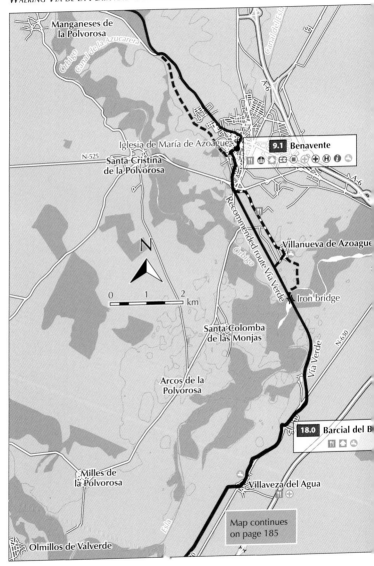

restaurant and turn left just before a roundabout to head for the **canal**, ignoring arrows on the road.

## Recommended route

Continue ahead on the Vía Verde, passing a turn-off for Villanueva de Azoague at the next junction, to reach a **canal** on the edge of **Benavente** (**3.3km**).

## Main route

Both options reunited, cross the **canal** onto Ctra. la Estación and pass under a bridge. For the albergue at the restored railway station, keep straight, following signs. For the centre, fork right onto Cl. los Carros, following a road sign for Torre del Caracol. Reach Plaza de Juan Carlos I, cross onto Cl. Santi Spíritu and turn first right onto Plaza de la Madera to the **Iglesia de María de Azoague**.

### 9.1KM BENAVENTE (ELEV 748M, POP 17,787) ⅰ⊕↻ℂ◉ℍ⊕⊕ℹ (328.3KM)

Strategically located upon a hill overlooking the Órbigo and Esla rivers, and first inhabited by the Romans, Benavente was repopulated in the Middle Ages by the kings of León, whose powers increased until the end of the 18th century. The 1176 **fortress** is thought to be where King Fernando II, founder of the town, died. During the Reconquest, two Romanesque churches were erected: **Santa María del Azoague** and **San Juan del Mercado**, both from the 12th century. In its courts, the powers of lords increased until the end of the 18th century. The **Hospital de la Piedad**, with a Renaissance facade and cloister, was, in its day, pilgrim accommodation.

Yet, the 'Fernando II de León' **Parador hotel** narrates the longest story. The Parador is based on the old 12th-century castle-palace of the Counts of Benavente. After many extensions and remodelling over subsequent centuries, it became one of the most sumptuous and important palaces of Spain. Alas, it was destroyed during the War of Independence. The impressive **Torre de Caracol**, in beautiful Gothic–Renaissance style with a Mudéjar coffered ceiling, is the only part that is preserved within the Parador hotel today.

⌂ **Albergue de peregrinos de Benavente** Ⓓ◉ⓀⓈ 2/12, €4, Ctra. de la Estación, tel 980 634 211, turismo@benavente.es. In the old railway station. Open 1 Mar–31 Oct. Keys from the albergue (Mon–Fri 12:30–22:00), the tourist office on Plaza Mayor (Sat–Sun 10:00–14:00) and the police station (Sat–Sun afternoons).

There are three options for leaving Benavente: the Vía Verde, the official Camino, or a recommended hybrid route (shown by a solid blue line on the map), which follows the official Camino as far as the Vía Verde bridge and then switches to the Vía Verde.

### Vía Verde

From the centre of Benavente, go back to Ctra. de la Estación, pass the albergue and turn right onto the **Vía Verde** (**0.5km**). Cross above the ZA-P-1511 (**3.4km**), where the official Camino passes below. Keep to the Vía Verde at the first junction with the official Camino (**2km**) but at the second junction turn left to join the official route (**0.5km**).

### Official Camino

From the **Iglesia de María de Azoague**, head onto Cl. los Herreros. At the big junction, turn left. At the roundabout, fork right onto Cl. Cañada de la Vizana (don't take Cl. de las Eras). Skirt a roundabout, proceeding uphill by a **modern mile marker** on tree-lined ZA-P-1511. Pass a service station (**2.9km**), reaching the **Vía Verde bridge** (**1km**). Continue on the road, then follow a **stone marker** (**1.5km**) to turn right onto a track. Soon, cross the **Vía Verde**. Keep left at the fork and immediately right. At the next junction, turn right twice to cross the **Vía Verde** again (**0.9km**).

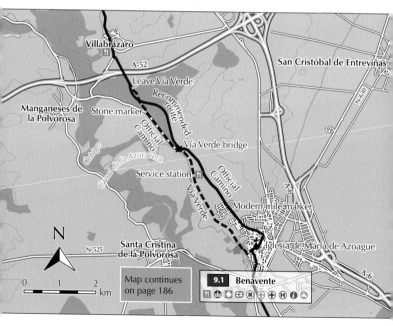

Map continues on page 186

### Recommended hybrid route

Take the official route out of Benavente, reaching the **Vía Verde bridge** over the ZA-P-1511. Instead of passing under it, take a right to climb up onto the bridge. Once atop, proceed right on the **Vía Verde**.

### Main route

With all route options reunited, **leave the Vía Verde** (which keeps straight) and turn left, go under the **A-52 (0.4km)** and turn right onto a road to a bar at **Villabrázaro (1.1km)**. Pass a mini-roundabout (drinking fountain), a **farm**, **wine caves** and a **cemetery** into **Maire de Castroponce (8.2km, ▯, park with drinking fountain). After town, the **road enters León** (announced by a road sign), the last council area of the Vía de la Plata, before crossing **Puente de la Vizana (2.8km)**.

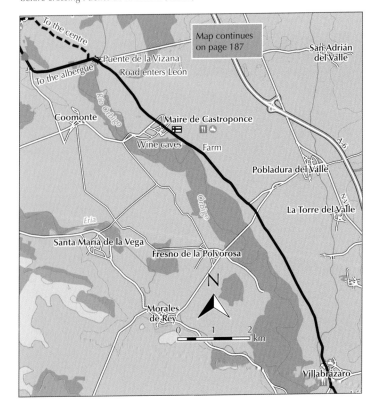

*The Camino enters León and crosses the medieval Puente de la Vizana before reaching Alija del Infantado*

The **Puente de la Vizana** over the Órbigo River is of medieval origin but was rebuilt in the second half of the 16th century. It was blown up by the Duke of Wellington's English troops in the War of Independence then repaired in 1917.

For the albergue, turn left on the road, passing a swimming pool. To shortcut to the centre, turn left and take the second track on the right into **Alija del Infantado** (drinking fountain on Plaza Mayor).

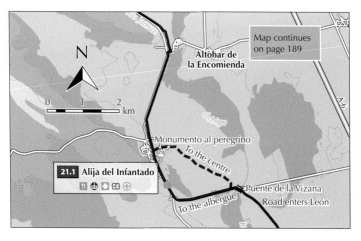

Map continues on page 189

## 21.1KM ALIJA DEL INFANTADO (ELEV 748M, POP 629) 🏨 ⊕ 🛆 🄲 ⊕ (307.2KM)

The **Pimentel castle** by the town hall is one of the oldest fortifications in León, dating from 931. Its purpose was initially defensive, but it later became the manor house of Alija, falling into ruin during the War of Independence. It was set on fire by English troops in 1810 due to the alliance between the Lord of Alija, 13th Duque del Infantado, and Napoleon Bonaparte, although it is said that in this region Napoleon recognized that his empire was threatened, and his good fortune began to fade. The castle's curse continued with an accidental fire in 1887, destroying it further.

Fortunately, four religious buildings still show the wealth of Alija's history: **Iglesia de San Verísimo** (12th–16th century), the parish church of Alija (1896), **Iglesia de San Esteban** (13th–16th century, and declared an Asset of Cultural Interest in 1993), and the **Ermita del Cristo** (mid 18th century).

🏠 **Albergue de peregrinos de Alija del Infantado** 🄾 🄳🄾 🄱🅁 🅂 2/12, €8, Ctra. de Benavente s/n, tel 660 068 794 or 987 667 201. Breakfast included.

Continue past the albergue to the centre of **Alija del Infantado**. Pass a petrol station and cemetery, spotting the **Monumento al Peregrino** on the hill to the right (**2km**). Santiago's cross recalls the San Mamés pilgrim hospital that used to be located here. Pass **wine caves** soon after and turn right over Río Jamuz (**2.2km**), immediately taking a **riverside path** on the left to a bar in **Quintana del Marco** (**5.4km**).

Embedded in the belfry of the Iglesia de San Pedro in **Quintana del Marco** is a bust that is said to represent Marcus Aurelius. The town's 15th-century Castle-Palace of the Quinones was declared a national monument in 1949.

Keep straight, passing opposite **Villanueva de Jamuz** (🏨), lying just off the Camino (**3.4km**). The path veers away from the river (**2.4km**), taking a diagonal right over **fields** to a more obvious track. The track edges back to the river then turns left, right and left to a wider track. Go across grass towards trees, with Santa Elena de Jamuz (no services) in sight. Arrive at a track junction (**1.4km**) and a route choice.

### Avoiding Santa Elena
Turn right, and after 280 metres take the first track on the left, then 530 metres later turn right onto the **LE-114** to rejoin the main route.

### Through Santa Elena de Jamuz
Go over the ford, turn right, then first left and right at the end to reach the main square (drinking fountain) in **Santa Elena de Jamuz**.

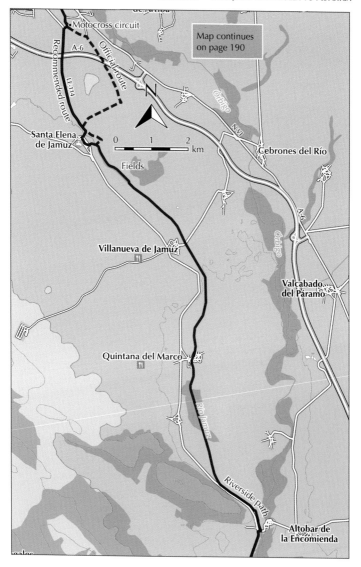

Map continues
on page 190

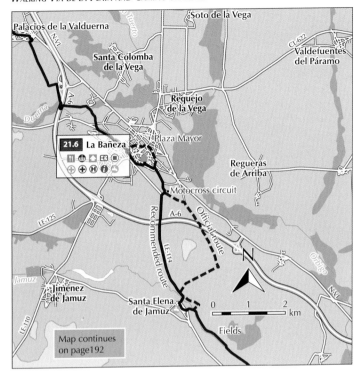

The hamlet of **Santa Elena de Jamuz** lies near the small reservoir of La Tabla, which irrigates its agricultural lands. The fields still display examples of traditional waterwheels (called *tablias*, from Arabic). The parish church conserves its original 16th-century Mudéjar coffered ceiling and a 17th-century altarpiece.

Proceed to take a right off the square to then go left onto the **LE-114**, where there are two options (**0.8km**).

### Official route
From the **LE-114**, turn right onto a track then take the third track on the left. After solar panels, turn right (no waymark) under the motorway. At the next junction, take the second track over on the left alongside a **motocross circuit** to turn right onto Cl. Santa Elena.

## Recommended route

Take the **LE-114** uphill over the **motorway**. Near town, turn right towards a **motocross circuit** (**3km**) on Cl. Santa Elena.

## Main route

At the next junction, now in **La Bañeza**, come to a choice (**0.8km**). For the albergue, go left then first right and turn right onto Cl. San Roque. For the centre, keep right on Cl. Santa Elena, turn left onto Plaza de los Reyes Católicos, fork right then left around the square (park) and turn right onto Cl. Juan de Mansilla to **Plaza Mayor**.

### 21.6KM LA BAÑEZA (ELEV 780M, POP 10,068) 🍴 🚌 🏠 🄲 Ⓘ Ⓗ ⊕ ⊕ 🛈 (285.6KM)

The first pre-Roman settlers in La Bañeza are believed to have been the Egurros Asturian tribe, and already in AD932 it was known as Vanieza. Destroyed by Almanzor at the end of the 10th century, it was then walled by Alfonso VII in the 12th century. Between the 15th and 17th centuries it saw the construction of hospitals, chapels and many churches, including that of San Antonio, which served as a pilgrim hospital. In the 18th century, the **Capilla de la Piedad** on Plaza Salvador also housed pilgrims. The Romanesque **Iglesia de El Salvador** (Pilgrim Mass) dates from 1085 and was formerly a monastery, the **Iglesia de Santa María** dates back to the 16th century, and the 14th-century **Iglesia de Santa Colomba de la Vega**, with a Mudéjar roof, was declared a national monument in 1943.

🏠 **Albergue de peregrinos Monte Urba** Ⓞ Ⓓₒ Ⓚ Ⓦ Ⓢ 2/36, €10, Cl. Bello Horizonte s/n, tel 987 640 992 or 649 332 087.

## From the centre

Take Cl. Reloj from **Plaza Mayor**, turn right onto Cl. Vía de la Plata and keep straight to Cl. José Marcos de Segovia.

## From the albergue

Turn right onto Cl. San Roque, right onto Cl. San Julián, then first left and first right onto Cl. Santa Lucía. Cross the roundabout onto Cl. Lope de Vega, pass the Santiago statue, a supermarket, and Iglesia del Salvador (with the Santiago cross) to turn right onto Cl. Vía de la Plata then left onto Cl. José Marcos de Segovia (**0.9km**).

## Main route

With both options reunited, fork right just before the street sign for Santiago de la Valduerna and cross over a road onto a track (**1.1km**). Veer left then right to the **disused railway** and cross the **iron bridge** (**0.5km**), then veer off left, turn left and left again

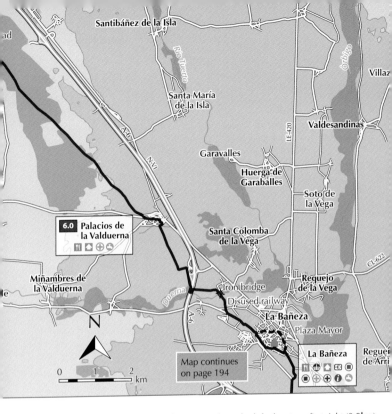

under the **A-6** (**1km**). Veer right and onto a track on the left, then turn first right (**0.9km**) to **Palacios de Valduerna**. Turn right, first left, then left and right to the church.

### 6.0KM PALACIOS DE LA VALDUERNA (ELEV 795M, POP 373) (279.6KM)

Nearby, to the south-east, lie unequivocal remains of the original Roman road: a small bridge and at least one culvert. Until the 16th century, Palacios knew great prestige and was the jurisdictional capital of the region (before La Bañeza). Now in ruins and declared a national monument, the **11th-century palace** used by the kings of León was rebuilt by Juan González Bazán during the first half of the 14th century. *Our hotel* is in the emblazoned house of the Bazán family.

⌂ **Hotel Rural Señorío de los Bazán** ◯ ᴘᵀ ᴿ ᴮʳ ᴳʳ ᔆ 8/16, €-/60–70/70/-/-, Av. Vía de la Plata 25, tel 987 665 628, email *reservas@senoriodelosbazan.com*, **www.senoriodelosbazan.com**.

Turn left, passing the town hall, then turn left by a square (drinking fountain) and pass a pilgrim statue (drinking fountain). Veer right and keep left to a track, then keep right, passing the cemetery (**0.9km**), into *dehesas*, where the Camino keeps continuously straight.

Visible in the distance to the left lies the **Santuario Virgen del Castro**, located on an ancient Asturian fort and later reused by the Romans as a surveillance point, looking out on the different communication routes that crossed the valley of the Duerna River. The Virgin of Castrotierra is considered the Leonese Goddess of Rain. It is believed that in the 5th century, facing prolonged drought, local farmers begged for help from the Bishop of Astorga. He advised them to find an image of Our Lady, bring it to Astorga Cathedral to be blessed and return it to the sanctuary. This tradition of local pilgrimage lives on today. The sanctuary that can be admired was in fact built in the 17th and 18th centuries.

Reach a **road** (**6.1km**), turn right onto it and then take a track ahead (**0.6km**) towards the **A-6**, where you turn left and right to pass under it (**3km**). Take the first left-hand track then cross a road. Turn immediately right and left to walk alongside the **N-VI** on its left-hand side. Soon cross it into **Estación de Valderrey**. If you are staying in the albergue, keep straight, otherwise turn left.

## 11.6KM ESTACIÓN DE VALDERREY (ELEV 833M, POP 25) 🛏 (268.0KM)

The albergue is set in the restored old railway station. With no services here, plan food in advance.

🛏 **Albergue de peregrinos Amigos Leopoldo Panero** Ⓞ Ⓓ Ⓡ Ⓚ Ⓦ Ⓢ
1/6, €Donation, Cl. Mercado 2, tel 686 199 380 or 679 178 596,
amigosleopoldopanero@gmail.com.

Continue ahead to soon go over the **Puente Valimbre** bridge (**0.7km**).

Both the Roman road and the Cañada de la Vizana crossed the **Puente Valimbre**. It was restored in 1786 by Joaquín Rodrígues, Master of Works of the Bishopric and Council Seminary of the city of Astorga.

After the bridge, ignore the option on the right (inadequately waymarked). Instead, turn left then cross the **N-VI** to take a parallel path on the left. From the bridge, you can also shortcut up the N-VI to Celada, saving 200 metres. Veer left away from the N-VI (**1.4km**), and before the motorway turn right onto a road into

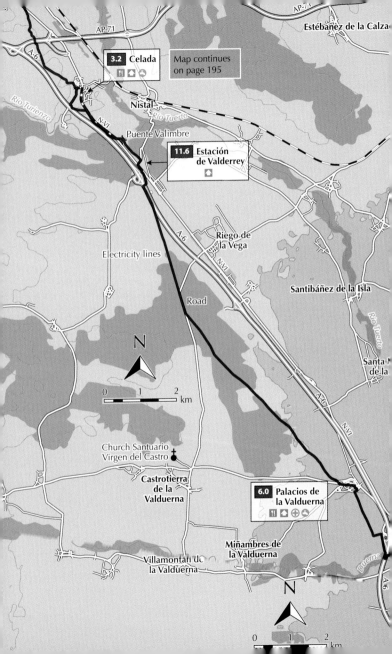

**AP-71**

**Estébanez de la Calza**

**A-6**

**3.2 Celada**

Map continues
on page 195

Río Turienzo

N-VI

**Nistal**

Río Tuerto

Puente Valimbre

**11.6 Estación
de Valderrey**

A-6

**Riego de
la Vega**

N-VI

Electricity lines

**Santibáñez de la Isla**

Río Tuerto

Road

Santa M
de la

N

0   1   2 km

Church Santuario
Virgen del Castro

**Castrotierra
de la
Valduerna**

**6.0 Palacios de
la Valduerna**

A-6

N-VI

**Miñambres de
la Valduerna**

Villamontán de
la Valduerna

duerna

A-6

N

0   1   2 km

**Celada (0.6km)**. Turn right for services, otherwise turn left then first right to the church (drinking fountain).

### 3.2KM CELADA (ELEV 840M, POP 105) 🍴 🏠 (264.8KM)

To the pride of its inhabitants, in 1964 Celada was the first town in this council area to have a public telephone. The facade of the **Iglesia de San Vicente** displays the date 1570, and the altarpiece of the Virgin dates from the 17th century.

🛏 Hostal La Paz Ⓞ⒫ⓇⓈ 35/70, €-/25/40/-/-, Ctra. N-VI km322, tel 987 615 277. Breakfast included.


Fork left and at the end turn left onto a track, then turn right, uphill, to views of Astorga (**0.9km**). Go under the **AP-71** (**1km**), turn right onto the next track, and turn left onto the N-VI into **Astorga** (**1km**). Soon cross the road and turn right, following signs for 'conjunto histórico' and 'parking'. Go up cobbled **steps** and under a bridge on the left, following the sign for 'oficina de turismo' past the **Basílica Nuestra Señora de Fátima**.

Reach **Plaza España** and traverse diagonally to Plaza Mayor and the **remains of the Roman Forum** that once stood here, marking the end of the Vía de la Plata. For the Catedral de Santa María, cross the square, turn left and keep straight past cafés, restaurants, souvenir shops and the Gaudí Palace.

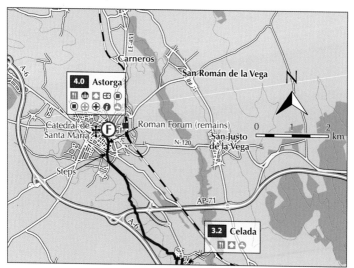

The last waymarks on the Vía take pilgrims to the Catedral de Astorga before they continue on the Camino Francés

**Astorga**

1 Albergue de peregrinos Siervas de María  2 Albergue San Javier
3 Albergue Só Por Hoje  4 Albergue MyWay

**4.0KM ASTORGA** (ELEV 872M, POP 10,553) 🏨 ⛲ 🏠 🎫 🏧 ℹ️ ✚ ⊕ ✱ (260.8KM)

Reaching Asturica Augusta marks the end of the Mérida to Astorga Roman road, the Vía de la Plata. It is here that pilgrims on the Vía greet those from the popular Camino Francés. At its peak in the 17th century, pilgrims from east and south stayed at one of 21 pilgrim hospitals, as did St Francis of Assisi in 1214. It is also believed that Santiago and St Paul visited Astorga. Although the Romans built extensive walls, the city saw both Visigoth (456) and Muslim (714) invasions, and only 2km of the walls remain. The park below the walls is an ideal spot for a relaxing picnic.

The **Catedral de Santa María**, with its varied stone, dates from the 15th and 16th centuries and has a main altarpiece by Michelangelo's student, Gaspar Becerra. The nearby **Bishop's Palace**, designed by Antoni Gaudí and completed in 1913, now houses the excellent **Museo de los Caminos**. To feed a pilgrim's appetite, Astorga is also known as the regional chocolate centre, and the **Museo del Chocolate** will delight those with a sweet tooth. If you need your Roman fill, visit

197

the **thermal baths**, the **Roman Museum** in the remains of an *ergastulum* (prison) on Plaza de San Bartolomé, and (also on Plaza San Bartolomé) a very important **mile marker**. This *miliario* commemorates all the different *vías* that converged here: the two Braga–Astorga routes, the roads from Zaragoza (including the one through the Cantabrian mountains), Tarragona, Bordeaux (France), and, of course, the Vía de la Plata from Mérida.

⌂ **Albergue de peregrinos Siervas de María** Ⓞ Ⓓⓞ Ⓚ Ⓦ Ⓢ 22/156, €7, Plaza San Francisco 3, tel 987 616 034 or 618 271 773, asociacion@ caminodesantiagoastorga.com. Sells the *credencial*.

⌂ **Albergue San Javier** Ⓓⓞ Ⓡ Ⓚ Ⓦ Ⓢ 5/65, €14, Cl. Portería 6, tel 987 618 532, alberguesanjavier@hotmail.com. Open 20 Apr–31 Oct.

⌂ **Albergue Só Por Hoje** Ⓟⓕ Ⓓⓡ Ⓓⓞ Ⓡ Ⓑⓡ Ⓦ Ⓢ 1/10 & 2/4, €28/-/69/-/-, Cl. Rodríguez de Cela 30, tel 690 749 853, info@alberguesoporhoje.com, **https://alberguesoporhoje.com**. Open Mar–Nov. Breakfast included.

⌂ **Albergue MyWay** Ⓟⓕ Ⓓⓡ Ⓓⓞ Ⓡ Ⓚ Ⓒⓕ Ⓦ Ⓢ Ⓩ 1/14 & 5/8, €14/40/55/75, Cl. San Marcos 7, tel 640 176 338 or 987 913 011, alberguemyway@gmail.com. Open Apr–Oct.

# SECTION 4:
# CAMINO SANABRÉS
# TO OURENSE

*Changes in scenery on the Camino Sanabrés make for a
wonderful contrast from the Vía (Stage 33)*

Two more stages along the Meseta, albeit with noticeable changes from previous days, bring pilgrims to the banks of the Tera River by the N-525 highway in Santa Marta de Tera. The Camino meanders through forests, open fields, pretty towns and villages to climb to the Padornelo Pass, hike down again, and ascend once more to enter Galicia.

Waymarking becomes even clearer, hills greener and waterproofs more regularly worn as pilgrims hike the Galician lands. Arriving in A Gudiña, pilgrims choose between going to Ourense through Laza or, alternatively, via Verín. The Laza option, described in Stages 35–38, takes pilgrims above the As Portas reservoir before a long descent into Laza, more lovely wandering through Galician villages and arrival in historical Ourense, where tired bodies can be cured at the natural hot springs. The longer alternative via Verín, described in Stages 35A–38A, joins the Laza option in Pereiras for a final short stretch to Ourense.

## PLANNING

1   The albergue in Puebla de Sanabria has been known to close without notice, and hotel costs vary depending on the season, so check in advance.

2   With more provisions along the way, mainly drinking fountains, packs will feel lighter, except on the 18km from Granja de Moreruela to Faramontanos de Tábara on Stage 28.

3   A night in an *albergue municipal* in Galicia (from Stage 34) has a set rate of €8.

For planning tips on the Verín option, see 'A Gudiña to Ourense: variant via Verín'.

## WHAT NOT TO MISS

The greener and leafier Camino Sanabrés offers more opportunities to picnic outdoors. Some serene spots include the Puente Quintos bridge (Stage 28); the natural swimming pool in Santa Croya de Tera (Stage 29); the shores of the Embalse de Agavanzal (Stage 30); the Tejedelo woods of Requejo (Stages 32 and 33); the wolf trap above Lubián (Stage 33); the pass entering Galicia (Stage 34); and the most magical rest spot above the reservoir of As Portas (Stage 35).

Visiting the church and Santiago statue in Santa Marta de Tera is essential, as are Puebla de Sanabria, Ourense Cathedral and a pilgrim lunch (with pilgrim prices) at Rionegro del Puente's famous restaurant. Enjoy an evening of laughter with José Almeida in Tábara, have a cosy chat with Craig and Dorothea in Villar de Farfón, and add your signed shell to the shrine in Alberguería.

# STAGE 28

*Granja de Moreruela to Tábara*

| | |
|---|---|
| **Start** | Granja de Moreruela |
| **Finish** | Tábara |
| **Distance** | 26.2km |
| **Total ascent** | 450m |
| **Total descent** | 305m |
| **Difficulty** | Hard |
| **Duration** | 6½hr |
| **Percentage paved** | 14% |
| **Albergues** | Tábara 26.2km |

Starting the lovely Camino Sanabrés certainly breaks some of the routine of previous days as it wanders across fields, over the Puente Quintos bridge spanning the Río Elsa, across rocks with spectacular views and through more gorgeous *fincas*. Importantly, there is no option via the Monasterio de Moreruela (even though there are signs for it), since it involves trespassing on private land. The first 18.3km are solitary, with no provisions until Faramontanos.

From the Bar Tele-Club, cross the N-630, pass the albergue, turn left onto Cl. Doctor Damián Gonzales Galíndo and right behind the church to the Camino split, where the Ourense option takes you left. Pilgrims heading for Astorga to join up with the Camino

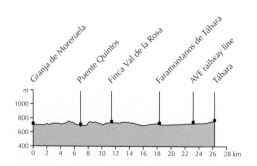

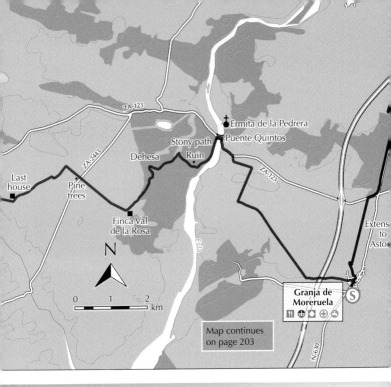

Map continues
on page 203

*A pilgrim admires outstanding views over Río Esla after having crossed Puente Quintos*

Francés will go right here. Following Camino signs for Ourense, go under the **A-66** (**1.2km**).

After a mile marker, turn right, uphill, and keep to the undulating track for 2.9km. Turn sharp right, uphill, before dropping down to turn left onto the **ZA-123** (**5km**), which crosses the **Puente Quintos**.

> Down the track on the right before crossing the bridge, the **Ermita de la Pedrera** houses the 1647 image of the Virgin of Montes Negros, named after the surrounding hills, and hosts an annual pilgrimage on 25 April. The bridge itself was built in 1920. It is 110 metres long and has nine arches.

Immediately over the bridge, take the **stony path** on your left by the cliffs. Cyclists are better off on the road, which is unsafe for pedestrians. After a short stretch over rocks, the Camino takes a riverside path through trees before a brief slope to a track at the top (**1.9km**). Turn right into *dehesas*, passing a **ruin**. Go downhill and then soon turn sharp left to eventually reach the entrance to **Finca Val de la Rosa** (**3.3km**). Turn right, away from the entrance, reach the **ZA-2443** (**1.5km**) and cross over it onto the track opposite, passing **pine trees**. Turn left then right and immediately left, with Faramontanos in sight. Pass houses and turn right at the **last house** to start the 2.4km track into the village.

Enter **Faramontanos de Tábara** (🏨 and bakery) on Cl. Benavente, keep right at the fork and turn right onto Cl. Pozo, reaching a drinking fountain by the Iglesia de San Martín (**5.4km**). Pass the church, take the track on the left parallel to Cl. Pozo next to a play park (drinking fountain), cross Cl. de Carretera then the **ZA-123** onto the track opposite (**0.7km**).

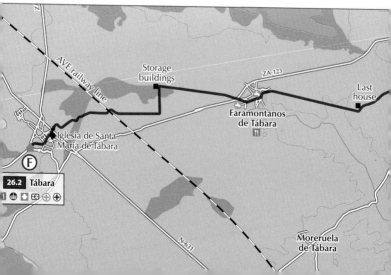

Keep straight for 2.2km and turn left just before two **storage buildings**. Take the next right leading over the **AVE railway line** (3.1km). Keep to the track, arriving in **Tábara** by the **Iglesia de Santa María de Tábara** (2.3km).

Cross the main road, turn left and immediately right onto Cl. Plaza Mayor, passing the town hall. Traverse the square diagonally, turn left onto Cl. Vistahermosa and next right onto Cl. Sol. Turn left onto Tr. Sol and immediately right onto Plaza Sol, past the library. When Plaza Sol becomes Cl. Calvo Sotelo, fork right, uphill, onto Camino Sotillo to the *albergue municipal*.

### 26.2KM TÁBARA (ELEV 749M, POP 740) 🔢 ⊕ 🏠 Ⓒ ⊕ ⊕ (349.6KM)

From the Middle Ages, Tábara was considered an important monastic centre. According to the Mozarabic Bible of the Cathedral of León, the **Monasterio de Santa María**, most likely erected on Visigothic remains, was founded by San Froilán at the end of the 9th century, at the request of King Alfonso III. The text also explains that the religious community of the monastery was made up of 600 monks and nuns.

The **Beato de Tábara** was crafted in the monastery's scriptorium, representing Spain's most valuable contribution to the history of medieval book illustration, now kept in the National Archive of Madrid. Begun by the painter-calligrapher Magius and completed by his disciple, the monk Emeterius, on 27 July 970, it is considered one of the most precious early medieval books in all of Spanish and even European history. The images, of a didactic nature, interpret the Apocalypse of the Bible through symbols, revelations, final catastrophes, fantastic beasts, angels and plagues. Difficult to understand for the people of the time, with imagery in violent outbursts of colour and harmonizing Carolingian and Islamic influences with a traditional background, they are anti-classical in nature. Within, the depiction of the painter and his disciples is the first preserved self-portrait of Hispanic art, while on the back, Emeterius tells us that his teacher Magius is buried in the monastery tower.

🏠 Albergue de peregrinos de Tábara Ⓞ Ⓓⓡ Ⓓⓞ Ⓚ Ⓑⓡ Ⓦ Ⓢ Ⓩ 4/28, €Donation, Camino Sotillo s/n, tel 637 926 068, alberguedetabara@gmail.com. It is run by Camino-inspired writer José Almeida, who is also an important figure in decision-making on all things Camino in the Zamora province, such as repainting arrows or better preserving the Santiago pilgrim statue in Santa Marta.

🏠 Albergue/Restaurante El Roble Ⓟⓡ Ⓓⓞ Ⓡ Ⓑⓡ Ⓖⓡ Ⓦ Ⓢ Ⓩ 1/14 & 15/28, €11/30/74/66, Cl. el Prado 3, tel 650 629 969 or 980 590 300, elrobletabara@gmail.com, www.turismoruralelroble.es. Closed 24 and 25 Dec.

# STAGE 29

*Tábara to Santa Marta de Tera*

| | |
|---|---|
| **Start** | Tábara |
| **Finish** | Santa Marta de Tera |
| **Distance** | 23.0km |
| **Total ascent** | 230m |
| **Total descent** | 260m |
| **Difficulty** | Easy |
| **Duration** | 5½hr |
| **Percentage paved** | 30% |
| **Albergues** | Villanueva de las Peras 14.3km; Santa Marta de Tera 23.0km |

Consider stocking up on food in Tábara, as the opening times of restaurants in Santa Marta de Tera are often undependable. The albergue in Santa Marta has a well-equipped kitchen, presenting a good opportunity to prepare a feast with fellow pilgrims. Otherwise, Santa Croya, 1km before Santa Marta, has a shop (with unreliable opening times) and some eateries. This stage of the Camino follows long tracks over a land that sadly suffered extreme wildfires in 2022. Villanueva is an ideal midway point for a rest and meal. At the church in Santa Marta, discover the Santiago pilgrim sculpture that has become a defining symbol of the Camino Sanabrés.

Turn right out of the albergue, up Camino Sotillo, and right onto Cl. Duernas before turning right onto Ctra. Ríofrío. Turn left onto Camino San Lorenzo, passing a drinking

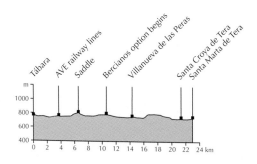

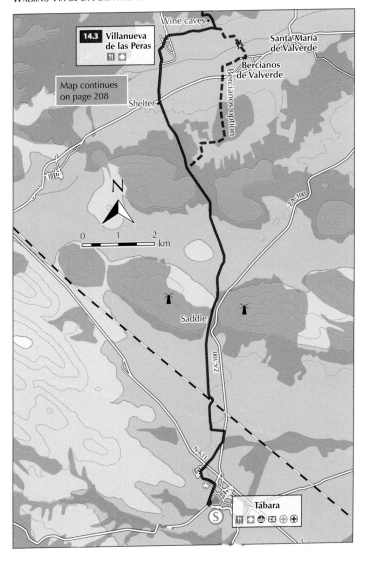

**14.3** Villanueva de las Peras

Map continues on page 208

Wine caves

Santa María de Valverde

Bercianos de Valverde

Bercianos option

Shelter

N

0    1    2 km

Saddle

ZA-100

ZA-100

N-631

Tábara

fountain by a cross on your right. Keep right at the fork and turn right onto Cl. Riego Primera. Cross the **N-631** to leave Tábara (**1.6km**) on a dirt track ahead towards the AVE railway line.

Turn left onto a road, left onto the next track and next right over the **AVE railway lines** (**2.2km**). The track makes its way uphill to a **saddle** between two hills and continues straight at the junction at the top (**2.9km**).

Wildfires continue to devastate the **Sierra de la Culebra**, and this particular section, in the low hills of the mountain range, suffered extremely in July 2022. The protected Sierra spans the most north-easterly corner of Portugal, bordering on sections of Castilla y León. It houses the highest concentration of wolves in all of Spain, as well as big populations of deer.

Head downhill, reaching two options (**3.9km**). The recommended route takes you into Villanueva de las Peras for services. An alternative option, via Bercianos de Valverde, follows the original Camino.

**Recommended route (5.4km)**

Take the left fork to reach a **road** and **shelter** (**2.1km**). With **Villanueva de las Peras** in sight to the right, reach it 1km later and proceed to the central square.

*Leaving Tábara, pilgrims walk up to the saddle before descending into Villanueva de las Peras*

## 14.3KM VILLANUEVA DE LAS PERAS (ELEV 743M, POP 79) ▯ ▯ (335.3KM)

In the past, all the houses in town had their own wine cellar, with approximately 50 still preserved today.

⌂ Albergue Alameda ▯ ▯ ▯ ▯ ▯ ▯ ▯ ▯ ▯ 1/12 & 3/7, €10/20/30/45, Cl. Alameda 21, tel 696 321 223 or 980 641 799, villanuevabar@yahoo.es. Keys from Bar Moña.

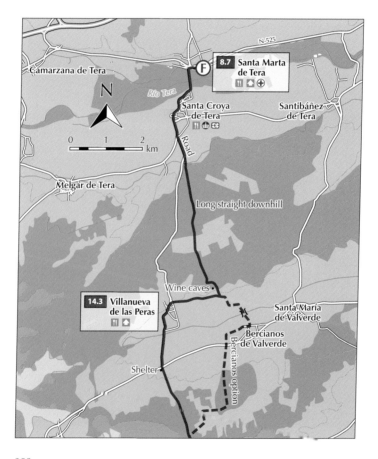

Continue onto Cl. Iglesia and fork immediately right onto Cl. Santa Croya. Take the fourth road on your right, leaving Villanueva on a track (**0.4km**), which after 1.3km joins the alternative route coming from Bercianos.

**Bercianos option (5.7km)**
At the junction, go right and keep left at the next fork. Turn right at the next junction, by a building, and turn left at the next crossroads of tracks. Cross over a **road** to keep to the track and at the end turn right. Head right to enter **Bercianos de Valverde** (no services) and follow arrows left onto Cl. Las Eras. Keep to the wide track over a **river** and then turn left at the next junction. Turn first right and then first left, connecting with the recommended route.

**Main route**
Turn left uphill past houses and **wine caves**, making sure to fork left soon after (**2km**). Head uphill then on a **long straight downhill** to a **road** (**3.4km**). Turn right onto it into **Santa Croya de Tera** (🄲). Keep to the same road to reach a shop (unreliable opening hours) and café/bars by the river, where locals enjoy dips in the refreshing natural swimming pool (**1.4km**).

Walk by a canal along a tree-lined pavement and cross **Río Tera** (**1km**) to **Santa Marta de Tera**. Turn right to the Iglesia Románica de Santa Marta and proceed on Cl. Iglesia to the albergue.

**8.7KM SANTA MARTA DE TERA** (ELEV 736M, POP 162) 🄸🄲🌀 (326.6KM)

The 10th-century **Iglesia Románica**, declared a monument of historic and artistic interest in 1931, was visited in 1129 by King Alfonso VII, who wished to thank Santa Marta for healing him following his illness. Tourists flock to the church twice a year on the equinoxes of spring and autumn to gaze in wonderment at the kaleidoscopic sunlight that floods in. The church is best known for its beautiful **sculpture of Santiago**, identifiable thanks to the scallop on his bag and his staff; his left hand, in which lies his main strength, is raised in greeting. It is regarded as the oldest sculpture of the apostle, dating from the 12th century, and is a well-known symbol of the Camino Sanabrés. The church includes a superb museum, where you can find photos of Pope John Paul II's pilgrimage to Santiago.

🏠 **Albergue de peregrinos de Santa Marta de Tera** 🄾 🄳🄾 🄺 🅆 🅂 2/16, €5, Cl. de la Iglesia 10, tel 980 649 006. Call ahead in winter.

# STAGE 30
*Santa Marta de Tera to Rionegro del Puente*

| | |
|---|---|
| **Start** | Santa Marta de Tera |
| **Finish** | Rionegro del Puente |
| **Distance** | 28.6km |
| **Total ascent** | 250m |
| **Total descent** | 200m |
| **Difficulty** | Hard |
| **Duration** | 6¾hr |
| **Percentage paved** | 43% |
| **Albergues** | Calzadilla de Tera 11.3km; Olleros de Tera 13.2km; Villar de Farfón 22.8km; Rionegro del Puente 28.6km |

A stupendously diverse stage makes this a memorable day, although it is sadly marked by wildfires. Calzadilla, Olleros and the cosy albergue of Villar de Farfón provide snacks. Offering a first-rate *menú del día* with a pilgrim discount, the Me Gusta Comer restaurant in Rionegro plates up a gastronomical experience unlike any other *menú*.

Return to the church, keep ahead, fork right onto Cl. Río and take the woodland track (**0.6km**). At the next fork, head left and soon left again. Turn left over a short **bridge** and fork right onto a **forest road** (**1.6km**).

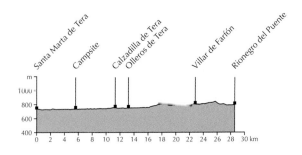

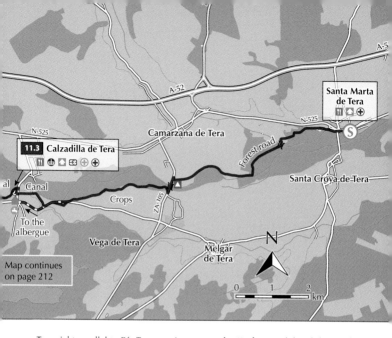

Turn right parallel to Río Tera, passing a **campsite** (**3.5km**), and then left onto the **ZA-105** to cross the river. Cross the road onto a path on the right into woods (**0.6km**). Follow the path as it skirts around **crops** to then turn right onto a road (**3.1km**). The Camino takes you on a swift detour on a track then returns you to the road, but you could also shortcut by keeping to the road.

Turn right onto a track below **Calzadilla de Tera** (or stick to the road for the albergue and drinking fountain), pass a fountain, go uphill and over a **canal**. Cross the road and turn right onto Cl. de la Iglesia to Romanesque church ruins.

### 11.3KM CALZADILLA DE TERA (ELEV 759M, POP 459) 🍴 ⊕ 🏠 🄲 ⊕ ⊕ (315.3KM)

In the 10th century, the town's patroness **La Virgen de la O** was brought from Sevilla on the Vía de la Plata.

🛏 **Albergue de Peregrinos de Calzadilla de Tera** 🄾 🄳🄾 🅂 1/6, €Donation, Cl. de las Eras s/n, tel 980 645 845.


This section can be confusing. Facing the church, take a path on your right down to the main road. Turn left onto it and then left onto a track to reach a junction of tracks. Don't follow the waymarkers, which send you to the right on a bizarre, pointless detour, but instead keep along the **canal** and turn left into **Olleros de Tera**.

### 1.9KM OLLEROS DE TERA (ELEV 752M, POP 129) 🏨 ⊕ 🏠 (313.4KM)

The **Vía Augusta XVII Roman road** between Astorga and Braga (Portugal) crossed Río Tera in this area.

🏠 Albergue/Restaurante La Trucha ⊙ 🔖 🔖 🔖 1/6, €7, Cl. de la Fuente 44, tel 673 910 592. Closed on Wednesdays. €18 for a half-board deal.

Turn left onto Cl. el Caño up to Iglesia de San Martín, then turn immediately right onto Cl. de la Fuente and left at the end (fork right for the albergue). Go next left onto Cl. de la Agavanzal and out of town. Turn right at the end (drinking fountain) then first left onto a lane to the **Iglesia Nuestra Señora de Agavanzal** (2.3km).

A legend tells of how the **Iglesia Nuestra Señora de Agavanzal** came to be built. Don Diego de Bustamante was riding towards Toro when a white dove began fluttering around him. The bird followed him, eventually allowing itself to be caught and caged. It escaped and repeated its game, only to be caught again. At this moment, Diego heard a voice saying 'Agavanzal, from Agavanzal I am', and he stumbled upon an image of the Queen of Heaven, inspiring him to build the chapel. Coins were sent from Toro for its construction, but the muleteers

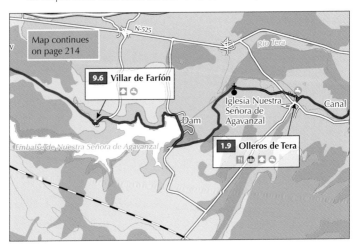

Map continues on page 214

greedily tried stealing them en route. However, the stubborn mules, like the dove, refused to change their course and delivered the coins to the chapel.

Turn left then keep right on the track at the fork. Reach a junction and turn right (**1.4km**). Proceed uphill until the Camino takes you over the **Presa de Agavanzal dam** on the Embalse de Nuestra Señora de Agavanzal.

Turn left at the end of the dam (**2.5km**), follow the reservoir around its northern shore and turn left onto a road. Turn right on Cl. de la Iglesia and then second right onto Tr. de la Iglesia to the albergue (drinking fountain) in **Villar de Farfón**.

### 9.6KM VILLAR DE FARFÓN (ELEV 805M, POP 14) 🛏 (303.8KM)

The construction of the dam flooded many parts of the village, and the 2022 wildfires caused more damage.

🏠 Albergue Rehoboth ⊠ 🄺 🅂 1/5, €Donation, Tr. de la Iglesia 25, tel 647 297 390, pilgrimmission@yahoo.co.uk. The hosts are Christian missionaries from South Africa who warmly offer refreshments to pilgrims. Check availability in winter.

Go past the albergue onto a track uphill and down to a **meadow**. Turn right (**4.1km**) to the **N-525**. Keep to the left of it and cross over Río Negro. Turn right, head through a tunnel and turn left up Cl. de la Plazuela to the albergue in **Rionegro del Puente**.

*An endearing statue of a pilgrim with a yellow backpack takes central stage in Rionegro del Puente's square*

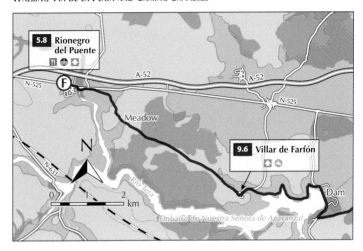

## 5.8KM RIONEGRO DEL PUENTE (ELEV 797M, POP 260) 🍴 ⊕ 🏠(298.0KM)

Rionegro is the birthplace of the famous 16th-century conqueror, Diego de Losada, who founded Venezuela's capital, Caracas, and another city on the Venezuelan coast which he named Nuestra Señora de la Carballeda. The **Santuario de la Virgen de la Carballeda** stands out, built on a small chapel of Romanesque origin, with chains in the entrance representing redemption. However, the only surviving remnant of the **Iglesia de Santiago Apóstol** is its bell tower.

🏠 Albergue de peregrinos Virgen de la Carballeda ⊙ ⊡ 🄺 🅆 🅂 3/28, €10, Ctra. N-525 49, tel 980 652 005 or 980 652 004, mozarabesanabres@gmail.com. Register at Me Gusta Comer restaurant.

# STAGE 31

*Rionegro del Puente to Asturianos*

| | |
|---|---|
| **Start** | Rionegro del Puente |
| **Finish** | Asturianos |
| **Distance** | 26.3km |
| **Total ascent** | 385m |
| **Total descent** | 210m |
| **Difficulty** | Moderate |
| **Duration** | 6½hr |
| **Percentage paved** | 45% |
| **Albergues** | Mombuey 9.1km; Entrepeñas 22.7km; Asturianos 26.3km |

The day starts on paths through fields, among deer, butterflies and bunnies. The trail enters Mombuey, where there are services, then roams through little villages with typical charming architecture in the style of mountain chalets. With not much shade, mercifully there are many drinking fountains.

Turn left out of the albergue and left up Cl. Vereda to a discreet grassy path on the right. Cross the **A-52** (**0.8km**) and turn left alongside it. Veer away towards the **N-525** and a track. Cross a road to take the track opposite (**2.8km**). A left turn down the road

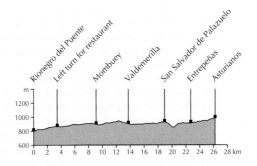

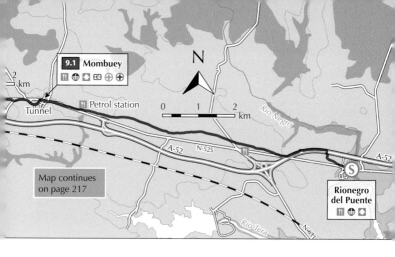

can swiftly take you to a **restaurant**. Enter fields and eventually reach a petrol station/restaurant (**4.4km**) and the road into **Mombuey**.

### 9.1KM MOMBUEY (ELEV 889M, POP 401) �️ �️ �️ �️ �️ �️ (288.9KM)

The **Iglesia de Nuestra Señora de la Asunción**, built in the 13th century and restored in the 18th, still preserves a Romanesque image of the Virgin and Child. The narrow Romanesque tower was declared a national monument in 1931, and its eastern and western walls are adorned with many motifs. Nevertheless, for the inhabitants of Mombuey, its most endearing feature is the figure of a cow, reputedly representing the ox that carried stone from the quarry to construct the tower.

🏠 **Albergue de peregrinos de Mombuey** �️ �️ 1/8, €Donation, Cl. de la Iglesia s/n, tel 980 642 711. Keys from the house across the road.

After services, turn left through a **tunnel**. Keep straight on Cl. Iglesia, pass the albergue and promptly spot the Iglesia de Nuestra Señora de la Asunción to the left. Turn right onto Cl. Rodrigo and immediately fork right to the **N-525 (0.6km)**. Keep on the left of it, with lovely views of the Sierra de Sanabria mountains on the right.

After the Pyrenees, the **Sierra de Sanabria** mountain range has the largest number of lagoons of glacial origin in Spain, with 35 lakes located at about 1600m altitude. Among them is the largest lake in the Iberian peninsula, Sanabria Lake, whose origins lie in the 20km glacier of 100,000 years ago. It is a fantastic day off from the Camino and accessible by bus from Puebla de Sanabria (Stage 32, tel 980 51 66 23 or 987 25 25 60).

The little village of Cernadilla has a welcome drinking fountain, distinguished by its on/off tap

The highest peak in the Sanabria range is Moncalvo (2044m). Hiking trails are fantastic and there are several mountain refuges. Because of its mixed Atlantic and Mediterranean climate, it is home to 1500 different species of plant.

Follow the Camino through trees, ignore a misleading arrow pointing ahead and keep to the path over the **motorway (2.4km)**. Take a sharp right (second track) then the road on the left across **railway lines (0.7km)**. Veer away from them, go left (poor

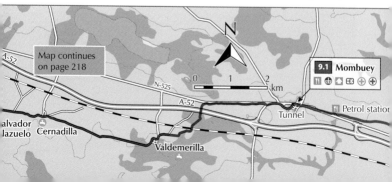

Map continues on page 218

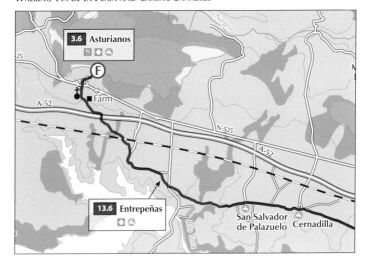

waymarking), then right at the fork and left onto a road into **Valdemerilla** (no services), reaching a drinking fountain (**1.1km**).

Skirt right around houses onto Camino de Valdemerilla, reaching the Ermita del Cristo (**3.4km**) in **Cernadilla** (no services), and turn left onto Cl. Ermita (drinking fountain). Turn left onto Cl. San Salvador de Palazuelo to a drinking fountain by an *ermita* (**1.7km**) in **San Salvador de Palazuelo** (no services). Take Av. De San Salvador past the Iglesia de la Transfiguración del Señor downhill to a track.

Cross a local road onto a path, reach another road and turn left onto it (**2.9km**). Pass an *ermita*, reaching the Iglesia de Nuestra Señora de la Asunción in **Entrepeñas** (drinking fountain).

### 13.6KM ENTREPEÑAS (ELEV 908M, POP 49) 🏠 (275.3KM)

The **Iglesia de Nuestra Señora de la Asunción**, partially destroyed by fire, preserves some Baroque pillars.

🏠 **Casa Las Peñas del Corredor** ⓞ Ⓟⓡ Ⓡ Ⓚ Ⓦ Ⓢ 4/6, €-/30/45/-/-, Cl. la Iglesia 6, tel 676 653 466. Transport to the restaurant in Asturianos is provided.

🏠 Casa Rural Azul Sanabria ⓞ Ⓖⓡ Ⓡ Ⓚ Ⓦ Ⓢ 1/3, €-/40/60/80/-, Cl. Escuela 20, tel 676 653 466, **https://casa-rural-azul-sanabria.negocio.site** Transport to the restaurant in Asturianos is provided. Whole house available.

Soon, take a track on the left under **railway lines** (**0.8km**) and over the **A-52** (**0.8km**). Pass a **farm** and go right at the fork past the **Iglesia de Nuestra Señora de la Asunción**. Cross over the N-525 into **Asturianos** (**1.2km**), with a bar/restaurant to the right.

Go up Cl. Carmen past the Iglesia de Nuestra Señora del Carmen (drinking fountain) and reach a waymark, from which you can either continue on the Camino by going left, or turn right for the albergue, which is up the road by the sports hall and a bar.

### 3.6KM ASTURIANOS (ELEV 972M, POP 260) 🍴 ⛲ (271.7KM)

Inhabited from pre-Roman times, modern Asturianos was part of the repopulation phenomenon that began in Covadonga in the year 718, and in the 10th century it saw its boom of new inhabitants from the Asturias region of Spain. The **Iglesia de Nuestra Señora de la Asunción** preserves 18th-century altarpieces and a 15th-century baptismal font.

🏠 Albergue de peregrinos de Asturianos Ⓞ 🔌 Ⓢ 1/10, €6, Cl. Castro Alto s/n, tel 679 819 360. Register at the bar opposite. Extra mattresses available.

# STAGE 32
*Asturianos to Requejo*

| | |
|---|---|
| **Start** | Asturianos |
| **Finish** | Requejo |
| **Distance** | 27.8km |
| **Total ascent** | 375m |
| **Total descent** | 365m |
| **Difficulty** | Moderate |
| **Duration** | 6¾hr |
| **Percentage paved** | 53% |
| **Albergues** | Puebla de Sanabria 15.7km; Requejo 27.8km |

This pleasant stage is made up of three parts: the gentle approach to historic Puebla de Sanabria, a riverside walk, and a ramble through a lovely primary forest to reach Requejo. The magnificence and liveliness of Puebla de Sanabria often tempts pilgrims to finish their stage here and splash out for a comfortable bed in a hotel.

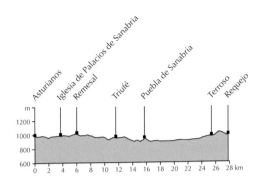

Return to the waymark out of Asturianos to reach the **N-525**. Turn right and promptly fork right, up a road. Take a track on the left (**1.2km**), which becomes a grassy **forest path**, to cross the **ZA-125**. For **Palacios de Sanabria** (■ ⊕), turn left down the road;

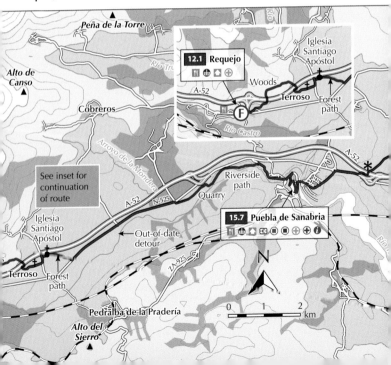

otherwise, stay above town, passing the **Iglesia de Palacios de Sanabria** (**2.5km**). Reach a road and cross over it onto a track to **Remesal** (**2.3km**, no services, drinking fountain).

> A monument in **Remesal** recalls events of June 1506, when Felipe, 'el Hermoso' (the Handsome), met here with his father-in-law, King Fernando II of Aragón, 'el Católico', to discuss the future of Castilla. Fernando renounced any right to the crown and instead put his daughter Juana (heir to the crown) and Felipe el Hermoso in charge of the government of Castilla from that day forward.

Keep to the track as it winds left and over the **A-52** (**1.8km**). Soon turn left onto a track, then keep left at the next fork and then right (but not back on yourself!). Turn left onto a road into **Otero de Sanabria** (no services) by the Iglesia de Santo Tomás Apóstol (**1.5km**). Go right, past the church, and turn right over the **A-52** into **Triufé** (no services) and the Iglesia de Triufé (**2.2km**). Turn left over the **motorway**, with Puebla de Sanabria now visible.

Turn right onto the **N-525** (**1.9km**) then left at the roundabout onto Av. del Padre Vicente Salgado. Pass the medical centre, closed albergue and supermarkets. Cross

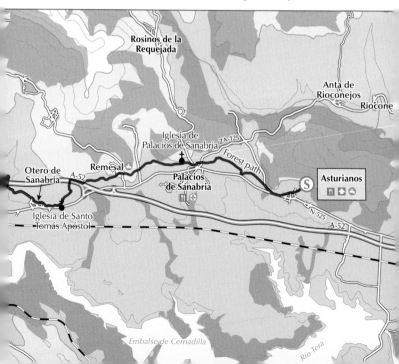

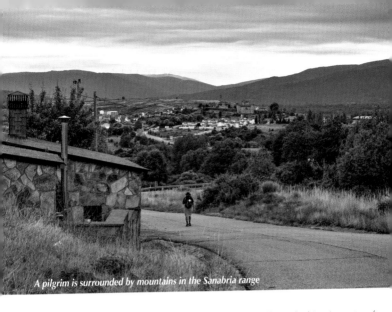

*A pilgrim is surrounded by mountains in the Sanabria range*

Río Tera and turn left. Go right, up cobbled Cl. de Costanilla, to the historic centre of **Puebla de Sanabria**.

### 15.7KM PUEBLA DE SANABRIA (ELEV 942M, POP 1356) 🍴 ⊕ ⌂ 🅒 ⊚ ⊙ ⊕ ⊕
ℹ️ **(256.0KM)**

Historical documents reveal that life in the region of Sanabria dates from the year 509, and that the town itself became a political centre in the 10th century. By the early 12th century, the **medieval castle** was built, and half a century later King Alfonso IX ensured its function as a fortress defending the Leonese border against Portugal, granting the town's charter in 1220. In 1451, half of the city and all the land was sold to Alonso de Pimentel, third Count of Benavente, and the Pimentel family acquired the other half soon after. The **castle of Puebla de Sanabria**, built on the ruins of the medieval fortress and tactically placed upon a hill surrounded by rivers, dates from the mid 15th century, under the mandate of the fourth Count of Benavente of the Pimentel family. In 1506, Juana I de Castilla and Felipe I de Castilla resided here.

During the 17th-century Portuguese wars, the castle and walls suffered deterioration and were classified as 'ruined'. In 1710, the Portuguese seized the town, although it was later recovered by the Spanish armies. The walls continued to fall into disrepair during the War of Independence against Napoleonic France and the 19th-century Carlist wars. Finally, in the peaceful years of the late 20th century, restoration began, and the castle and old town of Puebla are now classified as a site of historic and artistic interest.

For all hotels, prices fluctuate depending on the season, local holidays and festivals, so check ahead.

🏠 **Albergue Casa Luz** Do R K W S 34/7, €12, Cl. Padre Vicente Salgado 14, tel 980 620 268 or 619 751 762, info@alberguecasaluz.es, **www. alberguecasaluz.es**. Unpredictable closures which often last several months.

🏠 **Posada Real la Carteria** O Pr R Br G S 8/19, €-/75/94/140, Cl. Rúa 16, tel 980 620 312 or 980 620 009, posadareallacarteria@gmail.com, **www. lacarteria.com/index.html**. Free breakfast on mentioning this guidebook.

🏠 **Hotel Victoria** * O Pr R G W S 6/14, €-/45/57/77/97, Cl. Animas 20, tel 606 502 116, reservas@hotelvictoriapuebla.es, **https://hotelvictoriapuebla.es**.

🏠 **Hotel los Perales** ** O Pr R Br G S 25/53, €-/40/50/75/95, Av. de Galicia 22, tel 980 620 025, hotel.losperales@gmail.com, **https://hotelmania.net/hotel/ puebla-de-sanabria/hotel-los-perales**.

🏠 **Hostal Carlos V** ** O Pr R Br G W S 15/24, €-/45/59/85/115, Av. Braganza 6, tel 980 620 161 or 622 149 328, info@hostalcarlosv.es, **www. hostalcarlosv.es**. Takeaway breakfast and lunch options.

🏠 **Hostal Tribal** ** O Pr R G S 6/16, €-/65/65/85/106, Cl. Matadero 3, tel 634 825 625, complejolamajada@gmail.com, **www.hostaltribal.com**. Breakfast included.

🏠 **Hotel Tierra De Lobos** *** O Pr R Br G S 9/21, €-/-/75/-/-, Cl. Padre Vicente Salgado 24, tel 980 620 049 or 980 620 192, **www.tierradelobos.es**. Breakfast included.

🏠 **Posada Real La Pascasia** ***** O Pr R G S 7/14, €-/79/95/143, Cl. Costanilla 11, tel 980 620 242, lapascasia@gmail.com, **www.lapascasia.com**.

🏠 **Posada Real de las Misas** O Pr R Br G S 8/21, €-/79/86/142/172, Plaza Mayor 13, tel 980 620 358 or 639 665 066, posadareallacarteria@gmail.com.

🏠 **Apartamentos Turísticos Las Candelas** O Pr R G K W S 10/20, €-/69/73/81/81/182, Av. del Lago 3, tel 690 685 825 or 665 262 621, **https:// apartamentoslascandelas.com**. Whole apartments available.

Turn left down Plaza Castillo by streetlamps below the cemetery and turn left onto Av. Galicia over Río Castro. Facing the traffic, soon find a downhill path towards the river (**1.9km**). After heavy rain, keep straight and turn left onto the N-525 instead.

Follow the **riverside path** before veering away from the river to a small **quarry**, then turn right to the **N-525** (**2.9km**). Turn left onto it for a long stretch (ignoring an out-of-date detour to the left). Eventually, cross the N-525 onto an uphill **forest path** on the right (**3.3km**) to the **Iglesia Santiago Apóstol** and a fountain. Turn left down a path to cross a road and go right, passing the **Santiago pilgrim cross** and a play park to reach **Terroso** (**1.8km**, no services). Go over the **motorway** and take a path through **woods**, carefully following the yellow arrows with the shell symbol.

After 300 metres turn left, and 200 metres later keep left at the fork, following arrows on trees. Some 600 metres later, take a track across the **motorway** and cattle grid (**1.5km**) to enter **Requejo**. Cross over the N-525 to the Ermita Virgen de Guadalupe, town hall and bar (basic groceries). A **restaurant** with a pilgrim menu is located a little out of town along the N-525 on the right.

### 12.1KM REQUEJO (ELEV 990M, POP 149) 🍽 ⊕ 🛏 ⊕ (243.9KM)

Requejo is only 12.6km away from the Portuguese border, making it the closest town to Portugal along the entire Vía and Camino Sanabrés (except on the Verín alternative). The **Ermita Virgen de Guadalupe**, built in 1773, destroyed in the Civil War then rebuilt in 1988, faced more misfortunes recently, undergoing five years' work to eliminate woodworm, eventually reopening in 2021.

🛏 Albergue de peregrinos de Requejo ⓞ 🅓🅸 🆂 1/20, €5, Cl. Manonga s/n, tel 647 948 186.

🛏 Albergue Casa Cerviño ⓞ 🅓🅸 🅡 🅚 🆆 🆂 1/20, €15+, Av. Juan Seisdedos 45, tel 686 024 213, info@albergue-sanabria.com.

# STAGE 33
*Requejo to Lubián*

| | |
|---|---|
| **Start** | Requejo |
| **Finish** | Lubián |
| **Distance** | 16.2km |
| **Total ascent** | 505m |
| **Total descent** | 495m |
| **Difficulty** | Moderate |
| **Duration** | 4½hr |
| **Percentage paved** | 46% |
| **Albergues** | Padornelo 8.6km; Lubián 16.2km |

A change in scenery and more shade make for an extremely gratifying stage. It commences with a climb through an ancient forest to reach the highest point of the Vía de la Plata and Camino Sanabrés at the Padornelo Pass, where a striking white cross emerges at 1365m altitude among emerald-green hilltops. The Camino frequently crosses rivers, making paths slippery at times, so some care is required. Refreshments can be found in Padornelo.

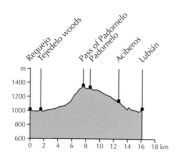

From the albergue, return to the town hall and bar and follow Cl. Carreira behind the bar, passing a **cemetery**. Cross the road onto a path ahead, follow the **riverside path** and go over a **bridge (1.7km)** into Tejedelo woods.

The enchanting **Bosque de Tejedelo** (Tejedelo woods) is one of the best-preserved yew forests in all of Spain, and many of the trees are more than 1000 years old.

The river's waterfalls on your left keep you company until a paved path on the right takes you uphill to **Requejo viaduct** (**3km**). The impressive Requejo railway viaduct is the longest (1718 metres) on the AVE Galicia–Madrid high-speed rail line. Promptly turn left down gravel to walk between the two railway lines before entering the forest again.

The grassy path narrows and can be muddy as it meanders over a wooden bridge and to a gravel track. Turn right towards a ruined building and reach a stony path in the woods to arrive at a **river crossing** (**1km**) where stepping stones take you onto a path ahead. Follow the path as it winds left, noting the wooden, yellow-topped waymarkers (essential tools for this section in poor weather) guiding you up a **steeper uphill climb** with regular switchbacks. Surprisingly, the Camino becomes very puddly for a while before it arrives at an opening with remarkable views over the valley. Soon take the wide grassy track on the left alongside the N-525 to the **Pass of Padornelo** (**2km**).

In the past, journeys through the Sanabrian mountains were difficult because of the force of the rivers and weak bridges. The **mountain passes** separating the Meseta plateau from Galicia added to the challenge, but not only because of extreme weather patterns: the mountains and dense forests were a perfect hiding spot for thieves. In 1506, when the royal entourage of King Felipe el

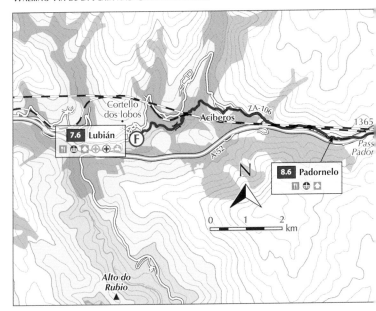

*A pilgrim discovers the dazzling white cross at the Pass of Padornelo*

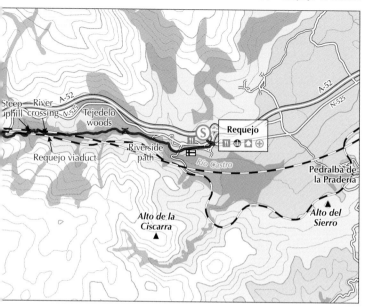

Hermoso passed through en route to Benavente, they were attacked by such bandits.

From the pass, beware of conflicting arrows and be sure to go left downhill on the track, then turn left onto the N-525 briefly. Just before **Padornelo**, fork left on a tree-lined lane.

### 8.6KM PADORNELO (ELEV 1305M, POP 27) ▮▮ ⊕ ⌂ (235.3KM)

The unique, quaint architecture of the tiny houses with thick granite walls in Padornelo is astonishing, even humorous, yet provides the most effective shelter for the cold and often snowy winter months.

⌂ Hotel/Restaurante Padornelo ◎ ▯ ▯ ▯ ▯ ▯ ▯ 21/38, €-/35/70/105/140, Ctra. N-525 km104, tel 652 077 319 or 980 567 939.

Follow Cl. Prieta and turn right on Cl. de Abajo, looking back to admire the views. Reach the N-525 again and turn left along it past a petrol station and hotel/

227

restaurant. After the N-525, turn right onto the **ZA-106** (**2.6km**). Soon abandon it onto a path on the left, which crosses a track and can also be a little flooded.

Turn left onto a paved track, pass the Ermita de Santa Ana, and enter the hamlet of **Aciberos** (no services) with its remarkable watermills and fountains. Proceed along Cl. Larga, turn left onto Cl. Consejo and then right on a lane (**1.9km**). Head downhill past beehives, over a bridge and through a tunnel under **railway lines**. Soon, turn left downhill in a switchback (**1.5km**) and onto a narrow path. Cross the river again and go uphill through woods to pass some ruins and arrive at the albergue in **Lubián**.

### 7.6KM LUBIÁN (ELEV 1023M, POP 304) (227.7KM)

The excitement of tomorrow's arrival in Galicia is truly felt in bilingual Lubián, where building and street names begin with the Galician 'O'. Only a 15min walk (signed) up the hill above the town lies a large circular enclosure with high stone walls, called a *cortello dos lobos*. It was used in the past to trap wolves: a goat or sheep would be positioned inside as bait, and although wolves could easily jump in they could not get back out. Nowadays, for pilgrims, the 'wolf trap' provides a wonderful spot for a rest among birch trees.

**Albergue de peregrinos de Lubián** O Do K S 2/16, €3, Cl. de la Cruz s/n, tel 980 624 003. Heating €2.

# STAGE 34

*Lubián to A Gudiña*

| | |
|---|---|
| **Start** | Lubián |
| **Finish** | A Gudiña |
| **Distance** | 24.5km |
| **Total ascent** | 635m |
| **Total descent** | 670m |
| **Difficulty** | Hard |
| **Duration** | 6¾hr |
| **Percentage paved** | 35% |
| **Albergues** | A Vilavella 10.8km; A Gudiña 24.5km |

Starting the day through forests, with a significant climb gaining 329m over 3.5km, pilgrims enter green Galicia and the region's delightful rolling hills. The

Camino heads to a pit stop in A Vilavella, before setting off with more ups and downs across a different terrain made up of rocks and shrubs sprinkled on the hills. At the stage end, it reaches A Gudiña and the Verín/Laza split.

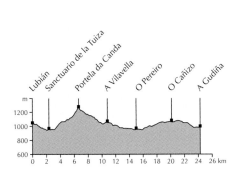

Out of the albergue, turn right and right again up Cl. da Cruz and left onto Cl. Forno Novo, reaching the Parroquia San Mamed, Martír (drinking fountain). Pass a shop and leave town on a lane. Continue on a paved path and under the A-52 to the **Santuario de la Tuiza** (**2.5km**).

The **Santuario de la Tuiza** dates from 1764, having been built using remnants of the former 16th-century chapel. Externally devoid of ornaments and in pure Baroque style, with elegant square granite ashlars and sombre black slates, its Galician and Portuguese influences are clear. In the past, many pilgrims would stay in an adjacent hostel before hiking the Portela da Canda hill pass. The sanctuary was declared an Asset of Cultural Interest in 1995.

Take the grassy path behind it, walking on top of stone slabs, and go over the bridge. A few metres further, commence a steeper **uphill climb** (**0.7km**). The path can

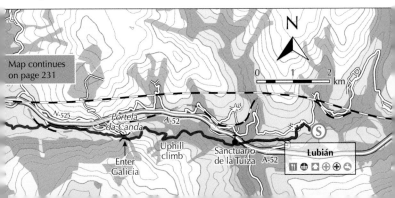

Map continues on page 231

be overgrown so look out for arrows, and 400 metres later fork slightly left where the waymarking is unclear (although the paths do reconnect). After 1km, cross a stream and follow the path as it zigzags uphill and meets a wider track to the top at **Portela da Canda** (3.5km).

Here, pilgrims greet **Galicia**, their final region of Spain on the Camino, where waymarking is exceptional. The individual style of the charming statue by Ourense-born sculptor Nicanor Carballo ensures that subsequent ones appearing en route to Ourense are easily identifiable.

Head down the gravel track to the left and keep right at the first fork, past farms. Take a local road lined by eucalyptus trees, leaving it on a little bridge to come alongside **railway tracks** and then under them (2.5km), before arriving in **A Vilavella**.

### 10.8KM A VILAVELLA (ELEV 1045M, POP 128) 🏨 ⊕ 🛏 (216.9KM)

During the Roman period, this territory, known as La Mezquita, was administered by its capital in Municipium Bracara Augusta (present-day Braga, Portugal). In medieval times, the lands belonged to the counts of Monterrei and the Pimentel family, with A Vilavella being the centre of the noble estate.

🏠 Hotel/Restaurante Spa Vilavella 🅾 🅿r 🆁 🅱r 🅶r 🆆 🆂 🆉 26/52, €-/-/69/- /-, Vilavella s/n, tel 988 594 242, reservas@hotelspavilavella.es, **https:// hotelspavilavella.es**.

🏠 Hostal Porta Galega 🅿r 🆁 🅱r 🅶r 🆂 38/50, €-/25/45/-/-, N-525 km118, tel 988 425 593, garciaestevezmiguel603@gmail.com, **www.hostalportagalega.es/ hostal**. Closed on Saturdays in winter, and for a fortnight from Christmas.

Take the road on the left (then first left for the café/bar), turn left down Rúa Cachon and onto some stepping stones to a grassy path and over a bridge. Pass a river and drinking fountain (2.4km) to reach the lovely 14th-century **Capela da Nosa Señora de Loreto**. Cross over the road and arrive in **O Pereiro** (no services) by a drinking fountain (1.9km).

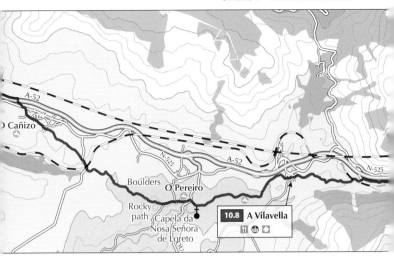

On a grassy path ahead, set foot into an entirely new landscape, scattered with boulders and where the Camino soon becomes rocky underfoot. Head uphill then briefly down to turn left and left again (**2.5km**) before a right turn along a road. Almost

*Pilgrims tackle a change in terrain before A Gudiña*

at once, cross **railway tracks** and take a track by the road. Soon cross the road onto a track opposite, then take a track on the left to a drinking fountain (**2.5km**) in **O Cañizo** (no services). Turn right shortly towards the N-525. Turn left onto it and cross it to go over the **A-52** (**1.1km**). Turn left and then head downhill towards town (**1.3km**). Turn right onto the N-525 past a **railway station** and services in **A Gudiña**. Cross over the road and keep ahead to the albergue.

*A delightful statue by Ourense-born Nicanor Carballo greets pilgrims upon their entrance into Galicia*

### 13.7KM A GUDIÑA (ELEV 979M, POP 1236) 🏨 ⊕ 🛒 🄲 ⊙ ⊙ ⊕ ⊕ 🛈 (203.2KM)

Now another decision has to be made. Which route to take to Ourense: Laza or Verín? While deliberating, visit the **Igrexa de San Martiño** (opposite the albergue), which was built in 1619, as revealed on the semicircular arch over the doorway. Next to it find a sculpture of Blessed Sebastián de Aparicio Prado. Born in A Gudiña and beatified in 1789, he was a 16th-century missionary who preached in Mexico. Because the town was divided between the council of Ourense and Astorga, it also has another church: **Igrexa de San Pedro** (16th–18th century).

🏠 **Albergue de peregrinos de A Gudiña** 🏠 🄾 🄳🄾 🅆 🅂 3/44, €8, Rua Beato Sebastián de Aparicio s/n.

# A GUDIÑA TO
# OURENSE VIA LAZA

## STAGE 35
*A Gudiña to Laza*

| | |
|---|---|
| **Start** | A Gudiña |
| **Finish** | Laza |
| **Distance** | 34.9km |
| **Total ascent** | 770m |
| **Total descent** | 1270m |
| **Difficulty** | Very hard |
| **Duration** | 8½hr |
| **Percentage paved** | 57% |
| **Albergues** | Campobecerros 20.2km; As Eiras 28.7km; Laza 34.9km |

Selecting the Laza option, the Camino winds up green hills among chestnut and pine trees. It passes several almost abandoned hamlets with no services and a deep blue reservoir. Steeply descending into Campobecerros, it drops 242m in 1.4km before the long progressive downhill to the Támega valley. Food is to be found only in Campobecerros, but there are several drinking fountains.

From the albergue, cross the N-525 road and go up by the church to the waymarked Laza/Verín split. Turn left up Rúa do Cima de Aldea, turn right and take a gravel track parallel to the road (**1km**). Wander atop the hill and then down towards **A Venda do Espino** (**3.2km**) to take a track parallel to the road. Soon turn right, away from the road, keeping to the track instead for marvellous views.

Follow the Camino as it crosses **railway lines** (**2km**), turns left, reaches a road and quickly leaves it on the right. Return to the road and take a track up on the left. After a farm, turn right on the road and then zigzag above into **A Venda da Teresa** (**1.4km**). Take the lane on the right above the **Embalse de As Portas**.

The source of Río Camba lies in the San Mamede mountains, at an altitude of 1480m. To control the flow, the **Embalse de As Portas** reservoir and dam were

built in 1972, flooding three towns and forcing 60 families to move. It is the largest reservoir in the Ourense province.

The Camino starts playing games now to avoid the road, taking three mini-detours on the left; however, shortcuts on the traffic-free road are perfectly fine. Go over

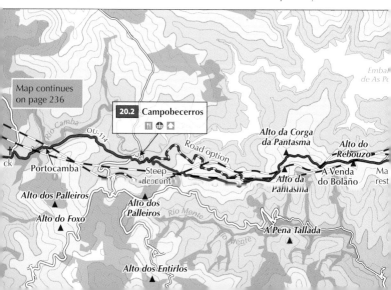

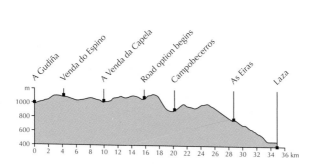

railway tracks to a drinking fountain in **A Venda da Capela** (**2.8km**). Stay on the road through the hamlet but soon take a left onto a track uphill, finding a **magical rest spot** (**1km**), before returning to the road into **A Venda do Bolaño**.

Keep to the road for 4.4km to reach a left turn up a track. If a steep descent on loose stones in rainy weather isn't your cup of tea, continue on the road, adding 1.2km. Keep straight on the wide ridge and start a **steep descent** into Campobecerros (**1.8km**) over rockier terrain, until you make inevitable contact with a gravel track and turn right. Turn left down the road (**1.5km**) to **Campobecerros**, past the Igrexa da Asunción with its modern Santiago statue, and fork left.

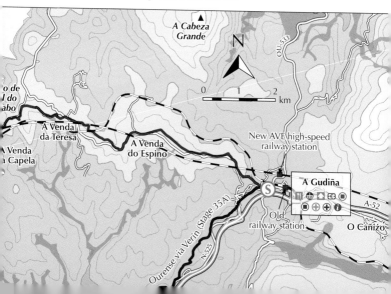

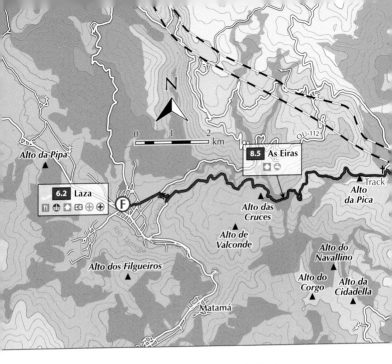

### 20.2KM CAMPOBECERROS (ELEV 898M, POP 82) 🍴 ⊕ 🏠 (183.0KM)

Campobecerros once had an active railway station. Opened in July 1957 to connect the city of Vigo on the Galician coast with Madrid, it closed in 2013. The statue in memory of Anton Vidal, who promoted the area, shows a traditional 'peliqueiro' outfit worn during the Laza Carnival, among the oldest in the world, the origins of which are disputed.

🏠 **Albergue da Rosario** Ⓞ Ⓓⓐ Ⓦ Ⓢ 1/20, €10, Cl. Cardenal Quiroga 9, tel 650 530 547 or 988 308 943, alberguedarosario18@gmail.com. Register at Bar Rosario.

Turn right down the second street and pass the bar on your right (for the albergue, turn right at the end of the road). Turn left onto the OU-114 to **Portocamba** (no services). Fork right, turn left, and arrive at a drinking fountain (**3.2km**). Proceed on the OU-114 to the **Cross of the Pilgrims** (**0.8km**). The Cross of the Pilgrims stands in memory of pilgrims who have lost their lives while on the Camino. Turn left onto a **track**, reaching a drinking fountain and shelter in **As Eiras** (**4.3km**).

236

### 8.5KM AS EIRAS (ELEV 769M, POP 11) 🏠 (174.5KM)

A *donativo* stand is regularly set up by a friendly group of youths from Laza. It is unmanned and offers snacks and refreshments in exchange for a donation to its honesty box.

🏠 **Casa Rural Terra Alma y Restaurante** Pr Dr R Br Cf S 7/17, €-/-70/95/-, Lugar das Eiras 1, tel 659 128 097, hola@terra-alma.es, **https://terra-alma. es**. Includes breakfast. Often closed over winter. 10% pilgrim discounts. Vegetarian meals only.

The subsequent long descent on the road reveals more outstanding views. Turn sharp right down a gravel path (**4.6km**), go over Río Cereixo, turn left and fork right to **Laza**, reaching the Protección Civil office on a roundabout. After registering and collecting the keys for the albergue, turn right out of the office and keep right on the roundabout to follow the road past the church and cemetery. Come alongside a field and take the next left, still by the field, reaching the albergue at the end of the road.

### 6.2KM LAZA (ELEV 470M, POP 1223) 🍴 ⊕ 🏠 C ⊕ ⊕ (168.3KM)

Nestled in a wide valley formed by Río Támega and its tributaries, and surrounded by mountains with peaks of up to 1550m, Laza was a natural place of transit to and from Portugal until modern highways were built. Roman ruins discovered in the vicinity prove that this was a stopping point on a secondary Roman road, the Vía do Támega. A local speciality is a sweet *bica blanca* cake, which is only made in three bakeries in the Laza district and nowhere else in Spain.

🏠 **Albergue de peregrinos de Laza** O Do S 5/36, €8, Rúa do Toural s/n, tel 988 422 112. Keys from the Protección Civil office.

# STAGE 36

*Laza to Albergería*

| | |
|---|---|
| **Start** | Laza |
| **Finish** | Albergería |
| **Distance** | 11.8km |
| **Total ascent** | 495m |
| **Total descent** | 75m |
| **Difficulty** | Easy |
| **Duration** | 3½hr |
| **Percentage paved** | 44% |
| **Albergues** | Albergería 11.8km |

This is a lovely short day, making up for yesterday, yet with a demanding uphill walk gaining 371m over 4km to reach an altitude of 911m. The pine forests provide some shade and the day ends in the pilgrim-themed hamlet of Albergería.

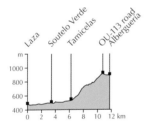

Return to the Protección Civil office to hand in the albergue keys. From there, go across the roundabout and continue slightly right and then left onto Rúa da Picota, meeting the **OU-113** (**0.9km**). Turn right onto it, soon forking right then left back onto it (to avoid a sharp corner on the road itself). Turn left onto a track to **Soutelo Verde** (bakery with unreliable opening hours) and a drinking fountain (**2.6km**). The hamlet of Soutelo Verde can be traced back to at least 1000BC, thanks to the discovery of a 2m high menhir in 2015.

Return to the OU-113, turn left onto it and immediately after a right bend take the gravel track on the right. Pass a fountain and take the lane into **Tamicelas** (no services). Turn left at the fork (**2.9km**) and left at the end of the road to a dirt track uphill.

The track bends left and right on a gentle **uphill climb** above the hamlet, then turns into a rocky path and a steeper uphill. Ignore the track on your right to keep to the rocky path. Soon it becomes a wider track through the forest, climbing more gradually. Reach the **top** and the **OU-113** (**4km**). The Camino turns right onto the road and forks left to reach the little village of **Albergería**.

Every passing pilgrim adds their shell to the shrine in the café/bar in Alberguería

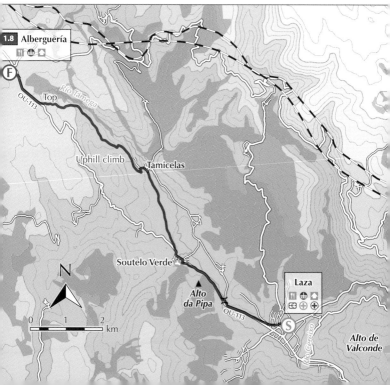

**11.8KM ALBERGUERÍA (ELEV 896M, POP 14)** 🏠 ⊕ 🏔 **(156.5KM)**

Alberguería is the location of the source of Río Támega. Giving its name to the **Plaza del Rollo**, a circular stone column (*rollo jurisdiccional*) stands as a reminder of the justice that was administered in earlier times. It once marked the limits of the Count of Monterrei's jurisdiction and served as a waymark for pilgrims. The column had been lost for many years until, in 1993, during one of his tours to research the Vía de la Plata, the historian Eligio Rivas spotted that a strange column in a private orchard was actually one of the lost *rollos jurisdiccionales*, and some residents recalled older villagers saying that it had once occupied the centre of the village square. So, in 2010, the column was finally returned to its original place.

Even if you're not staying here, pop into the café/bar to hang up your individual shell in the shell shrine.

🏠 **Albergue El Rincón del Peregrino** 🔤 🇰 🇼 🇸 2/15, €10, Alberguería s/n, tel 616 846 298, rolorivel@gmail.com. Open Mar–Nov.

# STAGE 37
*Alberguería to Xunqueira de Ambía*

| | |
|---|---|
| **Start** | Alberguería |
| **Finish** | Xunqueira de Ambía |
| **Distance** | 21.9km |
| **Total ascent** | 275m |
| **Total descent** | 635m |
| **Difficulty** | Easy |
| **Duration** | 5¼hr |
| **Percentage paved** | 45% |
| **Albergues** | Vilar de Barrio 7.0km; Xunqueira de Ambía 21.9km |

This stage starts in forests with shady sections before possible refreshments in Vilar de Barrio. The Camino then goes through fields and little villages with charming views until reaching the stage end in a bigger town.

Leave the albergue, taking a right turn. Take the first road on the left and turn left to a track. The Camino becomes a grassy path strewn with rocks and goes across a field. Cross the road (**1.6km**) onto a path ahead in a pine forest, reaching the **OU-113**.

The **Río Limia** is born here. It flows through Xinzo de Limia on the Verín variant of the Camino Sanabrés, then to Ponte de Lima on the Camino Portugués del Interior, and meets the Atlantic in Viana do Costelo on the Camino Portugués de la Costa – linking the Camino routes perfectly.

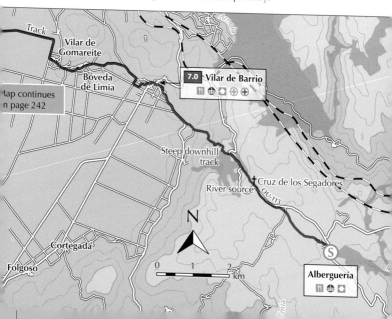

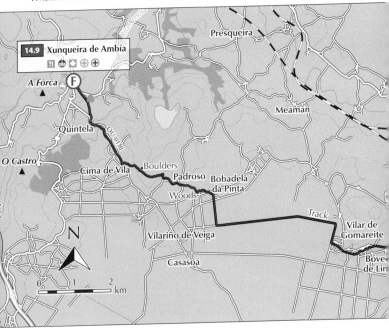

Cross over onto a downhill track to the **Cruz de los Segadores** on the Alto do Talariño (**1.3km**). The cross commemorates the harvesters from Galicia who travelled to work in Castilla for two months every year in the early 20th century. Turn right onto a road. Soon turn left on a **steep downhill track** and turn right as it flattens. Reach a road (**2.2km**), turn left downhill and take the track ahead before the road bends left. Turn right onto a road and then fork left into **Vilar de Barrio**, reaching the square.

### 7.0KM VILAR DE BARRIO (ELEV 665M, POP 1283) 🏠 ⊕ 🛏 ⊕ ⊕ (149.5KM)

The presence of Bronze Age cultures was found in the vicinity. Remains include gravestones, seemingly providing evidence of permanent inhabitants.

🏠 Albergue de peregrinos de Vilar de Barrio ⊙ ᴅᴏ ⓢ 3/24, €8, Av. de San Fiz s/n, tel 628 355 911 or 988 468 484.

242

Turn right immediately after the square and left onto Av. de San Feliz. Keep straight until you fork left and then head into **Bóveda de Limia** (no services) to a fountain and benches (**2.7km**).

Between the villages of Bóveda and Gomareite, atop the hill of **Monte do Castelo**, an important medieval castle once overlooked the region. Inside a cave on the hill, an image of a saint with a metal lamp in his hand was found and is now in the archaeological museum of Ourense.

Keep to the same road to immediately reach **Vilar de Gomareite** (unreliable bar) and leave by turning right onto a lane. Soon turn left onto a **track** by a bench (**1.6km**). After 3.4km, turn right and cross the road towards houses. Turn left onto a lane and immediately right into **Bobadela da Pinta** (**4.7km**, no services). Proceed uphill as the Camino zigzags through **woods**. Cross over a road, take the track opposite and reach another road where you turn left.

Fork right (**1.1km**) by farm buildings in **Padroso** (no services) and reach a path. Keep to the smaller path towards **boulders** (ignoring the downhill track), take the short rocky section and go downhill on a path. Pass a sign for a shortcut to **Cima de Vila** (no services) and nevertheless reach the village soon after (**1.7km**). Turn right onto a path crossing a lane and the **OU-0110** road to arrive in **Quintela** (**1.3km**, no services). Walk through and back up to the **OU-0110**.

Soon fork right onto a lane, pass a sign for the *albergue municipal* and reach it on the right (**0.9km**). For the centre of **Xunqueira de Ambía** and the private albergue, continue straight to the OU-0108 and follow it around to the Colexiata de Santa María.

*Bright pink and purple heather grows along the Camino before Xunqueira de Ambía*

**14.9KM XUNQUEIRA DE AMBÍA (ELEV 543M, POP 1374)** 🏨 ⊕ 🛒 ⊕ ⊕ **(134.6KM)**

Tradition maintains that in the 4th century the Virgin Mary appeared here in a bed of reeds (hence the town's name *Xunqueira*, from the Galician word for 'reed') and an *ermita* was built in that location. It first became a monastery between the 8th and 10th centuries. Its current Galician Romanesque style dates from the 12th century, and it achieved the rank of Colexiata by order of King Fernando II in 1164. The cloister dates from the 16th century, and in 1541 the prior of the monastery, Don Alonso de Piña, founded a pilgrim hospital next door. The monastery was declared a national monument in 1931.

⌂ Albergue de peregrinos de Xunqueira de Ambía Ⓞ Ⓓⓞ Ⓢ Ⓩ 3/24, €8, Cl. Asdrúbal Ferreiro s/n, tel 697 767 219 or 988 436 069.

⌂ Albergue/Cafetería Casa Tomás Ⓞ Ⓓⓞ Ⓡ Ⓑⓡ Ⓦ Ⓢ 3/9, €18, Plaza San Rosendo 13, tel 637 580 772 or 600 749 332, alberguecasatomas@outlook.es or reservas@pensioncasatomas.es, **http://pensioncasatomas.es**.

# STAGE 38
*Xunqueira de Ambía to Ourense*

| | |
|---|---|
| **Start** | Xunqueira de Ambía |
| **Finish** | Ourense |
| **Distance** | 22.2km |
| **Total ascent** | 220m |
| **Total descent** | 605m |
| **Difficulty** | Easy |
| **Duration** | 5¼hr |
| **Percentage paved** | 96% |
| **Albergues** | A Pousa 3.2km; Reboredo 15.2km; Ourense 22.2km |

Easy to follow, the OU-0102 road towards Ourense is pleasant enough before the unattractive *polígono industrial* (industrial estate). The Verín variant meets this stage in Perelras, along with the Camino Zamorano Portugués, which was last seen in Zamora. Together, pilgrims make their way to the delightful city of Ourense, where a feast for the eyes and the stomach awaits.

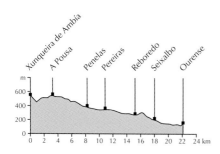

Facing the church, turn right along Rúa Colón, veer right (drinking fountain on the adjacent street) onto the OU-0102, fork left then right towards the medical centre, then left down a grassy slope (picnic spot). Turn left onto a path to the OU-0102, cross a **bridge** over Río Arnoia, and soon take a right-hand **forest path** (**1.1km**). After **San Xillao** (no services), cross a road onto a track to then turn right onto the OU-0102 and pass a bar before the village of **A Pousa**.

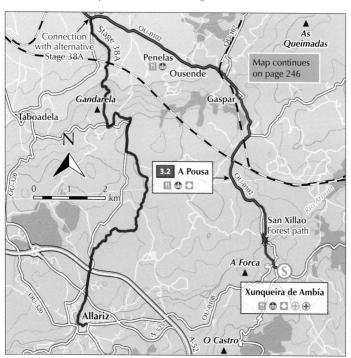

Map continues on page 246

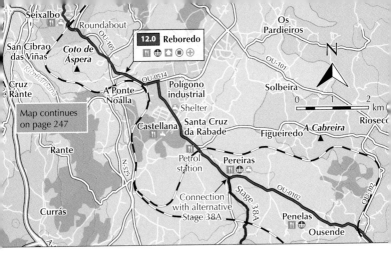

### 3.2KM A POUSA (ELEV 553M, POP 5)  (131.4KM)

🏠 **Pensión rural A Pousa** ⊙ Pr Br R 3/7, €-/15/30/-/-, A Pousa 6, tel 988 436 000, **www.pensionruralapousa.es**.

Continue to **Gaspar** (**2.6km**, no services), go among its houses and back to the OU-0102. Take another short detour on the left then cross **railway lines** (**1km**). Pass **Ousende** (no services) to bars and a shop in **Penelas** (**1.2km**) and then **Pereiras** (**2.8km**, 🍴 ⊕ and drinking fountain). Pass a petrol station (**0.9km**) and go under the **railway tracks**.

At the next junction, by a restaurant, ignore an arrow pointing right and follow a stone waymark to keep straight to **Castellana** (**1.5km**) and a bar (drinking fountain opposite). Cross the roundabout, fork left onto Rúa Número 3 (shelter and drinking fountain), turn left onto the **OU-0514** and at the roundabout go onto Estrada de Salgueiros, away from the OU-0514, to **Reboredo**.

### 12.0KM REBOREDO (ELEV 273M, POP 494) 🍴 ⊕ 🏠 ⊙ ⊕ (119.4KM)

🏠 **Hotel Eurostars Auriense** **** ⊙ Pr R Br G S 134/253, €-/55/60/80/-, Alto do Cumial 12, tel 988 234 900, reservas@exeauriense.com, **www. eurostarshotels.co.uk/exe-auriense.html**.

🏠 **Hostal Cid** ⊙ Pr R Br G S 30/52, €-/29/42/70/-, Rúa do Cumial 4, tel 988 246 178, info@hostalcid.com, **https://hostalcid.com**.

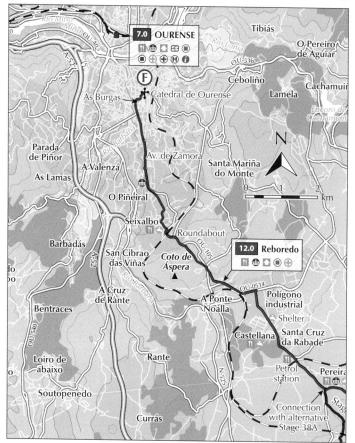

At the fork, go right to turn right onto the OU-105, then cross a road and take the first left to turn left onto the OU-105. Cross a **roundabout** and, after a right bend, take the road on the left to **Seixalbo** (🍴 and bakery) and its square (**2.7km**, drinking fountain). Turn right onto Rúa Maior, left opposite Igrexa de San Breixo de Seixalbo, left by a fountain and reach the OU-105 by a supermarket (**1.4km**). Turn left and cross a roundabout onto **Av. de Zamora in Ourense**.

At the next roundabout keep on Av. de Zamora among shops and cafés. Ignore the sign for the albergue but follow Camino signs instead for a more direct and intuitive

247

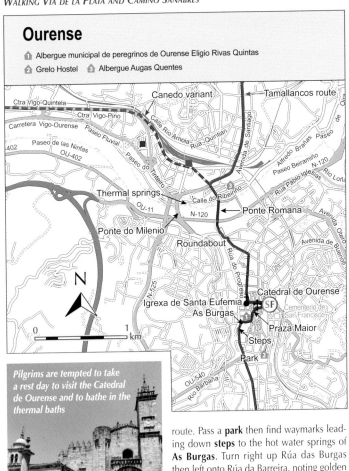

## Ourense

1. Albergue municipal de peregrinos de Ourense Eligio Rivas Quintas
2. Grelo Hostel  3. Albergue Augas Quentes

*Pilgrims are tempted to take a rest day to visit the Catedral de Ourense and to bathe in the thermal baths*

route. Pass a **park** then find waymarks leading down **steps** to the hot water springs of **As Burgas**. Turn right up Rúa das Burgas then left onto Rúa da Barreira, noting golden shells on the ground and a sign for the cathedral. The first house with green shutters on your left is the *albergue municipal*.

Reach **Praza Maior**, traverse diagonally, turn left and immediately right up Rúa Modesto Fernández to the **Catedral de Ourense**.

**7.0KM OURENSE (ELEV 143M, POP 105,643)** 🍴 ⊕ 🛏 ⒞ ⓢ Ⓗ ⊕ ⊕ **ⓘ**
**(112.4KM)**

From Neolithic times, nomadic tribes would travel through Ourense, and the As Burgas hot springs were a primitive settlement on which the Roman city originated in the 1st century AD. The Romans constructed the bridge over Río Miño (which flows through Portugal and into the ocean in Oporto), although the current structure is from the 13th century. After the 11th century, recovery from centuries of decline began, driven by the bishops of the diocese, and the current **Catedral de Ourense** was built. Visiting is recommended as a cooling relief from the scorching heat in summertime (Ourense has been nicknamed 'la sartén de Galicia', the frying pan of Galicia). It includes masterpieces such as the Pórtico del Paraíso, the Chapel of Santo Cristo and the High Altar, as well as a museum.

Another reason to stay an extra day is to visit the four **thermal baths**, only 2km from Praza Maior on the north bank of the river. To get there, you can walk, get a city bus or take the convenient Tren de las Termas (tourist train), which passes near Praza Maior and costs €0.85 one-way (see www.turismodeourense. gal/termalismo/tren-de-las-termas for information and timetable).

Dining on *pulpo a feira* (melt-in-your-mouth octopus with olive oil and paprika) and *pimientos de Padrón* (small green peppers with rock salt) may be the most tempting excuse for a rest day in the labyrinth-like historic quarter.

🛖 Albergue municipal de peregrinos de Ourense Eligio Rivas Quintas Ⓞ Ⓓⓞ Ⓦ Ⓢ 2/42, €8, Rúa da Barreira 12, tel 981 900 643. They sell the *credencial*.

🛖 Grelo Hostel Ⓞ Ⓓⓞ Ⓡ Ⓑⓡ Ⓦ Ⓢ 3/32, €15, Rúa Peña Trevinca 40 bajo, tel 988 614 564, info@grelohostel.com, **www.grelohostel.com**. Breakfast included.

🛖 Albergue Augas Quentes Ⓞ Ⓓⓞ Ⓡ Ⓑⓡ Ⓦ Ⓢ 3/36, €16, Rúa Vicente Risco 34, tel 988 061 322 or 679 958 780, info@albergueaugasquentes.com, **www. albergueaugasquentes.com**. Breakfast €3

# A GUDIÑA TO OURENSE: VARIANT VIA VERÍN

The variant through Verín boasts the many merits of Galicia: hilly evergreen landscapes; cascading rivers; well-preserved towns and villages; old monasteries, convents and pilgrim hospitals; beautiful churches in Gothic, Romanesque, Renaissance and Baroque styles; and very tasty food.

The Camino stays close to the N-525 and heads through hills and

*The Camino travels through hills and woods on its way to Verín (photo: Juan Carlos Medina Olid)*

woods towards the bigger town of Verín. It then hikes up to Monterrei castle, passes more woods, farms, hamlets and comfortably reaches Xinzo de Limia, after which the recommended option goes through restored wetlands on the site of a former lagoon. A few more villages and churches lead pilgrims into historical Allariz. Also recommended is a detour through Santa Mariña de Augas Santas, allowing pilgrims to taste the miraculous healing waters and, feeling better, reach the Laza connection to continue to Ourense.

## PLANNING

1   The Verín variant is 32.4km longer than going through Laza. The two options reconnect in Pereiras so follow Stage 38 from there, with 11.2km remaining to Ourense.
2   Stages 35A and 36A can both be easily split into two days.

3   Neither As Vendas da Barreira nor Allariz have pilgrim albergues so hotel options are provided, but (writing in 2023) there are plans for an albergue in Allariz.

## WHAT NOT TO MISS

Must-see recommendations include: a string of Romanesque churches in small hamlets (Stage 36A); the Areeiras de Limia wetlands after Xinzo de Limia, and the medieval Torre de Castro beyond Sandiás (both Stage 37A); and a restorative visit to the healing waters of Santa Mariña de Augas Santas (Stage 38A). The albergues in Verín, Vila de Rei and Xinzo de Limia are set in beautifully preserved buildings, and both Verín and Allariz have an abundance of historical buildings and monuments to see.

# STAGE 35A

*A Gudiña to Verín*

| | |
|---|---|
| **Start** | A Gudiña |
| **Finish** | Verín |
| **Distance** | 40.3km |
| **Total ascent** | 775m |
| **Total descent** | 1380m |
| **Difficulty** | Very hard |
| **Duration** | 10½hr |
| **Percentage paved** | 48% |
| **Albergues** | Mesón de Erosa 5.5km; As Vendas da Barreira 19.3km; Verín 40.3km |

Either as a marathon or perfectly split halfway, the Camino travels through hills and woods while taking full advantage of easy passages along the N-525 and breathtaking panoramic views. Most hamlets have no provisions, so plan carefully. Monterrei castle can be glimpsed from Fumaces onwards, before arrival in Verín where the Portuguese Caminos (Interior and Zamorano Portugués) meet the Sanabrés. Apart from a drinking fountain, there are no services along the 21km stretch between As Vendas and Verín.

Turn left out of the albergue on the N-525, leave the road by turning right at a restaurant, return to the road (**2.1km**) and veer right by **warehouses**. Wind left and right to a right-hand path before the **N-525** (**1.8km**). Return briefly to the N-525, turn right on a

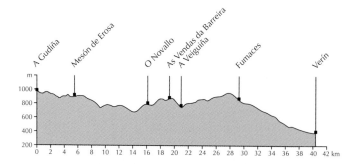

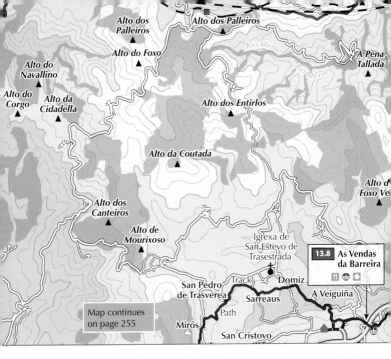

Labels on map: Alto dos Palleiros, Alto dos Palleiros, Alto do Foxo, A Pena Tallada, Alto do Navallino, Alto do Corgo, Alto da Cidadella, Alto dos Entirlos, Alto da Coutada, Alto d Foxo Ve, Alto dos Canteiros, Alto de Mourixoso, Igrexa de San Estevo de Trasestrada, **13.8** As Vendas da Barreira, San Pedro de Trasverea, Track, Domiz, A Veiguiña, Sarreaus, Map continues on page 255, Path, Mirós, San Cristovo, Río Mente, Río Mente

track, pass houses, turn right onto the N-525 (**1km**) to a not-so-obvious petrol station and hotel/restaurant at **Mesón de Erosa**.

### 5.5KM MESÓN DE EROSA (ELEV 912M) 🍴 ⌂ (230.1KM)

⌂ Hotel Mesón de Erosa *** ▢ Pr R Br Gr S Z 22/46, €-/25/50/75/100, A-52 Salida 132, tel 988 421 309, **www.mesonerosa.com**. Prices differ during holidays and festive seasons. Breakfast included.

Soon veer away from the N-525 on the right, quickly return to it, leave it on a track on the left (**2km**) and just before the A-52 turn left to go left on the **N-525**. Leave on a track, pass under the **A-52** (**2km**), wind right and left to turn right onto a lane back over the **motorway**.

Turn left on the **N-525**, make a detour on the left, return to the road (**2.3km**), cross immediately and take a **forest road** on the right, being sure to fork promptly right, Arrive at a sharp left bend (**1.6km**) then leave the forest road onto a track ahead under the **N-525** (**1km**) and into **O Novallo** (**1.7km**, no services). Leave on a track over the **A-52** (**0.8km**) then turn right.

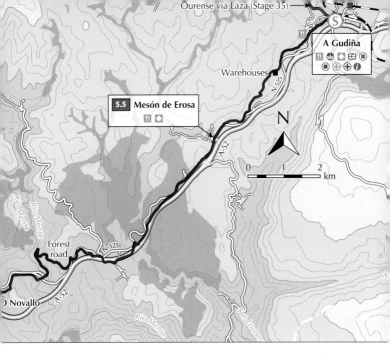

Proceed over a road into **As Vendas da Barreira** (**1.5km**). Turn right and left onto the N-525 (supermarket to the left), which heads over the motorway. Cross, stay on the N-525, then turn right onto a track by a chestnut and honey shop. For the hotel, continue on the N-525, where you will soon find it on the left-hand side.

## 13.8KM AS VENDAS DA BARREIRA (ELEV 846M, POP 96) 🍴 ⊕ 🏠 (216.3KM)

🏠 Hotel Bayona *** 🅿️ 🄶 🅆 🅂 🅉 16/32, €-/30/50/80/-, As Ferreiras 13, tel 988 425 094. Closed 24–25 Dec and 1 Jan.

Come to a local lane and go right, past a watermill, into **A Veiguiña** (**1.7km**, no services). Be sure to fork left by houses into **Domiz** (no services) and go straight through. Just after the last houses, the track on the right leads to the Igrexa de San Estevo de Trasestrada, where it is hoped that an albergue will reopen.

Fork right and turn right into **Sarreaus** (**1.9km**, no services). Turn right through town and fork left onto a **track**. Follow large stepping stones to the right and then a track to **San Pedro de Trasverea** (**1.3km**, no services). Turn left immediately onto a **path**,

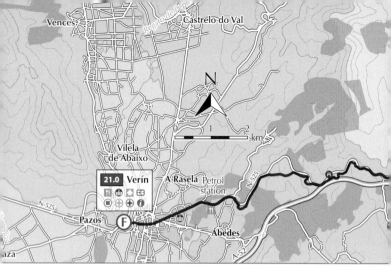

*Galicia's architecture is easily distinguishable from that of the rest of Spain (photo: Juan Carlos Medina Olid)*

then first right. Go uphill, veer left and left again into **Mirós** to a drinking fountain (**1.4km**).

Cross a road and take a **track** through woods over the hills. At the second junction, take not the first but the second track on the left (**2km**) to **Fumaces** (no services) and its parish church, the Parroquia de Fumaces e A Trepa (Santa María) (**1.6km**).

Turn right and left to head right on the **N-525**, crossing over to walk facing the traffic. Take the track on the left (**1.8km**) but swiftly return to the **N-525**. Leave it promptly on a forest road on the left that keeps mostly parallel to it. Pass a **picnic spot** and turn left onto the **N-525** (**2.5km**) as you enter the Támega valley.

The **Río Támega** which flows through Verín and its valley is surrounded by pine forests and scrubland. These highly fertile lands in a favourable climate enhance the quality of Monterrei's vineyards.

Leave the road on the left again and veer right at the next fork, coming parallel to it again (**2.1km**). Soon, turn right, then right and right again to the **N-525**. Turn left onto it, then pass a restaurant (**2.3km**) and petrol station, hotels, a supermarket and more restaurants on the way into **Verín**.

For the centre, turn right onto Tr. de Sousas (**1.5km**). For the albergue, continue straight then cross the river to find it opposite the Capela San Lázaro.

### 21.0KM VERÍN (ELEV 387M, POP 13,647) ▦ ⊕ ▣ 🅒 ▣ ⊕ ⊕ ❶ (195.3KM)

Verín arose from a Roman town upon the Monterrei hill, where remains of the 10th-century medieval fortress **Castillo de Cabreira** (destroyed in the 15th century) are located. During the Middle Ages, although Verín was a peaceful agricultural town, it was often involved in Spanish–Portuguese disputes. In 1506, it was the location for a meeting between King Felipe el Hermoso and Cardinal Cisneros to discuss the partial surrender of the troops of King Juan III el Piadoso of Portugal.

Verín has a rich cultural heritage. From the 11th to the 13th century it saw the coexistence of the **Convento de los Padres Franciscanos y de los Mercedarios** (founded in 1484 in Monterrei but moved two centuries later to Verín), the **Colegio de la Compañía de Jesús** and the **Hospital de San Lázaro**. The albergue, in beautifully preserved Baroque style, is located within the old Casa do Asistente.

🏠 **Albergue de peregrinos de Verín** Ⓞ Ⅾⓞ Ⓦ Ⓢ Ⓩ 3/38, €8, Av. de San Lázaro 26, tel 616 761 872.

# STAGE 36A

*Verín to Xinzo de Limia*

| | |
|---|---|
| **Start** | Verín |
| **Finish** | Xinzo de Limia |
| **Distance** | 37.2km |
| **Total ascent** | 820m |
| **Total descent** | 585m |
| **Difficulty** | Very hard |
| **Duration** | 9¾hr |
| **Percentage paved** | 53% |
| **Albergues** | Vila de Rei 21.2km; Xinzo de Limia 37.2km |

Another stage that can be neatly divided in two, it starts with a 140m climb up to beautiful Monterrei. The route passes through quaint Galician villages surrounded by rolling hills and agriculture. After Vila de Rei, visiting the Romanesque churches of Trasmiras, Zos and Boado is recommended.

Turn right out of the albergue and immediately left uphill, following Camiño Real signs up cobblestones to **Monterrei** and its castle (**1.1km**). Bizarrely, the Camino keeps straight, so detour to the castle following the pink signs.

'Are you from Verín or Monterrei?' Locals simply say they are from 'the valley', which can be admired from **Monterrei's fortress and towers**. The first

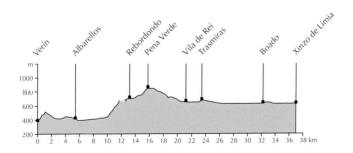

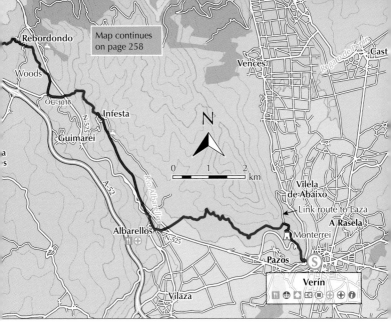

Map continues on page 258

printing press in the Kingdom of Galicia was installed here, and the scenery regularly inspired the writer and monk Tirso de Molina, who is best known for

Take a left off the Camino to see Monterrei's castle (photo: Juan Carlos Medina Olid)

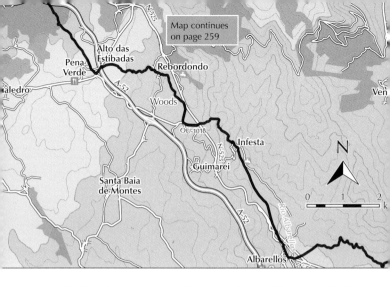

Map continues
on page 259

creating the infamous character of Don Juan in his play *El burlador de Sevilla y convidado de Piedra* (*The Trickster of Seville and the Stone Guest*).

During the **Irmandiño revolts** of the 15th century, the *irmandiños* (a brotherhood of groups rebelling against the nobility) had an army of 80,000 men at the ready to strike Monterrei castle. However, helped by Pedro Madruga, who had already freed Pontevedra, the castle remained secure and intact. It then played a strategic role as a military base in the wars with Portugal in the 17th century.

Retrace your steps from the castle, turn left and rejoin the Camino 400 metres later by turning left to two waymarking bollards. Here, the waymarker pointing right suggests a link route, which is only partially waymarked, to Laza, 18km away to the north along roads. To continue along the direct route, turn left and keep left onto a track.

Turn right onto a winding track (**1.8km**). At the junction, keep left (**2.5km**), then turn right opposite a car garage and swiftly left. Cross the **N-525**, turn right onto the OU-143 in **Albarellos** (🍴 ✚) and pass a bar (**1.3km**). Just before this, you can take a left to visit the Parroquia de Santiago. Opposite another bar, turn right towards a park/football pitch then follow the river to cross the **N-525**.

Following road signs for Infesta (no services), pass a drinking fountain in Parque Branco (**2.9km**). Keep straight through **Infesta**, uphill, to turn left onto a track. Soon turn right, fork left and cross a junction to the N-525 (**2.3km**).

Cross over onto the **OU-1018**, promptly turn right onto a road through **woods** and turn left onto a track by the N-525, coming into **Rebordondo** (**2.3km**, drinking fountain and rest spot). Walk through and leave town on a road to the left, then take an uphill track to the top of **Alto das Estibadas** (**1.7km**, 854m). Descend, turn right then left over the motorway and turn right through **Pena Verde** (**0.8km**, 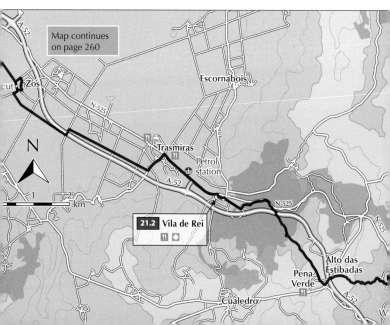). Turn right onto a track, fork left over the **motorway** (**2.4km**) and turn left twice onto a forest road parallel to the **N-525**.

Turn left, leaving the N-525, then promptly right past the Parroquia San Salvador, bending right to the N-525. For all services, turn right into **Vila de Rei**; to continue the Camino, turn left.

**21.2KM VILA DE REI** (ELEV 653M, POP 105) (174.1KM)

Vila de Rei is a perfect example of Galician architecture, with its delicate, precise lime-mortar pointing and balconies that let in an abundance of light, and the albergue is no exception. The **Parroquia San Salvador** dates from the 16th century, but has undergone subsequent reforms.

🏠 Albergue de peregrinos de Viladerrei ⊙ Do W S Z 2/30, €8, Cl. Vicente Risco 89.

After a petrol station (**1.1km**), continue into **Trasmiras** (), turn left opposite the Ermita de Trasmiras (continue straight for a drinking fountain in a park), pass the Igrexa de San Xoán and take the next right to a track (**1.5km**).

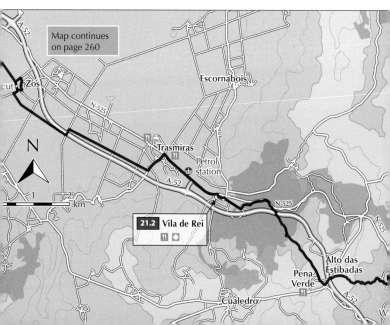

Map continues on page 260

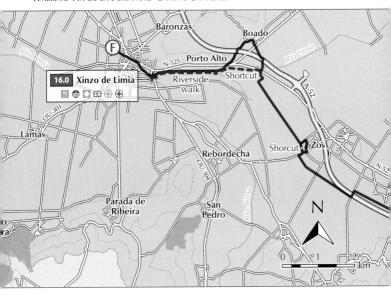

Turn left onto a road under the **motorway** (**2.6km**), immediately go right onto a track, cross a road and turn right towards **Zos** (**2.1km**, no services). Bend right to the houses. To save 230 metres, keep straight instead of bending right. In the hamlet, take the first left and at the end of the road turn left.

The Romanesque 13th-century **Igrexa de Santa María** in Zos has two portals: one adorned with geometric motifs and a pelican carved on a capital, and the other with a unique carved interlace. To visit, keep straight upon entering the village.

Joining the shortcut, take the first track on the right and follow it to the end. Turn right (**2.8km**) and then left opposite the **N-525**, coming to two options.

**Shortcut (3.2km)**
Turn left along the south shore of the river on a **riverside walk**, crossing a bridge then another, now in **Xinzo de Limia**.

**Official route through Boado (4.2km)**
Cross **Río Limia**, pass under the **A-52**, turn left and cross a road into **Boado** (no services). Go right then left through the village to the end of the road (**1.4km**). Turn right to

visit the 13th-century Parroquia San Pedro, otherwise go left and fork left out of town. Pass over the **A-52** into **Porto Alto** (no services). Cross the **N-525** (**1km**) and turn right along Río Limia into **Xinzo de Limia** (**2.2km**).

**Main route**

Both options reunited, turn right onto Av. de Portugal, left onto Rúa Rosalía de Castro, passing the school, left onto the N-525 and immediately keep left on Rúa de Lepanto. Pass the Igrexa Nova, then Praza Maior to take Rúa Galicia to the albergue.

**16.0KM XINZO DE LIMIA** (ELEV 626M, POP 9637) ⬛ ⊕ ⬛ Ⓔ ⊕ ⊕ (158.1KM)

The **Igrexa de Santa María** has a medley of architectural styles from different eras, with the Romanesque present in the western doorway and parts of the tower. Take a restful stroll through **Parque do Toural** and try the local speciality of frogs' legs.

🏠 Albergue de peregrinos de Xinzo de Limia Ⓞ 🅳🅾 🆆 🆂 🆉 2/15, €8, Rúa Serra de San Mamede 2.

# STAGE 37A

*Xinzo de Limia to Allariz*

| | |
|---|---|
| **Start** | Xinzo de Limia |
| **Finish** | Allariz |
| **Distance** | 22.3km |
| **Total ascent** | 270m |
| **Total descent** | 425m |
| **Difficulty** | Easy |
| **Duration** | 5½hr |
| **Percentage paved** | 66% |
| **Albergues** | Sandiás 9.3km; Allariz 22.3km |

Straight away, a recommended variant takes you through a landscape of restored wetlands and pretty lakes, before the trail continues its familiar wandering through small Galician villages, presenting another interesting alternative via a 12th-century tower. With places to stock up, the day is easy and thoroughly enjoyable.

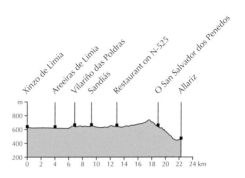

By the albergue, veer left onto Rúa da Se then left onto Rúa Sta. Mariña to a round-about. Exit onto the **OU-531** past a supermarket. Cross the next roundabout, and at the next one arrive at a choice of two routes (**1.1km**).

**Official route via the road (3.8km)**
Keep on the **OU-531**.

**Recommended route via Areeiras de Limia (5km)**
Turn left at the roundabout then right, passing a **football pitch** (**1km**), to a track. Turn right at the end and immediately left onto a track to the **Areeiras de Limia** wetlands (**2.1km**).

> The former **Antela Lagoon** that once covered this area was the largest fresh-water lagoon in Spain, 7km long and more than 5km wide. It was drained to make way for agriculture in the early 1960s, after which many birds disap-peared. Now recognized as a protected area, the restored wetlands are home to an array of birdlife once again, especially between mid April and late June.

> Cross the first junction then wind left and right to turn right at the next one. Cross a **canal** (**1km**), pass farms, keep left, turn right onto a road and left onto the **OU-531** (**0.9km**), where the official road route rejoins.

**Main route**
Both options land in **Vilariño das Poldras** (🏠). Turn right onto Rúa San Mateo, pass Capela de San Mateo and turn right onto the OU-1116, passing a bar. Turn second right after the bar to see three original Roman mile markers from the Braga–Astorga Vía. Proceed to **O Couso de Limia** (**1.4km**, unreliable services) and keep following the same road to the albergue in **Sandiás**.

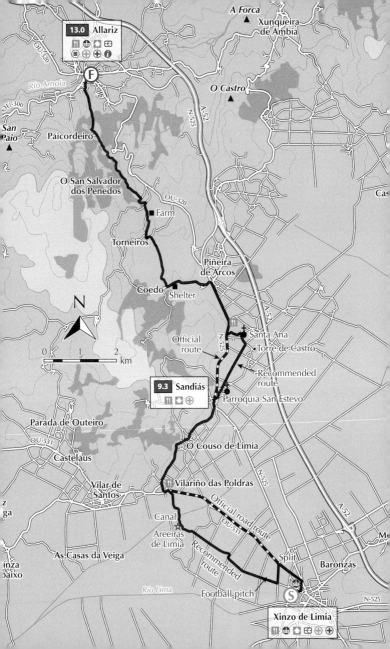

## 9.3KM SANDIÁS (ELEV 644M, POP 1198) ⏸️ 🏔️ ⊕ (148.8KM)

The **Torre de Sandiás**, locally known as the **Torre de Castro**, was most likely constructed in the early 12th century to help control the Limia region. It was destroyed during the anti-seigneurial revolt in 1467, and legend tells that the besiegers were assisted by a servant within. The insurrection forced part of the nobility to flee towards Portugal.

🏠 **Albergue de peregrinos de Sandiás** ⓞ ⒹⓄ Ⓢ Ⓩ 3/22, €8, Ctra. de Couso s/n, tel 988 465 001.

*The Parroquia de San Estevo in Sandiás reflects the transition from Gothic to Renaissance architecture (photo: Juan Carlos Medina Olid)*

Turn left onto the N-525, pass a pharmacy and café/bar, reaching Rúa da Carreira and two options (**0.3km**).

**Official route/ Shortcut (1.9km)**
Stay on the **N-525**.

**Recommended route via Torre de Castro (2.9km, not waymarked)**
Turn right onto Rúa da Carreira, fork left onto Tr. da Carreira and turn left onto Rúa da Igrexa to the **Parroquia San Estevo**. The church wonderfully reflects the transition from Gothic to Renaissance architecture. Follow a sign towards the **Torre de Castro**, visible ahead, and under the hill turn left (**2.1km**) into **Santa Ana** (unreliable services). Cross

the junction and at the next fork go left, then left again on a road, soon turning right onto the **N-525** (**0.8km**) to join the official route.

## Main route

Both options reunited, pass a restaurant just before entering **Piñeira de Arcos** and turn left following signs for Coedo (**1.5km**). Pass a **shelter** just before **Coedo** and turn right onto a track (**1.3km**) to **Torneiros** (**1.7km**, no services). Turn right and keep right to take a right-hand path. Pass a **farm** then turn right onto a road. At the end, turn right and quickly turn left into woods (**1.1km**), before returning to the road and turning left to **O San Salvador dos Penedos** (**1.1km**, no services). Go straight through woods to **Paicordeiro** (**1.6km**, no services).

Keep ahead and cross the main road on the outskirts of **Allariz** (**1.2km**). Turn right at the next junction and at the next one cross onto Rúa do Hospital, passing the Igrexa San Pedro. Proceed onto Rúa da Cruz to the Praza Maior and Igrexa de Santiago.

### 13.0KM ALLARIZ (ELEV 453M, POP 6245) 🍴 ⊕ 🛖 🅒 ⊚ ⊕ ⊕ ❶ (135.8KM)

Named the 'Key to the Galician Kingdom' by King Sancho IV in the 13th century, Allariz, with its well-preserved medieval walls, manor houses, churches and palaces, was declared an area of historic and artistic interest in 1971. In the 11th century, King Alfonso VI had the **castle and walls** built, giving the city its fortified appearance. His successor, Alfonso VII, turned it into a **Villa Real** (Royal Town) in 1154, a popular place for members of the Castilian–Leonese royalty. Builders of the Romanesque **Igrexa de Santiago** used formulas derived from Maestro Mateo's style in the Catedral de Santiago. The old **pilgrim hostel** on Rúa das Hortas displays a coat of arms with a pilgrim's gourd. The cloister of the **Monasterio Real de Santa Clara** is the largest in Spain, boasting 72 arches, but unfortunately cannot be visited.

Accommodation prices may vary depending on local and national holidays.

🛏 Hotel O Portelo Rural ** 🅟🅣 🅡 🅑🅡 🅒🅣 🅩 13/30, €-/42/52/-/-, Rúa do Portelo 20, tel 606 943 530, reservas@hoteloportelorural.com, **www.hoteloportelorural. com**. Closed 24 and 25 Dec.

🛏 Hostal/Restaurante Alarico * 🅟🅣 🅡 🅑🅡 🅒🅣 🅢 14/28, €-/35/35/55/-, Rúa Alarico 4, tel 988 440 790, info@hostalalarico.com, **www.hostalalarico.com**. Check ahead for dates.

🛏 Hotel OCA Vila de Allariz **** 🅞 🅟🅣 🅡 🅑🅡 🅒🅣 🅦 🅢 39/78, €-/-/70/-/-,

Paseo do Arnado 1, tel 988 55 40 40, reservas.viladeallariz@ocahotels.es, **www. ocahotels.com/hoteles/hotel-oca-vila-allariz**.

⬥ Pensión/Restaurante Pallabarro *** **Pr R Gr** 4/8, €-/-/55/-/-, Rúa Sur 1, tel 988 554 027, **www.pallabarro.com/index.html**. Closed 7 Jan–7 Feb.

⬥ Hotel/Restaurante Torre Lombarda *** **O Pr R Br Gr S Z** 9/16, €-/59/65/- /-, Rúa Alfredo Nan s/n, tel 988 554 005, info@torrelombarda.com, **www. torrelombarda.com**.

⬥ Hostal/Restaurante Limia ** **Pr R Gr S** 7/14, €-/30/46/-/-, N-525 km216, tel 988 440 247. Closed 24 Dec–15 Jan.

# STAGE 38A

*Allariz to Pereiras*
*(connection with Stage 38 to Ourense)*

| | |
|---|---|
| **Start** | Allariz |
| **Finish** | Pereiras (connection with Stage 38 to Ourense) |
| **Distance** | 12.2km to Pereiras (23.4km to Ourense) |
| **Total ascent** | 205m to Pereiras (370m to Ourense) |
| **Total descent** | 310m to Pereiras (755m to Ourense) |
| **Difficulty** | Easy |
| **Duration** | 3¼hr to Pereiras (6hr to Ourense) |
| **Percentage paved** | 57% to Pereiras (77% to Ourense) |
| **Albergues** | Santa Mariña de Augas Santas 7.6km (Reboredo 16.4km; Ourense 23.4km) |

Today's stage connects with the Laza option (Stage 38) in Pereiras before reaching wonderful Ourense, with its historical and gastronomical delights. Apart from drinking fountains, there are no other services until Pereiras, unless the recommended route through Santa Mariña de Augas Santas is taken. The detour, adding only 700 metres, is unwaymarked although popular and easy to follow. It takes pilgrims via a 12th-century church, where healing waters flow in memory of Ourense's patron saint, Santa Mariña.

From Praza Maior, go left, veer right to the Igrexa de Santa María de Vilanova and cross **Ponte de Vilanova**. Four old mills stand by the 15th-century Vilanova and 18th-century Frieira bridges that span Río Arnoia.

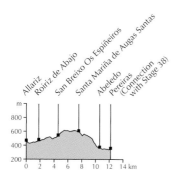

Proceed to the N-525 (**1km**), turn left onto it and, following the road sign for Santa Mariña de Augas Santas, go right onto the **OU-0101** then under the **motorway**. Turn first left to **Roiriz de Abajo** (**0.9km**, drinking fountain) then fork right, cross over the OU-0101 and turn first right into **Roiriz de Arriba** (no services). Turn right and fork left onto a grassy track to **Rubiás** (**1.2km**, no services). Turn right onto another grassy path into woods, arriving in **San Breixo Os Espiñeiros** (**1.5km**, drinking fountain). Follow the road as it bends left and take a right-hand path. This route coincides with the Braga–Astorga Roman road number XVIII, known as the Vía Nova.

Land in **Turzas** (**1km**, no services), fork left and turn left onto a forest road. Arrive at the **OU-0101** opposite a **shelter and stone cross** (**1.2km**), where there are two options: a recommended route via Santa Mariña de Augas Santas, and a shortcut on the official route.

*An old water mill is reflected in the waters of Río Arnoia in Allariz (photo: Juan Carlos Medina Olid)*

### Official route (990 metres)
Take the forest track straight ahead to **A Vila** (no services) and proceed to the **OU-0101**. Turn left then cross onto a path into woods.

### Recommended route (1.6km, unwaymarked)
Turn right and continue to **Santa Mariña de Augas Santas**, arriving 800 metres later. Fork right into the village and turn left at the end of the road by the hotel.

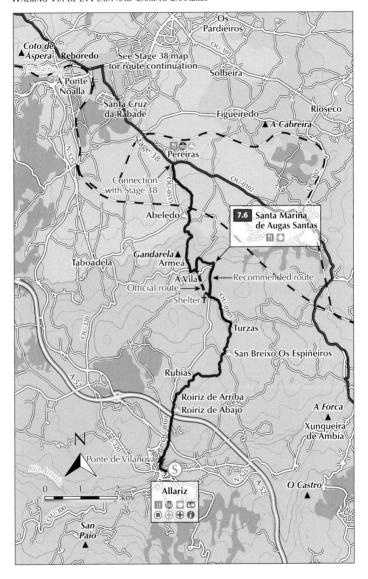

Turn left, reaching the sacred fountain and Parroquia de Augas Santas. Turn left behind the church and take a woodland path. Soon veer left and cross the **OU-0101** onto a path ahead to rejoin the official route.

### Main route

With both options united, the path arrives back on the **OU-0101** (**0.9km**). Turn right onto it to **Armeá** (no services) and leave on a track. Keep left at the fork to **Abeledo** (**2.1km**, drinking fountain) then take the first track on the right and fork left under **railway tracks**. Pass a storehouse, veer right at the fork to turn right onto the **OU-0515** (**1.2km**), uniting with Stage 38 in **Pereiras** (🍴 ⊕ and drinking fountain). To continue to Ourense, see Stage 38.

### 7.6KM SANTA MARIÑA DE AUGAS SANTAS (ELEV 590M, POP 53) 🍴 🏠 (128.2KM)

Two stories tell of **Mariña of Augas Santas** and her martyrdom. According to the traditional account, she was born in the highly Romanized Limia region (Forum Limicorum). Her mother died in childbirth so Mariña was educated by her nurse, choosing a Christian life but keeping it secret from her father, with his Roman views. She tended to the household and farm until one day a young Roman prefect approached her, wanting to make her his wife, which she refused. In response, he accused her of being a Christian. She was imprisoned and condemned to die if she did not renounce her Christian beliefs. Again, she refused. She was taken to an open field to be beheaded, and where her head touched the ground, water started to flow.

Another account tells of how she was born as one of nine sisters to Lucius Catilius Severus, Roman governor of Gallaecia and Lusitania, and Calcia, his wife. Mariña's mother was frightened that her husband would see this multiple birth as possible infidelity, so she ordered her servant, Sila, to drown her daughters. Sila was a secret Christian and instead put them in the care of other families. The daughters were baptized and brought up Christian. Upon reaching the age of 20, they were accused of being Christian and their father, the governor, asked them to renounce their faith; the sisters refused. They ran away but were caught and beheaded, and water started to flow in that location.

Other versions combine the two stories. The current church was built at the end of the 12th century.

🏠 Restaurante/Casa das Augas Santas Ⓞ Ⓟⓡ Ⓡ Ⓑⓡ Ⓖⓡ Ⓦ Ⓢ 5/10, €-/47/59/-/-, Sta. Mariña Augas Santas 15. Prices may vary.

*Ourense's streets are quiet during siesta before locals go out in the evenings*

Pilgrims, locals and tourists queue for Mass at the Catedral de Santiago de Compostela (Stage 43)

Ourense is the most popular starting point on the Vía de la Plata and Camino Sanabrés, since the final stretch of 112km from Ourense meets the 100km requirement for pilgrims to receive their *compostela*. Nevertheless, it remains quiet when compared to the Caminos Norte, Francés, Inglés and Portugués.

After the preceding endurance sections with their scant services, the stages on this section are a breeze. Charming villages, forests, churches, albergues and cafés lead to the outskirts of Santiago de Compostela, where the Vía takes a very pleasant route into town. The city's Cidade da Cultura de Galicia Museum appears brightly on the horizon and, moments later, the cathedral's spires start to beckon.

## PLANNING

1   The *albergue municipal* in Castro Dozón is currently (in 2023) closed, although perhaps this is a blessing as it encourages pilgrims to stay at the exquisite Monasterio de Oseira. (The albergue may reopen in future.)

2   Comparatively, this is by far the easiest section, with an abundance of pit stops, drinking fountains and lodgings.

3   It is best to book ahead for accommodation in Santiago de Compostela.

## WHAT NOT TO MISS

Although this is a short section, it does not disappoint. Try the famous artisan bread in Cea, then attend vespers at the Monasterio de Oseira prior to an overnight stay there (Stage 39); avoid the mosquitoes in A Laxe, but get a bite to eat in the local restaurant on the N-525 before continuing on your way to the impressive Ponte Taboada (Stage 41); and, finally, have a fabulous last night in the Albergue Reina Lupa (Stage 42). In Santiago, drop your bag, claim your *compostela* and distance certificates, then marvel at the intricate restoration work outside and within the magnificent cathedral. Mass is open to all, and the singing and acoustics make the heart soar. Head to the Mercado de Abastos (food market) for fresh seafood cooked for you on the spot.

*A young pilgrim crosses the bridge into Ponte Ulla (Stage 42)*

# STAGE 39
*Ourense to Oseira*

| | |
|---|---|
| **Start** | Ourense |
| **Finish** | Oseira |
| **Distance** | 31.9km |
| **Total ascent** | 940m |
| **Total descent** | 435m |
| **Difficulty** | Very hard |
| **Duration** | 8hr |
| **Percentage paved** | 72% |
| **Albergues** | Tamallancos 12.5km; Cea 22.6km; Oseira 31.9km |

The Tamallancos option to Cea passes tranquil farms, villages and woods, whereas the Canedo variant, although 3km shorter and passing a much-loved bar run by a pilgrim, has perilous traffic whizzing by so is not recommended and is less popular. Currently (in 2023) the albergue in Castro Dozón is closed; however, the Oseira alternative is both blessed and practical. Do plan ahead, as the only restaurant in Oseira closes on Mondays, and the albergue only has a microwave.

Facing the cathedral entrance, turn right around it onto Rúa Cardenal Cisneros and left down Rúa San Juan de Austria to the **Igrexa de Santa Eufemia**. The Galician Baroque church was an old Jesuit school. Turn right onto Rúa Lamas Carvajal, left onto Rúa Juan

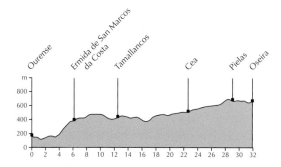

Manuel Bedoya, cross the roundabout and the **Ponte Romana** (**1.3km**) and go up Av. das Caldas to the two options (**0.4km**).

### Canedo variant

Keep straight on Av. das Caldas, turning left past **Ourense railway station** to the N-120. Take a right fork onto the OU-0520 road signposted to Castro de Beiro. Pass under the AVE viaduct and start the **ascent up the Canedo road**. At the top, cross a road, pass a restaurant and turn left onto the **OU-0526**. Some 1.3km later, take a right-hand **path** and cross a road into **Reguengo** (**3.5km**, bar run by a pilgrim). Take the track ahead, then a forest path, and cross a **bridge** into **Mandrás** (🏠). Keep straight along the road and then a track to **Pulledo** (no services). Turn right at a junction and cross the N-525 into **Casas Novas**, rejoining the recommended route coming from Tamallancos.

### Recommended route via Tamallancos

Turn right up **Av. de Santiago**, after a petrol station/restaurant go right down a lane (**1.3km**), cross the N-525 and climb steeply up to **Cudeiro** (**1.2km**, unreliable cafés). After the Igrexa de San Pedro, cross the OU-150 to the **Ermida de San Marcos da Costa** then a drinking fountain. At the next crossroads, veer right on a track, turn left onto a road (**2.9km**), fork right onto a track, pass a big **house** by the OU-526 and enter the forest on the right.

Pass a **retirement home** then turn left to a drinking fountain (**1.3km**). Eventually, cross the OU-0525, pass a **factory** (**3.6km**), turn left onto the **N-525**, cross it and take a right-hand lane to a drinking fountain and **Tamallancos**. Turn left for services.

#### 12.5KM TAMALLANCOS (ELEV 441M, POP 217) 🏠 ⊕ 🛏 ⊕ (99.9KM)

🏠 Hotel Via Stellae ⊙ Ⓟ Ⓡ Ⓖ Ⓢ 5/10, €-/-/55–65/-/-, Ctra. de Santiago 48, tel 988 279 649, info@viastellae.com, **http://viastellae.com**.

Back on the Camino, reach **A Ermida** and a bar (**0.8km**), cross the **N-525**, turn right and take a left-hand lane into **Bouzas** (no services). Down the hill, fork right to a road ahead. Pass **Sobreira** (no services), cross a **medieval bridge** (**2.7km**) and **Faramontaos** (no services), then fork left to an uphill track to a drinking fountain and supermarket. Turn right then left into **Biduedo** (**2.1km**, no services).

Keep straight to the **N-525**, turn left, pass another supermarket and cross to a path, which becomes a delightful series of **stepping stones** through a tunnel of trees. After a short uphill bank, head into **Casas Novas** (**2.2km**, 🏠).

### Main route

Both options reunited, keep straight to cross the OU-405 (**1.1km**), pass a restaurant, cross another road and veer right uphill (turn left for the albergue). Then turn left to the main square of **Cea** with its impressive clock tower and fountain.

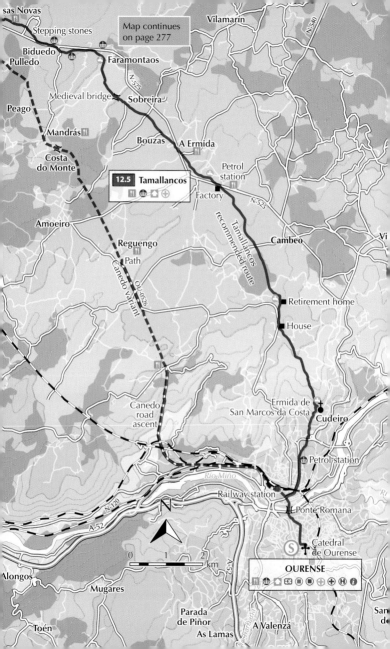

sas Novas

Stepping stones

Biduedo
Pulledo

Faramontaos

N-525

Peago

Medieval bridge

Sobreira

Mandrás

Bouzas

A Ermida

Costa
do Monte

Petrol
station

**12.5** Tamallancos

Factory

N-525

Amoeiro

Reguengo

Path

Cambeo

Vi

OU-0525

Canedo variant

Retirement home

House

Canedo
road
ascent

Ermida de
San Marcos da Costa

Cudeiro

Petrol station

Río Miño

Railway station

N-120

Ponte Romana

Alongos

N

Tamallancos recommended route

Catedral
de Ourense

**OURENSE**

0    1    2
km

Mugares

A-52

Toén

Parada
de Piñor
As Lamas

A Valenzá

San

Map continues
on page 277

Vilamarín

N-540

**10.1KM CEA** (ELEV 527M, POP 569) 🔵 🔵 🔵 🔵 🔵 **(89.8KM)**

Best known for its famous **artisan bread**, Cea maintains the same baking traditions as those established by the original bakers of Oseira Monastery. Key characteristics include a laborious kneading process followed by baking the dough in circular granite stone ovens.

🏠 Albergue de peregrinos de Cea 🔵 🔵 🔵 🔵 1/42, €8, Cl. Santo Cristo 5, tel 600 878 289 or 988 282 000.

Traverse the square diagonally, keep straight, and cross the OU-0405 onto Rúa Lodairo, reaching a baker statue. Turn left here for the direct route to Castro Dozón (see 'Direct route to Castro Dozón' below). Follow the road past the sports complex (ignoring arrows for the Castro Dozón variant, unless you are going that way) and take a right-hand path after the big **bakery** into woods (**0.7km**).

After 3.4km, turn left onto a road into **Silvaboa** (no services) followed by an uphill stretch (**4.6km**). Go downhill and turn right to a drinking fountain (**1km**) in **Pielas** (no services). With views of Oseira, bend left, taking in the magnificence of the monastery. On arrival in **Oseira**, ignore the first entrance to the monastery and instead go left, pass the restaurant and go through the main entrance. Beyond the first trees on the right, turn right, following rows of little lights on the ground to the albergue.

*The Monasterio de Oseira offers guided tours, participation in vespers and a chance to buy its local Eucaliptine liqueur*

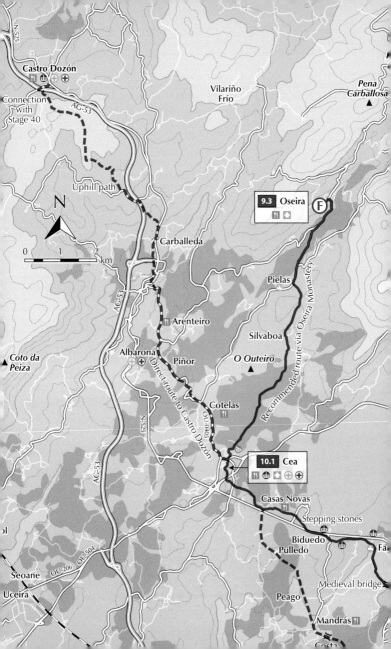

**9.3KM OSEIRA (ELEV 662M, POP 37)** 🔟 🛏 **(80.5KM)**

An overnight stay at **Oseira Monastery** provides an opportunity to participate in vespers and take a guided tour through lavender-scattered cloisters. The name Oseira is derived from the Latin *ursus*, meaning 'bear', alluding to the monastery's location in a valley of Sierra Martiña, where bears were once common. In 1137, several monks founded a little church here to live in solitude with God, joining the Cistercian order in 1141. The church transformed into a monastery during the late 12th and early 13th centuries, and became one of the largest of the order in Spain. In 1142 it was home to San Famiano, a German pilgrim who, at the age of 18, gave his life to God and set off on a pilgrimage to Christian sanctuaries, including Santiago; in Oseira, he was ordained a priest. Oseira benefited hugely from the splendour of the Baroque centuries, with enlarged rooms, new facades and a third cloister.

To satisfy your thirst, try **Eucaliptine**, a liqueur developed by the Cistercian monks using medicinal plants such as eucalyptus, melissa, chamomile, peppermint, elderflower and clove. The alcohol volume, much too high to abide by Spanish alcohol regulations, was recently lowered!

🏠 **Albergue de peregrinos del Monasterio de Oseira** ◉ ⊠ 🅂 1/42, €8, Monasterio de Oseira, tel 988 282 004, info@mosteirodeoseira.org, **http://mosteirodeoseira.org**.

**Direct route to Castro Dozón (15km)**

From the baker statue in Cea, turn left onto the **OU-0405** to reach **Cotelas** (**1.7km**, 🔟). After two short detours from the road, first on the right, then on the left over a river, enter **Piñor** (no services) then **Albarona** (**2.1km**, ⊕ ⊕). Pass a bar and Capela da Peregrina in **Arenteiro** (**1.1km**) and leave the road on a right-hand lane. Immediately keep left on a track over the OU-154 to the N-525 (**1.6km**). Cross over, turn left then right uphill to a track. Cross a road and soon reach **Carballeda** (no services) on the N-525 (**1km**).

Cross, turn left, cross again, take a track to the motorway, turn right to a road over the **motorway** (**1.5km**) then take an **uphill path** on the right. Fork left, turn right and left then right to the end of the track, reaching a road (**4.9km**). Turn right then left by the motorway, turn right onto the OU-223 over the **motorway**, turn left onto the N-525 (joining Stage 40 coming from Oseira) and enter **Castro Dozón** (🔟 ⊕ ⊕ ⊕).

# STAGE 40

*Oseira to Botos (Estación de Lalín)*

| | |
|---|---|
| **Start** | Oseira |
| **Finish** | Botos (Estación de Lalín) |
| **Distance** | 23.4km |
| **Total ascent** | 585m |
| **Total descent** | 760m |
| **Difficulty** | Moderate |
| **Duration** | 6¼hr |
| **Percentage paved** | 55% |
| **Albergues** | Botos (Estación de Lalín) 23.4km |

The Camino enjoys another splendid typical Galician day of steady ups and downs through picturesque hamlets, woods and pastures, with provisions and water easily accessible.

Leave the monastery and turn left uphill just after the restaurant to a **viewpoint**. Ensure you take the path just before the viewing platform (often overlooked, especially in poor visibility).

Keep uphill, cross a **track**, turn right then immediately left up a **cobblestone path**. Ignore a blue-and-white cross painted on stones (local route) and keep ahead to a **road** (**1.6km**). Soon, take a shortcut downhill on the left to turn left on the road again. Pass **Vilarello** (no services) and take a path on the right over a river and back to the road.

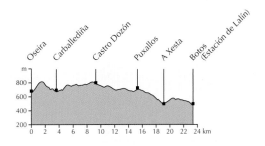

Cross over into **Carballediña** (**1.8km**, drinking fountain) and **O Outeiro** (**1.1km**, no services), where a right-hand uphill track goes into **woodland**.

Follow the track into **A Gouxa** (**1.9km**, no services), turn left onto the road, take a grassy path on the right and cross over the road into **Bidueiros** (no services). Turn left on the road, take a track on the right and return to the road. Turn right to the farms and church in **San Martín** (no services) and the N-525 (**2km**). Cross over it and turn right downhill into **Castro Dozón** (**1.9km**, 🍴 ☕ ✚ ⊕). The direct route from Cea to Castro Dozón rejoins here.

Head along the N-525 and opposite the school take a right up Parque Pozón to the **Igrexa de San Salvador de la O**. The parish church of O Castro, the Igrexa de San Salvador de la O, was built at the beginning of the 19th century in neoclassical style. Turn left to walk parallel to the **N-525** (**1km**), promptly fork right onto a forest path then turn right and go through a **tunnel** (**1.5km**) to the other side of the N-525.

Detour on a left-hand path, return to the N-525, cross over, turn left and cross again,

Map continues on page 282

*Eucalyptus trees aim for the sky in Galician forests*

passing a restaurant (**1.4km**). Soon, turn left up a track and at the fork turn left to a lane into **Puxallos** and its drinking fountain (**2.3km**).

Keep ahead and take a downhill track to cross the **AP-53** (**1.7km**). Head right, parallel to the motorway, until a left fork leads into the forest then into **Pontenoufe** (no services). Continue ahead, promptly take a left-hand path then turn right on a road to a drinking fountain (**2.1km**) by the Capela do Carmen in **A Xesta** (no services).

Cross the **PO-902** onto a track, turn left on a road, cross **railway tracks** (**1.4km**) and take the PO-534, now in **Botos**. Turn left to cross the roundabout, finding the hotel on the left.

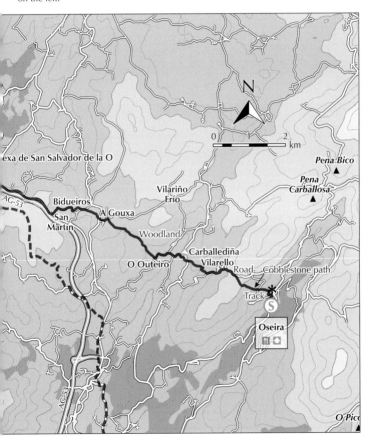

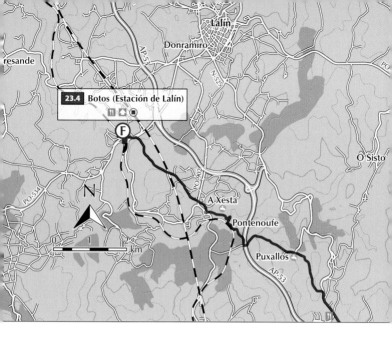

### 23.4KM BOTOS (ESTACIÓN DE LALÍN) (ELEV 476M, POP 18)  (57.1KM)

The town of Lalín, 3.7km up the road (waymarked), is the final town on the **Camino del Invierno** (the Winter Way), which joins the Camino Sanabrés tomorrow. The Invierno connects Ponferrada with Santiago along an alternative to the Camino Francés. In the past, it was used during the winter by Roman legions, Napoleon's troops and pilgrims as it was easier than going through O Cebreiro (on the Camino Francés). As the only Camino to cross every one of the four Galician provinces, it is known as the most Galician of all Caminos and is becoming more and more popular as a short, 10-day Camino option.

🏠 Hostal/Restaurante A Taberna de Vento ⊙ 🅿️ 🆁 🅶 🆂 8/18, €-/30/40/55/55, Estación de Botos 38, tel 629 306 679, **https://a-taberna-de-vento. marketinghotelero.top**.

# STAGE 41

*Botos (Estación de Lalín) to Dornelas*

| | |
|---|---|
| **Start** | Botos (Estación de Lalín) |
| **Finish** | Dornelas |
| **Distance** | 27.6km |
| **Total ascent** | 550m |
| **Total descent** | 730m |
| **Difficulty** | Moderate |
| **Duration** | 7hr |
| **Percentage paved** | 62% |
| **Albergues** | A Laxe 5.9km; Bendoiro de Abaixo 7.4km; Silleda 15.4km; Bandeira 22.6km; Dornelas 27.6km |

With many stopping places for pilgrims, Santiago de Compostela's proximity is felt more than ever. A long but easy-going day through Galician towns and villages, accompanied by fields and forests of eucalyptus trees, makes for highly enjoyable walking.

Go back to the roundabout. Turn left and left again into **Baxán** (no services). Take a right-hand path under **railway tracks** (**0.9km**). Turn left uphill, fork right, cross a road, and take a forest track. At the end, turn right to the **Igrexa de Santa Baia de Donsion** and drinking

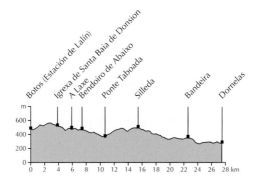

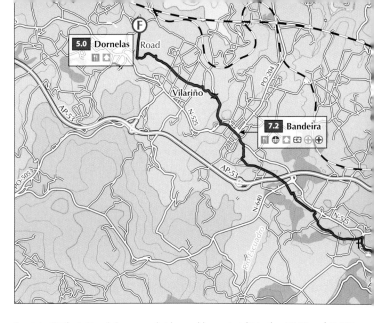

fountain (**2.9km**). Turn left, cross a bridge and keep straight to the **AP-53** and N-525 (**1.5km**), then turn left into **A Laxe**. For the albergue, cross the N-525 and turn left.

### 5.9KM A LAXE (BENDOIRO) (ELEV 470M, POP 93) ⓘ⌂ (51.2KM)

The Camino del Invierno joins the Sanabrés here. Although the albergue is convenient, with good facilities, pilgrims must be aware that an ongoing mosquito infestation that has been noticed throughout the seasons (at the time of writing in spring 2023) makes rest difficult. The issue has been raised with the Galician government so look out for updates.

⌂ **Albergue de peregrinos de A Laxe (Bendoiro)** Ⓞ Ⓓ Ⓦ Ⓢ 2/30, €8, A Laxe 21.

Follow the N-525, pass a restaurant and turn left into **Bendoiro de Abaixo**.

### 1.5KM BENDOIRO DE ABAIXO (ELEV 472M, POP 4) ⓘ⌂ (49.7KM)

⌂ **Hotel & Spa Pazo de Bendoiro** Ⓞ Ⓟ Ⓡ Ⓑ Ⓖ Ⓦ Ⓢ 10/20, €-/64/75/-/-, Bendoiro de Abaixo, tel 986 794 289 or 687 462 785, info@pazodebendoiro. com, **www.pazodebendoiro.com**.

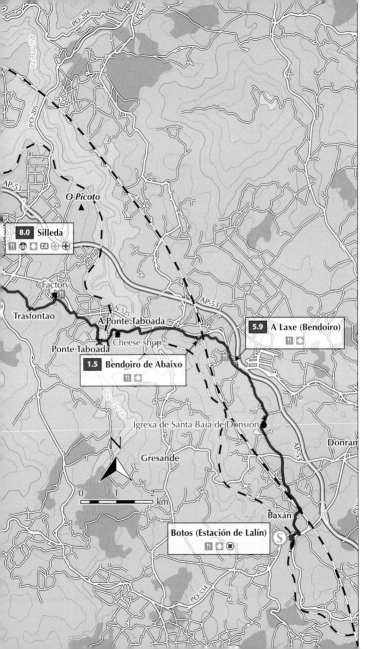

RÍO DEZA

PO-204

PO-2

PO-205

AP-53

*O Picoto* ▲

**8.0 Silleda**
🍴 ⊕ 🏠 ⊕ ⊕

Factory 🏠

Trasfontao

N-525

A Ponte Taboada

Ponte Taboada

Cheese shop

AP-53

**5.9 A Laxe (Bendoiro)**
🍴 🏠

**1.5 Bendoiro de Abaixo**
🍴 🏠

Igrexa de Santa Baia de Donsion

**N**

Gresande

0    1    2 km

Donra

AP-53

Baxán

**Botos (Estación de Lalín)**
🍴 🏠 ◉   Ⓢ

PO-534

Reach the N-525, turn left and soon veer left away from it, turning right then left to a cheese factory and **cheese shop** (**2.5km**). Turn left downhill to cross the **Ponte Taboada** and head up to the village of **A Ponte Taboada**.

It is most likely that this high stone bridge, the **Ponte Taboada**, replaced a wooden one constructed in 912. The current bridge dates from the 17th century, is 9m high and is engraved with crosses.

Turn left at the road to a grassy path, then right towards the **N-525** and a path on the left. Then turn left uphill to **factory buildings** (**2km**) and left at the road (bar to the right) to a forest track between drystone walls, forking right into **Trasfontao** (no services).

Keep downhill and turn right onto a path to cross the **PO-2205** (**1.1km**), reaching a road. Now in **Silleda**, turn left onto Rúa Carballeira do Chousiño to the Igrexa de Santa Eulalia.

### 8.0KM SILLEDA (ELEV 493M, POP 8845) 🔢 ⊕ ⬚ 🄲 ⊕ ⊕ (41.7KM)

It was not until 1853 that Silleda became the capital of its local council area.

🏠 Albergue Santa Olaia ⓞ ⒹⓄ Ⓡ ⓀⓌⓈ 18/70, €10, Av. del Parque 17, tel 679 508 709 or 619 521 475, alberguesantaolaia.info@gmail.com, **www. alberguesantaolaia.es.**

🏠 Albergue Turístico Silleda ⓞ ⒫⒯ ⒹⓄ Ⓡ ⓀⓌⓈ 11/28, €10/20/30/30/-, Cl. Venezuela 38 2º–3º–4º izq., tel 643 898 693, reservas@ albergueturisticosilleda.es, **www.albergueturisticosilleda.es.**

🏠 Albergue Trabazo ⓞ ⒹⓄ ⓇⓌⓈ 3/24, €15, Cl. Alfonso Trabazo 8–2º, tel 722 129 401, alberguetrabazo@gmail.com, **www.alberguetrabazo.com.**

🏠 Green Hostel Galicia ⒹⓄ Ⓡ ⓀⓌⓈ 9/29, €15, Cl. Antón Alonso Ríos 18, tel 986 580 156 or 615 604 393, elgranalberguedesilleda@gmail.com. Open 1 Apr–31 Oct.

Turn right after the church, then left onto the **N-525**. Leave it on the left, return to it briefly and fork left up a path to a drinking fountain (**1.3km**). Return to the N-525 and then turn sharp left to a drinking fountain (**1km**). Pass a **cross**, turn right and immediately left into woods.

Cross a road and go left onto a downhill track, keeping left under the **N-640** (**2.5km**) and over the **motorway**. Turn right, immediately fork left then keep right into **Bandeira**.

## 7.2KM BANDEIRA (ELEV 355M, POP 864) 🏨 ⊕ 🛒 € ⊕ ⊕ (34.5KM)

The **Parroquia de San Tirso de Mánduas** is named after one of the town's patron saints, the other being San Antonio de Padua. Of the original 1171 parish church, only the main doorway and two Baroque altarpieces have been preserved. In the 17th century the town was called O Fortín (stronghold), alluding to a house with very thick walls and small windows for defensive purposes. The house was a warehouse, storing the income from grain sales. A big market takes place in town on the 14th and 29th of each month, maintaining a custom dating from the Middle Ages.

⌂ Albergue de peregrinos de Bandeira ◎ ⅅ S 2/36, €8, Cl. Agro do Balo s/n.

Go through town and take a right-hand road signposted to A Caselas. Cross a **bridge** (**1.5km**) to **Vilariño** (no services) where you turn right, then fork left twice. Eventually, turn right, then left downhill and right on the **road** to the albergue in **Dornelas**.

## 5.0KM DORNELAS (ELEV 285M, POP 58) 🏨 🛒 (29.5KM)

The **Igrexa San Martiño de Dornelas** is considered an example of rural Compostela Romanesque from the 12th century.

⌂ Albergue Casa Leiras 1866 ⅅ ⅅ R B W S 1/10, €15, Dornelas 8, tel 620 483 603 or 634 613 690, casaleiras1866@yahoo.es. Open all year except Christmas.

Dornelas albergue has an adorable bouncer

# STAGE 42
*Dornelas to Deseiro (Sergude)*

| | |
|---|---|
| **Start** | Dornelas |
| **Finish** | Deseiro (Sergude) |
| **Distance** | 18.8km |
| **Total ascent** | 500m |
| **Total descent** | 575m |
| **Difficulty** | Easy |
| **Duration** | 5hr |
| **Percentage paved** | 89% |
| **Albergues** | Ponte Ulla 8.0km; O Outeiro 12.3km; Lestedo 15.4km; Deseiro (Sergude) 18.8km |

Wandering along country lanes leads to a descent (dropping 160m in 1.5km) into Ponte Ulla which, compared to the rest of Galicia, appears tropical with its palm trees. The subsequent two options involve a climb back out of the valley before a charming ramble from one village to another. There are no services in O Outeiro so plan accordingly if staying the night there.

Turn right out of the albergue, pass the **Igrexa San Martiño** and at the end of the road, turn left. After 2km, turn right, then turn left over the CP-2017 to the road ahead (following a road sign for Castro). Pass a timber workshop and a vending machine (**2.2km**) in **A Caballeira** (no services), and continue to the **Capela de las Angustias** (**1km**) and

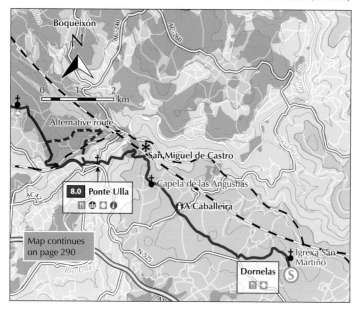

then **San Miguel de Castro** (no services). Turn right, pass a dry fountain, and start the long descent (**1km**) into Ponte Ulla. Here a swift detour leads to a lovely viewpoint/shelter.

The road flattens and soon a right turn crosses a bridge into **Ponte Ulla**, entering the province of A Coruña, the final one of the pilgrimage. Arrive at the Igrexa Santa María Magdalena, with the tourist office opposite it.

### 8.0KM PONTE ULLA (ELEV 85M, POP 48) 🍴 ⊕ 🏠 ℹ️ (21.5KM)

The **Igrexa Santa María Magdalena**, founded in the 8th century by Odario, Bishop of Lugo, preserves Romanesque elements, such as the semicircular arches within its southern chapel and a star-shaped vault with five keys, which is thought to be from the 16th century.

🏠 **Albergue-Pensión O Cruceiro da Ulla** O Pr Do R K Br W S Z 8/18 & 6/11, €15/25/45/60, Vista Alegre s/n, tel 981 512 099, info@ocruceiro.es, **www.ocruceiro.es**.

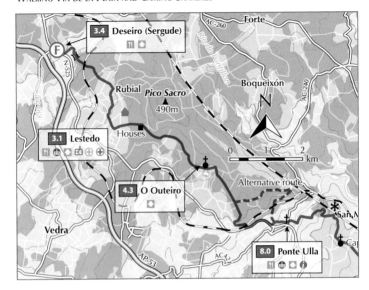

Continue ahead then turn left, passing a stone fountain, to reach a square with a stone cross. For the albergue, go straight then turn right, up steps, before the bridge. Just at the end of the square, alongside a stone wall, go up some grass on the right. Turn left, then 500 metres later arrive at two options. The recommended route is shorter and easier to navigate, particularly in poor weather.

### Alternative route (3km)
Go right, uphill, into the woods, passing houses and the **railway tracks** after 560 metres. Take a sharp left 690 metres later and reach a road. Turn right, ignore the first road on the left and at the next crossroads turn right, rejoining the official route.

### Recommended official route (2.1km)
Proceed ahead to turn right uphill onto the N-525 (**0.7km**), briefly go right into the forest before returning to the N-525, then turn right into the forest again, leaving the N-525 for the time being. Go under **railway tracks** (**1km**) to take the track on the left. Turn right onto a road and first right onto another to soon take a track on the left.

### Main route
Both options reunited, keep straight. After a left turn onto another road (**2.2km**), arrive at the beautiful stone drinking fountain with its carved Santiaguiño pilgrim beside the 1676 Iglesia de Santiago in **O Outeiro**. Keep straight to the albergue.

The carved Santiaguiño pilgrim statue on the fountain sits opposite the 1676 Iglesia de Santiago in O Outeiro

### 4.3KM O OUTEIRO (ELEV 288M, POP 40) ⬜ (17.2KM)

O Outeiro has an old Jacobean heritage, and is surrounded by legends telling how the body of James the apostle was brought to Galicia. The chapel holds an image of Santiago Matamoros.

⌂ **Albergue de peregrinos de Outeiro** ⓞ 🅳ⓞ 🆂 2/32, €8, Outeiro s/n, tel 689 352 875 or 683 331 961.

Continue ahead to wind through a forest with views of the Pico Sacro mountain. Reach a local road by wheatfields (**2.2km**), turn left onto it, come to **houses**, cross over the first road, and at the next junction turn right. Turn left for services in **Lestedo**; for the hotel, turn first right, then first left.

### 3.1KM LESTEDO (ELEV 260M, POP 34) 🔢 ⊕ ⬜ ⓒ ⊕ ⊕ (14.1KM)

In addition to its 20th-century **Igrexa de Santa María**, Lestedo is also home to the **Santuario da Nosa Señora de Lourdes**.

⌂ **Hotel Rural Casa de Casal** 🅿r 🅳ⓞ 🆁 🆆 9/23, €-/-/65/80, Lugar de Cachosenande 7, tel 698 148 323, **www.casadecasal.com**.

Keep straight on the Camino, then turn right, passing a fountain (**1km**) in **Rubial** (no services). Turn right to another fountain by a cross, turn left, go under **railway tracks** and cross a **bridge** (**1.7km**). Walk among houses, now in **Deseiro**. After the vines, turn left towards the **N-525**. About 100 metres later, the Camino turns right, but for the albergue, proceed across the N-525.

### 3.4KM DESEIRO (SERGUDE) (ELEV 197M, POP 55) 🔢 ⬜ (10.7KM)

Albergue Reina Lupa is named after **Queen Lupa**, who is also remembered in the name of the fountain in O Outeiro: the fountain of Queen Lupa. According to legend, the lady lived on the Pico Sacro mountain, having converted to Christianity. She is said to have provided oxen to carry Santiago's body to the cemetery on which the current Compostela Cathedral is located.

⌂ **Albergue Reina Lupa** 🅿r 🅳ⓞ 🆁 🆆 1/14 & 2/4, €15/-/45/-, Deseiro N-525, tel 981 511 803 or 679 842 829, info@albergereinalupa.com, **http:// albergereinalupa.com**. Closed 15 Dec–15 Jan

# STAGE 43

*Deseiro (Sergude) to Santiago de Compostela*

| | |
|---|---|
| **Start** | Deseiro (Sergude) |
| **Finish** | Santiago de Compostela |
| **Distance** | 10.7km |
| **Total ascent** | 295m |
| **Total descent** | 240m |
| **Difficulty** | Easy |
| **Duration** | 2¾hr |
| **Percentage paved** | 86% |
| **Albergues** | Santiago de Compostela 10.7km |

Take advantage of a short day to let your heart sing. Some run, while others decide to take very slow steps, uncertain as to what feelings will take over at the end of their Camino.

Go back across the N-525 and up the road to turn first left then right, uphill and down. Turn left then left again onto the AC-960. Reach the N-525 (**1.6km**) in **A Susana** (🏨 🌐 ⊕). Cross, go between houses and onto a track. Pass a picnic spot, go under the highway, turn left then right over **railway tracks** (**1.1km**) and turn left downhill. Turn left again by fields, right by a *lavadero* (old communal wash house, **1.1km**) and left under **railway tracks**. Turn right and fork left then go right and left again to the **Ermida Santa Lucía** (**1.9km**) and onwards to **Piñeiro** (🏨).

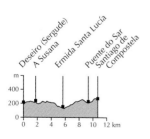

Take the track uphill under the **motorway** (**1.6km**), turn left onto Rúa do Limpiadoiro then right over **railway tracks**, with views towards the towering, modern curved buildings of Cidade da Cultura de Galicia. Turn right then left uphill onto Rúa de Angrois, entering the city of **Santiago de Compostela**. Keep straight and cross Rúa de Santiago, pass a *cruceiro* (crucifix) and go down cobblestoned Calzada do Sar on the left (**1.1km**), as the cathedral's spires start to appear in the distance.

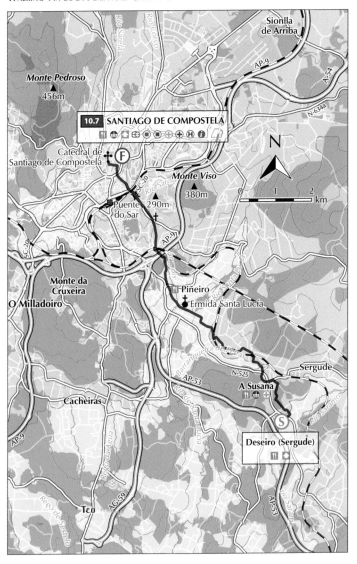

*Pilgrims head down cobblestones on Calzada do Sar as views of the cathedral appear*

Turn right onto Rúa da Ponte do Sar, go over the Roman **Puente do Sar**, under busy highways and **railway tracks** and up Rúa do Sar. After a steep climb (the last!) on **Patio de las Madres**, reach the **Convento de las Mercedarias Descalzas** and Rúa da Enseñanza (**1.6km**).

Cross to the paved road on the right (by a car park) and follow it as it bends to the left through the **Arco de los Mazarelos** and onto Praza de Mazarelos. Keep straight, passing the **Faculdade de Xeografía e Historia** library building. Cross over Praza de Entrepraciñas onto **Rúa do Castro**, and turn left onto **Rúa de Xelmírez** to the Fonte dos Cabalos statue and the steps up to the southern entrance of the cathedral (which is the entry for Mass).

Turn right at the end of the road and arrive at **Praza do Obradoiro** in front of the facade of the marvellous **Catedral de Santiago de Compostela**: a glorious finish to a beautiful journey. Well done!

### 10.7KM SANTIAGO DE COMPOSTELA (ELEV 261M, POP 97,858) ⊞ ⊕ △ Ⓒ ◉ ◉ Ⓗ ⊕ ⊕ ❶ (0KM)

On the **Praza do Obradoiro**, multitudes of pilgrims embrace and share memories of their adventure with joy, laughter and tears. Santiago's historical old town, a UNESCO World Heritage site, bustles with locals and tourists discovering its many fabulous monuments and delicious eateries. On the north side of the square, facing the cathedral, stands the stunning **Hospital de los Reyes Católicos**. It was built in 1501 by King Ferdinand and Isabela to care for pilgrims, and is now the grandiose Parador hotel. Next door is the 18th-century **town hall** and, beside it, within a 16th-century building, the library of the University of Santiago de Compostela.

The splendid **Catedral de Santiago** is the third most important place of Christian pilgrimage after Jerusalem and Rome, and devoted pilgrims have journeyed here since King Alfonso II walked the Camino Primitivo from Oviedo. Founded in 899 as a church, it was extended and elevated to a cathedral in 1075. A century later, King Fernando II converted it into a burial place for kings, increasing its grandeur further. Thus, between the years 1168 and 1211, Maestro Mateo was placed in charge of the project, which saw the Romanesque style replaced by the Gothic. The 17th-century changes and additions included Baroque elements such as the new Quintana facade and the Clock Tower, as well as the main chapel. The following century, the new western Obradoiro facade was built by Fernando de Casas, where, surrounded by spiritual figures and masterful intricate stonework, Santiago Peregrino stands highest of all.

A tour of the **cathedral rooftops**, the **Torre de la Carraca** and the 12th-century **Pórtico de la Gloria** includes museum access and is an absolute must (http://catedraldesantiago.es/visitas for information and bookings). Views over Santiago unlike any other allow you to admire the city away from the crowds. Look over the red rooftops and identify the many treasures waiting to be visited: the **Mosteiro de San Martiño Pinario**, the **Convento de San Francisco**, university buildings such as the **Biblioteca da Facultade de Xeografía e Historia**, and the dozens of squares.

A **Pilgrim Mass** to make the soul soar is held in the cathedral daily at 07:30, 09:30, 12:00 and 19:30. With sufficient demand from pilgrims, priests will swing the smoking *botafumeiro*, dispersing clouds of incense in an age-old ceremony whose original purpose may have been to mask the odour of countless pilgrim bodies (botafumeiro@catedraldesantiago.es for requests and information). Importantly, there is no access to the cathedral at any time with a backpack. For the *compostela* (pilgrim certificate), head to the Pilgrim Office on Rúa das Carretas. Booking your night's stay in Santiago is recommended.

⌂ Albergue A Fonte de Compostela Ⓞ Ⓟ Ⓓ Ⓡ Ⓖ Ⓚ Ⓦ Ⓢ 1/30 & 1/2, €14–18/30/40/-, Rúa de Estocolmo 172, tel 604 019 115, **https://alberguesafonte.com**.

⌂ Albergue Alda O Fogar de Teodomiro Ⓞ Ⓓ Ⓡ Ⓖ Ⓚ Ⓦ Ⓢ 5/24, €14+, Rúa Praciña Algalia de Arriba 3, tel 001 092 981, **www.aldahotels.es/alojamientos/albergue-alda-o-fogar-de-teodomiro**.

⌂ Albergue Azabache Ⓞ Ⓓ Ⓡ Ⓖ Ⓚ Ⓦ 4/20, €15–25, Rúa Acibechería 15, tel 981 071 254, **https://albergueazabache.com**.

⌂ **Albergue Basquiños 45** `O` `Do` `R` `Gr` `W` `S` 1/6, €10, Rúa dos Basquiños 45, tel 661 894 536.

⌂ **Albergue Blanco** `O` `Pr` `Do` `R` `Gr` `W` `S` `Z` 2/20 & 4/9, €15–20/-/40/50, Rúa das Galeras 30, tel 881 976 850 or 699 591 238, **www.prblanco.com**.

⌂ **Albergue Dream in Santiago** `Do` `R` `K` `W` `S` `Z` -/60, €18–25, Rúa de San Lázaro 81, tel 981 943 208, **https://dreaminsantiago.com**. Open 1 Mar–31 Oct.

⌂ **Albergue Fin del Camino** `Do` `K` `W` `S` 8/112, €14, Rúa de Moscova 110, tel 981 587 324, **https://alberguefindelcamino.com**. Open Easter–Oct.

⌂ **Albergue La Credencial** `Do` `R` `Gr` `K` `W` `S` 3/36, €14–20, Rúa Fonte dos Concheiros 13, tel 639 966 704, **www.lacredencial.es**. Open 1 Mar–Nov. Groups accepted in winter.

⌂ **Albergue La Estación** `Do` `R` `K` `W` `S` 2/24, €15–17, Rúa de Xoana Nogueira 14, tel 981 594 624, **www.alberguelaestacion.com**. Open Easter–16 Oct.

⌂ **Albergue La Estrella de Santiago** `Do` `R` `Gr` `W` `S` 1/20, €10–16, Rúa dos Concheiros 36–38, tel 881 973 926, **www.laestrelladesantiago.es**. Open 1 Mar–Dec.

⌂ **The Last Stamp** `Do` `R` `Gr` `K` `W` `S` 8/62, €19–22, Rúa do Preguntoiro 10, tel 981 563 525, **www.thelaststamp.es**. Closed 15 Dec–15 Jan inclusive.

⌂ **Albergue Linares** `O` `Do` `R` `Gr` `W` `S` `Z` 2/14, €16+, Rúa da Algalia de Abaixo 34, tel 981 943 253, **www.linaresroomssantiago.com**.

⌂ **Albergue LoopINN Santiago** `Pr` `Do` `R` `Gr` `W` `S` 12/60 & 19/21, €21+/38+/53+/87+, Rúa Tras Santa Clara, tel 981 585 667, **https://loopinnhostels.com/santiago**. Closed mid Dec–mid Jan.

⌂ **Meiga Backpackers Hostel** `Do` `R` `Gr` `K` `W` `S` 5/30, €14–21, Rúa dos Basquiños 67, tel 981 570 846, **www.meiga-backpackers.es**. Open 1 Mar–30 Nov.

⌂ **Albergue Monterrey** `Do` `R` `Gr` `W` `S` 3/36, €14–17, Rúa Fontiñas 65, tel 655 484 299, **www.alberguemonterrey.es**. Open 1 Mar–30 Nov.

⌂ **Mundoalbergue** `O` `Do` `R` `W` `S` 1/34, €19, Rúa de San Clemente 26, tel 981 588 625, **www.mundoalbergue.es**.

⌂ **Albergue Porta Real** `O` `Do` `R` `K` `W` 1/20, €16–20, Rúa dos Concheiros 10, tel 633 610 114.

- 🏠 Albergue Santiago Km.0 **Do** **R** **Gf** **K** **W** **S** 10/51, €25–30, Rúa Carretas 11, tel 881 974 992, **https://santiagokm0.es**. Open 1 Mar–8 Dec. Groups accepted at other times.

- 🏠 Albergue Santos **Pr** **Do** **R** **K** **W** **Z** 3/24 & 1/2, €15+/30+/40+/-, Rúa dos Concheiros 48, tel 881 169 386, **https://albergue-santos.negocio.site**. Open 1 Mar–30 Nov.

- 🏠 Albergue Santo Santiago **O** **Do** **R** **W** **S** 3/38, €12–16, Rúa do Valiño 3, tel 657 402 403, **www.elsantosantiago.com**.

- 🏠 Albergue SCQ **Do** **R** **K** **Br** **W** **S** 4/24, €18–22, Rúa da Fonte dos Concheiros 2C, tel 622 037 300, **www.alberguescq.com**. Open 1 Mar–15 Dec.

- 🏠 Albergue Seminario Menor La Asunción **Pr** **Do** **R** **K** **W** **S** 12/173 & 81/81, €16–19/18–24/36–44/-, Av. Quiroga Palacios, tel 881 031 768, **www.alberguesdelcamino.com/santiago**. Open Apr–Oct inclusive.

- 🏠 Albergue SIXTOS no Caminho **Pr** **Do** **R** **Gf** **W** **Z** 1/40 & 1/2, €15–20/-/45–60/-, Rúa da Fonte dos Concheiros 2A, tel 682 721 194, **www.sixtosnocaminho.com/albergue-sixtos-0-home**. Open 1 Apr–20 Nov.

*A place of unions, reunions, laughter and tears, the Praza do Obradoiro welcomes hundreds of thousands of pilgrims each year*

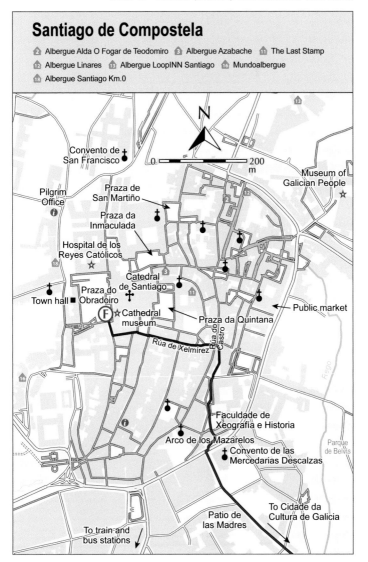

# Santiago de Compostela

- 🄫 Albergue Alda O Fogar de Teodomiro
- 🄫 Albergue Azabache
- 🄫 The Last Stamp
- 🄫 Albergue Linares
- 🄫 Albergue LoopINN Santiago
- 🄫 Mundoalbergue
- 🄫 Albergue Santiago Km.0

Convento de San Francisco

Pilgrim Office

Praza de San Martiño

Praza da Inmaculada

Museum of Galician People

Hospital de los Reyes Católicos

Catedral de Santiago

Town hall

Praza do Obradoiro

Cathedral museum

Praza da Quintana

Public market

Rúa de Xelmírez

Rúa do Castro

Faculdade de Xeografía e Historia

Arco de los Mazarelos

Convento de las Mercedarias Descalzas

Parque de Belvís

To train and bus stations

Patio de las Madres

To Cidade da Cultura de Galicia

0 ___ 200 m

# APPENDIX A
*Stage planning tables*

Distances between accommodation intervals are provided in the table below for the route from Sevilla to Santiago de Compostela on the Vía de la Plata and Camino Sanabrés via Laza. The Verín variant and extension to Astorga are also shown. Some helpful calculations for day averages of 20km, 25km, 30km and 40km are given. These exclude any alternatives or detours.

| Stage no. | Name | Distance from Santiago (km) | Distance from start (km) | Distance from previous place (km) | Itinerary at 20km stage average (km) | Guidebook itinerary: 25km stage average (km) | Itinerary at 30km stage average (km) | Itinerary at 40km stage average (km) | My itinerary |
|---|---|---|---|---|---|---|---|---|---|
| 1 | Sevilla | 995.3 | 0.0 | 0.0 | | | | | |
| | Santiponce | 986.0 | 9.3 | 9.3 | | | | | |
| 2 | Guillena | 973.5 | 21.8 | 12.5 | 21.8 | 21.8 | 21.8 | | |
| 3 | Castilblanco de los Arroyos | 955.3 | 40.0 | 18.2 | 18.2 | 18.2 | 18.2 | 40.0 | |
| 4 | Almadén de la Plata | 925.8 | 69.5 | 29.5 | 29.5 | 29.5 | 29.5 | | |
| 5 | El Rea de la Jara | 911.9 | 83.4 | 13.9 | 13.9 | 13.9 | | 43.4 | |
| | Hotel Compejo Leo | 900.0 | 95.3 | 11.9 | | | 35.1 | | |
| 6 | Mone terio | 890.7 | 104.6 | 9.3 | 21.2 | 21.2 | | | |
| | Fuente de Cantos | 869.9 | 125.4 | 20.8 | 20.8 | | | 42.0 | |

| Stage no. | Name | Distance from Santiago (km) | Distance from start (km) | Distance from previous place (km) | Itinerary at 20km stage average (km) | Guidebook itinerary: 25km stage average (km) | Itinerary at 30km stage average (km) | Itinerary at 40km stage average (km) | My itinerary |
|---|---|---|---|---|---|---|---|---|---|
| 7 | Calzadilla de los Barros | 863.4 | 131.9 | 6.5 | | 27.3 | 27.3 | | |
| | Puebla de Sancho Pérez | 849.1 | 146.2 | 14.3 | | | | | |
| 8 | Zafra | 845.1 | 150.2 | 4.0 | 20.8 | 18.3 | | | |
| | Los Santos de Maimona | 840.7 | 154.6 | 4.4 | | | | | |
| | La Almazara | 831.8 | 163.5 | 8.9 | 17.3 | | 31.6 | 38.1 | |
| 9 | Villafranca de los Barros | 824.3 | 171.0 | 7.5 | 7.5 | 20.8 | | | |
| 10 | Torremejía | 797.0 | 198.3 | 27.3 | 27.3 | 27.3 | 34.8 | 34.8 | |
| 11 | Mérida | 780.6 | 214.7 | 16.4 | 16.4 | 16.4 | | | |
| | El Carrascalejo | 766.9 | 228.4 | 13.7 | | | 30.1 | | |
| 12 | Aljucén | 764.3 | 231.0 | 2.6 | 16.3 | 16.3 | | 32.7 | |
| 13 | Alcuéscar | 745.0 | 250.3 | 19.3 | 19.3 | 19.3 | | | |
| 14 | Aldea del Cano | 729.7 | 265.6 | 15.3 | 15.3 | 26.5 | 37.2 | 34.6 | |
| | Valdesalor | 718.5 | 276.8 | 11.2 | 23.2 | | | | |
| | Cáceres | 706.5 | 288.8 | 12.0 | | | | | |
| 15 | Casar de Cáceres | 695.2 | 300.1 | 11.3 | 11.3 | 23.3 | 34.5 | 34.5 | |

| Stage no. | Name | Distance from Santiago (km) | Distance from start (km) | Distance from previous place (km) | Itinerary at 20km stage average (km) | Guidebook itinerary: 25km stage average (km) | Itinerary at 30km stage average (km) | Itinerary at 40km stage average (km) | My itinerary |
|---|---|---|---|---|---|---|---|---|---|
| 16 | Cañaveral | 662.0 | 333.3 | 33.2 | 33.2 | 33.2 | 33.2 | | |
| | Grimaldo | 653.5 | 341.8 | 8.5 | 8.5 | | | 41.7 | |
| 17 | Galisteo | 633.3 | 362.0 | 20.2 | 20.2 | 28.7 | 28.7 | | |
| 18 | Carcaboso | 622.5 | 372.8 | 10.8 | 10.8 | 10.8 | | 31.0 | |
| | Arco de Cáparra (hotel transfer) | 604.5 | 390.8 | 18.0 | 18.0 | | 28.8 | | |
| 19 | Hotels Asturias and Jarilla | 594.1 | 401.2 | 10.4 | | 28.4 | | | |
| | Aldearrueva del Camino | 582.7 | 412.6 | 11.4 | 21.8 | | | 39.8 | |
| | Baños de Montemayor | 573.1 | 422.2 | 9.6 | | | 31.4 | | |
| 20 | Puerto de Béjar (Colonia la Estación) | 569.9 | 425.4 | 3.2 | | 24.2 | | | |
| | Albergue Puente de la Malena | 566.4 | 428.9 | 3.5 | | | | | |
| | La Calzada de Béjar | 560.6 | 434.7 | 5.8 | 22.1 | | | | |
| | Valverde de Valdelacasa | 552.0 | 443.3 | 8.6 | | | | | |

| Stage no. | Name | Distance from Santiago (km) | Distance from start (km) | Distance from previous place (km) | Itinerary at 20km stage average (km) | Guidebook itinerary: 25km stage average (km) | Itinerary at 30km stage average (km) | Itinerary at 40km stage average (km) | My itinerary |
|---|---|---|---|---|---|---|---|---|---|
| 21 | Fuenterroble de Salvatierra | 540.1 | 455.2 | 11.9 | 20.5 | 29.8 | 33.0 | 42.6 | |
| 22 | San Pedro de Rozados | 512.3 | 483.0 | 27.8 | 27.8 | 27.8 | | | |
| | Morille | 508.2 | 487.1 | 4.1 | | | 31.9 | 31.9 | |
| 23 | Salamanca | 487.0 | 508.3 | 21.2 | 25.3 | 25.3 | | | |
| | Castellanos de Villiquera | 474.6 | 520.7 | 12.4 | | | 33.6 | | |
| 24 | Calzada de Valdunciel | 470.3 | 525.0 | 4.3 | 16.7 | 16.7 | | 37.9 | |
| 25 | El Cubo de Tierra del Vino | 449.6 | 545.7 | 20.7 | 20.7 | 20.7 | 25.0 | | |
| | Villanueva de Campeán | 436.0 | 559.3 | 13.6 | 13.6 | | | 34.3 | |
| 26 | Zamora | 417.7 | 577.6 | 18.3 | 18.3 | 31.9 | 31.9 | | |
| 27 | Montamarta | 398.1 | 597.2 | 19.6 | 19.6 | 19.6 | | 37.9 | |
| | Fontanillas de Castro | 386.3 | 609.0 | 11.8 | | | 31.4 | | |
| 28 | Granja de Moreruela | 375.8 | 619.5 | 10.5 | 22.3 | 22.3 | | | |
| 29 | Tábara | 349.6 | 645.7 | 26.2 | 26.2 | 26.2 | 36.7 | 48.5 | |

| Stage no. | Name | Distance from Santiago (km) | Distance from start (km) | Distance from previous place (km) | Itinerary at 20km stage average (km) | Guidebook itinerary: 25km stage average (km) | Itinerary at 30km stage average (km) | Itinerary at 40km stage average (km) | My itinerary |
|---|---|---|---|---|---|---|---|---|---|
| | Villanueva de las Peras | 335.3 | 660.0 | 14.3 | | | | | |
| 30 | Santa Marta de Tera | 326.6 | 668.7 | 8.7 | 23.0 | 23.0 | | | |
| | Calzadilla de Tera | 315.3 | 680.0 | 11.3 | | | 34.3 | | |
| | Olle os de Tera | 313.4 | 681.9 | 1.9 | | | | | |
| | Villar de Farfón | 303.8 | 691.5 | 9.6 | 22.8 | | | 45.8 | |
| 31 | Rionegro del Puente | 298.0 | 697.3 | 5.8 | | 28.6 | | | |
| | Mombuey | 288.9 | 706.4 | 9.1 | 14.9 | | 26.4 | | |
| | Entrepeñas | 275.3 | 720.0 | 13.6 | | | | | |
| 32 | Asturianos | 271.7 | 723.6 | 3.6 | 17.2 | 26.3 | | | |
| | Puebla de Sanabria | 256.0 | 739.3 | 15.7 | 15.7 | | 32.9 | 47.8 | |
| 33 | Requejo | 243.9 | 751.4 | 12.1 | | 27.8 | | | |
| | Padornelo | 235.3 | 760.0 | 8.6 | 20.7 | | | | |
| 34 | Lubián | 227.7 | 767.6 | 7.6 | | 16.2 | 28.3 | | |
| | A V lavella (A Mezquita) | 216.9 | 778.4 | 10.8 | 18.4 | | | 39.1 | |
| 35 | A Cudiña | 203.2 | 792.1 | 13.7 | 13.7 | 24.5 | 24.5 | | |

## Via Laza (90.8km to Ourense)

| Stage no. | Name | Distance from Santiago (km) | Distance from start (km) | Distance from previous place (km) | Itinerary at 20km stage average (km) | Guidebook itinerary: 25km stage average (km) | Itinerary at 30km stage average (km) | Itinerary at 40km stage average (km) | My itinerary |
|---|---|---|---|---|---|---|---|---|---|
| | Campobecerros | 183.0 | 812.3 | 20.2 | 20.2 | | | | |
| | As Eiras | 174.5 | 820.8 | 8.5 | | | | 42.4 | |
| 36 | Laza | 168.3 | 827.0 | 6.2 | 14.7 | 34.9 | 34.9 | | |
| 37 | Alberguería | 156.5 | 838.8 | 11.8 | | 11.8 | | | |
| | Vilar de Barrio | 149.5 | 845.8 | 7.0 | 18.8 | | | | |
| 38 | Xunqueira de Ambía | 134.6 | 860.7 | 14.9 | | 21.9 | 33.7 | 39.9 | |
| | A Pousa | 131.4 | 863.9 | 3.2 | 18.1 | | | | |
| | Reboredo | 119.4 | 875.9 | 12.0 | | | | | |
| 39 | Ourense | 112.4 | 882.9 | 7.0 | 19.0 | 22.2 | 22.2 | | |
| | Tamallancos | 99.9 | 895.4 | 12.5 | | | | | |
| | Cea | 89.8 | 905.5 | 10.1 | 22.6 | | | 44.8 | |
| 40 | Oseira | 80.5 | 914.8 | 9.3 | 9.3 | 31.9 | 31.9 | | |
| 41 | Botos (Estación de Lalín) | 57.1 | 938.2 | 23.4 | 23.4 | 23.4 | | | |
| | A Laxe | 51.2 | 944.1 | 5.9 | | | | | |
| | Bendoiro de Abaixo | 49.7 | 945.6 | 1.5 | | | | | |

| Stage no. | Name | Distance from Santiago (km) | Distance from start (km) | Distance from previous place (km) | Itinerary at 20km stage average (km) | Guidebook itinerary: 25km stage average (km) | Itinerary at 30km stage average (km) | Itinerary at 40km stage average (km) | My itinerary |
|---|---|---|---|---|---|---|---|---|---|
| | Silleca | 41.7 | 953.6 | 8.0 | 15.4 | | | 38.8 | 48.1 |
| | Banceira | 34.5 | 960.8 | 7.2 | | | | | |
| 42 | Dormelas | 29.5 | 965.8 | 5.0 | | 27.6 | | | |
| | Ponte Ulla | 21.5 | 973.8 | 8.0 | 20.2 | | | | |
| | O Outeiro | 17.2 | 978.1 | 4.3 | | | | | |
| | Lestedo | 14.1 | 981.2 | 3.1 | | | | | |
| 43 | Deseiro (Sergude) | 10.7 | 984.6 | 3.4 | | 18.8 | 31.0 | | |
| | Santiago de Compostela | 0.0 | 995.3 | 10.7 | 21.5 | 10.7 | 10.7 | 41.7 | |
| | **Total stages to Santiago** | | | | **52** | **43** | **33** | **25** | |

## Variant via Verín (123.2km to Ourense)

| Stage no. | Name | Distance from Santiago (km) | Distance from start (km) | Distance from previous place (km) | Itinerary at 20km stage average (km) | Guidebook itinerary: 25km stage average (km) | Itinerary at 30km stage average (km) | Itinerary at 40km stage average (km) | My itinerary |
|---|---|---|---|---|---|---|---|---|---|
| 35A | A Cudiña | 235.6 | 792.1 | 13.7 | 13.7 | 24.5 | 24.5 | | |
| | Mesón de Erosa | 230.1 | 797.6 | 5.5 | | | | | |
| | As Vendas da Barreira | 216.3 | 811.4 | 13.8 | 19.3 | | | 33.0 | |
| 36A | Verín | 195.3 | 832.4 | 21.0 | 21.0 | 40.3 | 40.3 | | |

| Stage no. | Name | Distance from Santiago (km) | Distance from start (km) | Distance from previous place (km) | Itinerary at 20km stage average (km) | Guidebook itinerary: 25km stage average (km) | Itinerary at 30km stage average (km) | Itinerary at 40km stage average (km) | My itinerary |
|---|---|---|---|---|---|---|---|---|---|
| | Vila de Rei | 174.1 | 853.6 | 21.2 | 21.2 | | | 42.2 | |
| 37A | Xinzo de Limia | 158.1 | 869.6 | 16.0 | 16.0 | 37.2 | 37.2 | | |
| | Sandiás | 148.8 | 878.9 | 9.3 | | | | | |
| 38A | Allariz | 135.8 | 891.9 | 13.0 | 22.3 | 22.3 | | 38.3 | |
| | Santa Mariña de Augas Santas | 128.2 | 899.5 | 7.6 | | | 29.9 | | |
| | Pereiras (Connection with Stage 38) | 123.6 | 904.1 | 4.6 | | | | | |
| 39 | Ourense | 112.4 | 915.3 | 11.2 | 23.4 | 23.4 | 15.8 | 23.4 | |
| | **Total stages to Santiago** | | | | **53** | **43** | **34** | **25** | |

### Extension to Astorga

| Stage no. | Name | Distance from Astorga (km) | Distance from Santiago (km) | Distance from start (km) | Distance from previous place (km) | Itinerary at 20km stage average (km) | Guidebook itinerary: 25km stage average (km) | Itinerary at 30km stage average (km) | Itinerary at 40km stage average (km) | My itinerary |
|---|---|---|---|---|---|---|---|---|---|---|
| Extension | Granja de Moreruela | 94.6 | 355.4 | 619.5 | 10.5 | 22.3 | 22.3 | | | |
| | Barcial del Barco | 76.6 | 337.4 | 637.5 | 18.0 | 18.0 | | 28.5 | 40.3 | |
| | Benavente | 67.5 | 328.3 | 646.6 | 9.1 | 9.1 | 27.1 | | | |

| Stage no. | Name | Distance from Astorga (km) | Distance from Santiago (km) | Distance from start (km) | Distance from previous place (km) | Itinerary at 20km stage average (km) | Guidebook itinerary: 25km stage average (km) | Itinerary at 30km stage average (km) | Itinerary at 40km stage average (km) | My itinerary |
|---|---|---|---|---|---|---|---|---|---|---|
| | Alija del Infantado | 46.4 | 307.2 | 667.7 | 21.1 | 21.1 | 21.1 | 30.2 | 30.2 | |
| | La Bañeza | 24.8 | 285.6 | 689.3 | 21.6 | 21.6 | 21.6 | | | |
| | Palacios de la Valduerna | 18.8 | 279.6 | 695.3 | 6.0 | | | 27.6 | | |
| | Estación de Valderrey | 7.2 | 268.0 | 706.9 | 11.6 | | | | 39.2 | |
| | Celada | 4.0 | 264.8 | 710.1 | 3.2 | | | | | |
| | Astorga | 0.0 | 260.8 | 714.1 | 4.0 | | | 18.8 | 7.2 | |
| | **Total stages to Astorga** | | | | | 5 | 4 | 3½ | 3 | |

# APPENDIX B

*Spanish–English glossary of key terms*

**Intonation**

As in English, when asking a question raise your voice at the end. For example, 'You like to go walking' is an affirmation so the tone of voice remains level, but 'You like to go walking?' is a question so the voice rises at the end. The same happens with the Spanish *Te gusta andar* and *¿Te gusta andar?*

**Grammar**

Adjectives end in 'o' for masculine nouns, and 'a' for feminine nouns.

**Pronunciation**

In Spanish, every letter is pronounced, except 'h', which is a silent letter. So *tomates* is pronounced 't-oh-m-ah-t-eh-s' but *hotel* is 'oh-t-eh-l'.

'Z' sounds like an 's' or 'f'. 'S' is always a soft sound like 's' in '**s**nake'. 'Ch' is the same as 'ch' in '**ch**eese', 'ñ' sounds like 'ny' in the words 'ca**ny**on' or 'o**ni**on', and 'j' sounds like 'h' in the English word '**h**at'.

'C' sounds like 'k' before consonants and the vowels 'a', 'o' and 'u', but like 's' or 'f' before 'e' and 'i'. 'G' follows the same pattern as 'c': it sounds like 'g' in **g**ate before 'a', 'o' and 'u', but like 'h' for '**h**ouse' before the vowels 'e' and 'i'.

**On the trail**

| Spanish | English | Spanish | English |
|---|---|---|---|
| abejas | bees | arcén | pavement |
| acequia | water channel | arco | arch |
| acueducto | aqueduct | arroyo | stream |
| agua no tratada | untreated water | autovía | motorway |
| agua potable | drinking water | avenida | avenue |
| águila | eagle | aves | birds |
| alameda | promenade, usually in a park or by a river | ayuntamiento | town hall |
| | | banco | bank |
| albergue | pilgrim hostel | barranco | gorge |
| alcázar | fortress | barrio | neighbourhood |
| alcornoque | cork oak | bodega (de vino) | warehouse/storehouse/cellar (winery) |
| alojamiento | accommodation | | |
| alto | peak | bosque | forest/woods |

| Spanish | English |
|---------|---------|
| caballo | horse |
| cajero automático | ATM |
| calle | street |
| calzada (romana) | (Roman) footpath |
| camino | path/route |
| campo | field |
| cañada | drover's road or transhumance route |
| canal | canal |
| capilla | chapel |
| carnicería | butcher's |
| carretera | main/major road |
| carretera nacional | equivalent of a British A road, but quieter in Spain as a motorway almost always runs parallel to it and is preferred by drivers |
| casa | house |
| castillo | castle |
| catedral | cathedral |
| cementerio | cemetery |
| central fotovoltaica | solar panel plant |
| cerdo | pig |
| cerro | hill |
| ciervo | deer |
| cigüeña | stork |
| ciudad (amurallada) | (walled) city |
| claustro | cloister |
| colada | drover's road or transhumance route |
| colina/collado | hill |
| columna | pillar |
| concello | local council |

| Spanish | English |
|---------|---------|
| concha | shell |
| conjunto histórico | historical centre |
| consejo | local council |
| consultorio | doctor's surgery |
| cordel | drover's road or transhumance route |
| cordillera | mountain range |
| cortijo | farmhouse |
| coto (de caza) | hunting reserve |
| cruce | junction |
| cruz | cross |
| cuesta | uphill slope |
| cueva | cave |
| dehesa | pastureland with oak trees that are spread out evenly for grazing livestock, especially cows, bulls and the Iberian pig |
| embalse | reservoir |
| encina | holm oak |
| entrada | entrance |
| eólicos | wind turbines |
| ermita | hermitage/chapel |
| estación (de tren/ bus) | (railway/bus) station |
| estación de servicio | petrol/service station |
| eucaliptos | eucalyptus trees |
| farmacia | pharmacy |
| ferrocarril | railway line |
| finca | estate/property, usually dedicated to farming |
| flecha (amarilla) | (yellow) arrow |
| frontera | border |
| fuente | fountain/spring |
| ganadería | livestock |

| Spanish | English |
|---------|---------|
| *granja* | estate/property, usually dedicated to farming |
| *hórreo* | traditional granary (in Galicia) |
| *hospital* | hospital |
| *hostal* | hotel |
| *hostel* | hostel (different from 'hostal', which is a hotel) |
| *hotel* | hotel |
| *huerto* | orchard/plot |
| *iglesia/igrexa* | church |
| *indicador* | cairn/milestone/waymark |
| *laguna* | lake |
| *lavadero* | wash house |
| *línea (de tren)* | (railway) line |
| *llano* | plain/flatlands |
| *mansio* | (Latin) Roman stopping point on the Vía de la Plata |
| *médico* | doctor's surgery |
| *mesón* | restaurant |
| *miliario romano* | Roman mile marker |
| *mirador* | viewpoint |
| *mojón* | cairn/milestone/waymark |
| *molino (de agua/ viento)* | (water/wind) mill |
| *monasterio* | monastery |
| *monte* | mountain |
| *municipio* | municipality |
| *museo* | museum |
| *nacimiento* | source (of a river) |
| *oficina de turismo* | tourist office |
| *otero* | hillock/knoll |
| *oveja* | sheep |
| *palacio* | palace |

| Spanish | English |
|---------|---------|
| *panadería* | bakery |
| *pantano* | reservoir |
| *parada (de tren/ bus)* | (train/bus) stop |
| *Parador* | hotels in preserved historic buildings, owned by the state |
| *parcela* | estate/property, usually dedicated to farming |
| *parroquia* | parish |
| *parque* | park |
| *paseo* | promenade, usually in a park or by a river |
| *paso* | walkway |
| *pensión* | hotel |
| *pilar* | pillar |
| *pinos* | pine trees |
| *piscina* | swimming pool |
| *pista (de tierra)* | (dirt) track |
| *plaza (mayor)* | (main/central) square |
| *población* | town |
| *polígono industrial* | industry and warehouses, usually on the outskirts of a big town or city |
| *pozo* | well |
| *pueblo* | village |
| *puente* | bridge |
| *puerta* | door |
| *puerto* | col/mountain pass |
| *prohibido* | forbidden |
| *refugio* | shelter |
| *roble* | oak |
| *río* | river |
| *rotonda* | roundabout |

| Spanish | English |
|---------|---------|
| *rúa* | street |
| *ruinas* | ruins |
| *salida* | exit |
| *santuario* | sanctuary |
| *señalización* | waymarking |
| *sendero* | footpath/trail |
| *sierra* | mountain range |
| *supermercado* | supermarket |
| *templo romano* | Roman temple |
| *tienda* | shop |
| *toro* | bull |
| *torre* | tower |
| *travesía* | side street |
| *túnel* | tunnel |
| *urbanización* | a residential new-build area, usually just outside a town or city (typical of Spain) |
| *vaca* | cow |
| *valle* | valley |
| *venado* | deer |
| *vera* | bank, for example of a river |
| *vereda* | footpath/drover's track |
| *vía* | road/path/way/track |
| *viaducto* | viaduct |
| *vía pecuaria* | cattle road |
| *vía verde* | disused railway (literally 'green way'), now a walking and cycling path |
| *villa* | town |

### In town and accommodation

| Spanish | English |
|---------|---------|
| *hola* | hello |
| *por favor* | please |
| *gracias* | thank you |
| *adiós* | goodbye |
| *ayuda* | help |
| *Tengo un problema* | I have a problem |
| *No hablo español* | I don't speak Spanish |
| *¿Qué significa…?* | What does…mean? |
| *No entiendo* | I don't understand |
| *¿Cuánto/ Cuántos…?* | How much/many…? |
| *¿Cuándo…?* | When…? |
| *¿Hay…?* | Is there/Are there…? |
| *¿(Salamanca) está lejos?* | Is (Salamanca) far? |
| *¿(Ourense) está cerca?* | Is (Ourense) near? |
| *¿Cuántos kilómetros quedan para (Zamora)?* | How many kilometres are left until (Zamora)? |
| *Estoy perdido/a* | I am lost |
| *¿Qué tiempo hará hoy?* | What will the weather be like today? |
| *¿A qué hora es la misa?* | What time is the Mass? |
| *¿Dónde puedo comprar…?* | Where can I buy…? |
| *…unas banderitas/ tiritas* | …some plasters |
| *…unas pilas* | …some batteries |
| *…unas compresas* | …some sanitary towels |
| *…un sello* | …a stamp |
| *¿Dónde está (el albergue)?* | Where is (the pilgrim hostel)? |
| *a la derecha* | to the right |
| *a la izquierda* | to the left |
| *cerca* | close |
| *lejos* | far |
| *todo recto* | straight on |
| *delante* | in front of |

| Spanish | English |
|---|---|
| *detrás* | behind |
| *al lado* | next to |

## Places in town

| Spanish | English |
|---|---|
| *un/el albergue* | a/the pilgrim hostel |
| *un/el bar* | a/the bar |
| *un/el café* | a/the café |
| *el centro* | the centre |
| *una/la comisaria* | a/the police station |
| *una/la embajada* | an/the embassy |
| *una/la farmacia* | a/the pharmacy |
| *una/la fuente de agua potable* | a/the drinking fountain |
| *una/la guardia civil* | a/the police station |
| *un/el hospital* | a/the hospital |
| *un/el hostal/hotel* | a/the hotel |
| *una/la iglesia* | an/the church |
| *un/el médico* | a/the doctor |
| *un/el museo* | a/the museum |
| *una/la pensión* | a/the hotel |
| *la plaza mayor* | the main square |
| *un/el restaurante* | a/the restaurant |
| *un/el supermercado* | a/the supermarket |
| *una/la tienda* | a/the shop |

## At the hostel

| Spanish | English |
|---|---|
| *un/el hospitalero* | a/the volunteer host at a pilgrim hostel |
| *una/la cocina* | a/the kitchen |
| *una/la lavadora* | a/the washing machine |
| *una/la sábana* | a/the blanket |
| *una/la secadora* | a/the dryer |

| Spanish | English |
|---|---|
| **Food and drink** | |
| *agua* | water |
| *un/el bocadillo (con…)* | a/the sandwich (with…) |
| *carne* | meat |
| *cerdo* | pork |
| *ensalada* | salad |
| *jamón* | ham |
| *pescado* | fish |
| *pollo* | chicken |
| *queso* | cheese |
| *ternera* | beef |
| *tomate* | tomato |
| *tortilla* | tortilla (Spanish omelette) |
| *verduras* | vegetables |
| *un café (con leche)* | a coffee (with milk) |
| *una cerveza* | a beer |
| *un vino tinto/ blanco* | a red/white wine |
| *No puedo comer/ beber…* | I can't eat/drink… |
| *…gluten* | …gluten |
| *…leche* | …milk |
| *…alcohol* | …alcohol |
| *Soy vegetariano/a* | I'm vegetarian |
| *Tengo una alergia a…* | I have an allergy to… |
| *…cacahuetes/ frutos secos* | …peanuts/nuts |

# APPENDIX C
*Useful contacts and links*

Telephone numbers are provided in their local form. If you are calling from outside Spain, use the international access code for the country you are calling from, followed by the country code for Spain (34) and then the number provided. For example, to call 654 504 390 from the UK, use 00 34 654 504 390.

**Useful phone numbers**

All emergencies 112

Local police 092

Civil guard 062

Fire department 080

Emergency dentist 961 496 199

Tourist helpline 902 102 112

**Pilgrim offices and pilgrim information**

**Full details and locations**

Asociaciones de Amigos del Camino de Santiago
tel 654 504 390
info@editorialbuencamino.com
www.editorialbuencamino.com/mapa-del-camino-de-santiago

**Sevilla**

Sevilla Cathedral
tel 954 335 274 or 696 600 602
www.viaplata.org/atencion-al-peregrino

**Mérida**

Albergue Molino de Pancaliente
tel 682 514 366

**Fuenterroble de Salvatierra**

Albergue parroquial Santa María
tel 923 151 083
alberguefuenterroble@gmail.com
https://alberguedefuenterroble.wordpress.com

### Salamanca

Albergue de peregrinos Casa la Calera
tel 652 921 185

### Zamora

Albergue de peregrinos de Zamora
tel 980 534 097

### Astorga

Albergue de peregrinos Siervas de María
tel 987 616 034 or 618 271 773
asociacion@caminodesantiagoastorga.com

### Santiago de Compostela

Asociación Galega de Amigos do Camiño de SantiagoAv. Coimbra 1
info@amigosdelcamino.com

Pilgrim Reception Office
Rúa das Carretas 33
tel 981 568 846
oficinadelperegrino@catedraldesantiago.es
https://oficinadelperegrino.com

### Transport

Trains
www.renfe.com

Buses
www.alsa.es

Planes
www.skyscanner.net

### Vía de la Plata and Camino Sanabrés online information resources

Gronze pilgrim guide and online updates (Spanish)
www.gronze.com/via-plata

Gerald Kelly's online updates (English)
www.viadelaplataguide.net

Eroski Consumer guide (Spanish)
https://caminodesantiago.consumer.es/los-caminos-de-santiago/via-de-la-plata

All Caminos (Spanish)
www.caminosantiago.org/cpperegrino/comun/inicio.asp

Sections in Galicia (Spanish)
www.amigosdelcamino.com/caminos/via-de-la-plata

Blog (Spanish)
https://viadelaplataelcamino.blogspot.com

Stingy Nomads (English)
https://stingynomads.com/via-de-la-plata-camino-de-santiago

Spanish–English dictionary
www.wordreference.com

Silver Way BASIC Peregrino Online app (English, Spanish, French, German and Italian)
www.peregrino.online/en/app-guide-silver-way

Accommodation (English)
www.booking.com

Weather (Spanish)
www.aemet.es
(AEMET app available)

**Social media**

www.facebook.com/ciceronecamino (English)

www.facebook.com/groups/viadelaplatapilgrimsgroup
(Gerald Kelly's page, English)

www.facebook.com/groups/viadelaplataelcamino (multilingual)

www.facebook.com/groups/421177385161547
(Camino Vía de la Plata Mozárabe Sanabrés, multilingual)

www.facebook.com/alberguetabara (Spanish)

www.facebook.com/Asociación-caminos-vía-de-la-plata-106919914418997 (Spanish)

www.facebook.com/groups/CaminoJournals (mainly English)

# APPENDIX D
*Bibliography*

This guidebook would never have materialized without the following devoted authors, to whom an immense debt of eternal gratitude is due.

ALONSO, Joaquín, and PÉREZ, Miguel, *La Vía de la Plata*, Everest, León, 2010: excellent information on the original Roman road, providing in-depth historical data.

ANDERSON, Bloo, *Camino Mozárabe – a time travelling pilgrimage in Iberia*, 2018, www.cicerone.co.uk/camino-mozarabe-a-time-travelling-pilgrimage-in-iberia

BARREDA FERRER, Ángel Luis, ARRIBAS CASTRILLO, Mª del Carmen, and MEDIAVILLA, Hugo, *Guía del peregrino en la Vía de la Plata*, Fundación Siglo para el Turismo y las Artes de Castilla y León, 2020: good, accessible information; available as a PDF, downloadable from www.turismocastillayleon.com (type the book title into the Search box).

BROWN, Sandy, *Camino de Santiago: Camino Francés*, Cicerone, Cumbria, 2022: the must-have guidebook to completing the route from Astorga to Santiago, as well as stages for Fisterra and Muxía. Sandy is most definitely the modern pioneer of pilgrimage guidebooks, and the breadth of his historical, cultural and practical knowledge is key to the understanding of the Camino.

COSMEN ALONSO, María Concepción, *Arte y liturgia en Santa Marta de Tera*, Centro de Estudios Astorganos, 2008: a good article on the history of the region.

DENNETT, Laurie, *2000 Years of the Pilgrimage*, www.csj.org.uk/2000-years-of-the-pilgrimage, 2005: a good overview of the history of the Camino.

DOPICO CALVO, María José, *La gran obra de los Caminos de Santiago. Iter Stellarum*, Hércules de Ediciones, 2008: a multi-volume extravaganza on all Caminos, with the Vía de la Plata, Camino Sanabrés and Camino Francés covered in volumes I–VIII.

ENRÍQUEZ, Adolfo, *Hasta Santiago*, Xunta de Galicia, 2003: a beautiful collection of Camino photography.

FÁBREGA, Fernando, and team, *El Camino de Santiago*, Espasa Calpe, Madrid, 2004: superb background information on the Camino.

HAYES, John, *Cycling the Ruta Vía de la Plata*, Cicerone, Cumbria, 2022: the essential guidebook covering on- and off-road options for cyclists, it also includes details of continuation to Gijón as well as more lavish accommodation options and recommendations for fantastic restaurants.

HERNÁNDEZ, Filiberto, and DELGADO MORÁN, Uxúa, *A caballo hacia Santiago por la Ruta Vía de la Plata*, Concejalía de Turismo del Ayuntamiento de Zamora, 2019: an indispensable guidebook for horse-riding pilgrims, it includes information on accommodation for humans as well as their four-legged swishy-tailed companions. Filiberto is the president of the Asociación de Caminos de la Vía de la Plata and runs the Torre de Sabre albergue in El Cubo de Tierra del Vino.

KELLY, Gerald, *Walking Guide to the Vía de la Plata and the Camino Sanabrés*, www. viadelaplataguide.net, 2022: concise practical information. The website contains a great FAQ section, which Kelly updates meticulously along with his addictive Facebook page (see Appendix C).

MUÑOZ HIDALGO, Diego M, 'Sobre el topónimo "Camino de la Plata"', *El nuevo miliario* (vol. 11, pp. 5–36), 2010: this fabulous, dedicated historian has written many articles on the Vía and has worked half his life to protect and promote it. Bump into him at the Van Gogh albergue in Zafra and say hello!

RAJU, Alison, *The Way of Saint James*, Cicerone, Cumbria, 2018: an inspiration to pilgrims and pilgrimage writers, Alison was Vice Chair of the Confraternity of Saint James in the UK (www.csj.org.uk).

ROLDÁN HERVÁS, José Manuel, and CABALLERO CASADO, Carlos, 'Itinera Hispana', *El nuevo miliario* (vol. 17, pp. 10–253), 2014: a tremendous, detailed article on Roman *vias*, *mansios* and emperors, covering Roman itineraries across the entire Iberian peninsula.

# DOWNLOAD THE ROUTES
# IN GPX FORMAT

All the routes in this guide are available for download from:

### www.cicerone.co.uk/1080/GPX

as standard format GPX files. You should be able to load them into most online GPX systems and mobile devices, whether GPS or smartphone. You may need to convert the file into your preferred format using a conversion programme such as gpsvisualizer.com or one of the many other such websites and programmes.

When you follow this link, you will be asked for your email address and where you purchased the guidebook, and have the option to subscribe to the Cicerone e-newsletter.

## CICERONE
www.cicerone.co.uk

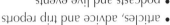